The Braided Dream

The Braided Dream

Robert Penn Warren's Late Poetry

Randolph Paul Runyon

THE UNIVERSITY PRESS OF KENTUCKY

I would like to express my gratitude to Leonard Simutis,
Dean of the Graduate School of Miami University,
and Stephen Day, Dean of the College of Arts and Science,
for their generosity in making funds available
to support the publication of this book.

for ELIZABETH

Contents

Introduction
Buried Narrative and the Parody of Time

Robert Penn Warren, until his death on 15 September 1989, had been generally acknowledged to be this country's greatest living poet. For Harold Bloom he was "our most eminent man of letters"; Peter Stitt found him "the most important American poet of the second half of the twentieth century, and one of the five most important of the entire century" (review of *New and Selected Poems*, 648). He twice received the Pulitzer Prize for poetry, for *Promises* and *Now and Then*, and the list of his other awards was extensive. The publication of *New and Selected Poems: 1923-1985* on the occasion of his eightieth birthday was a literary event, and the announcement in early 1986 that Warren had been named the nation's first poet laureate was generally greeted with the feeling that the man dignified the office, not the other way around.

One of the most remarkable qualities of Warren's poetry is its accessibility. Beyond its immersion in America's past, and the poetry's intrinsic greatness, the fact that it can be read by everyman (and everywoman)—even *People* exhorted its readers to "check it out!" (17 March 1986, p. 66)—with no special preparation made the laureate announcement especially welcome. It is not particularly difficult poetry, at least not on the surface, though it richly rewards close rereading. There is no reason why anyone who enjoys poetry at all cannot find immense pleasure in reading the recent sequences that have so enhanced Warren's steadily rising reputation, and it is to such a reader that this book is addressed.

It was perhaps not always so accessible. Warren began his poetic career under the influence of T.S. Eliot and the seventeenth-century English Metaphysicals, and such early works as "Bearded Oaks" and "Terror"[1] with their borrowed rhetoric and occasional archaic language, though in fashion at the time, would appear somewhat offputting to a present-day reader. Yet the kind of close reading championed by the New Critical movement of which Warren was a prime mover owes something to these same influences, and certainly the close reading I will attempt here is itself indebted to the way Warren and Cleanth Brooks taught a whole generation to read in *Understanding Poetry*.

There have been three major phases in the poetic career of Robert Penn Warren. The first began in 1922, when he published poems in the *Fugitive* while he was still an undergraduate at Vanderbilt, and concludes in 1944 with the appearance of *Selected Poems, 1923-1943*. This was his third published volume of poetry, preceded in 1935 by *Thirty-Six Poems* and in 1943 by *Eleven Poems on the Same Theme*. The *Selected Poems* of 1944 included all eleven of the preceding year and all but two of the 1935 collection. Three appeared for the first time in 1944, of which "The Ballad of Billie Potts," consistently reprinted in the three subsequent *Selected Poems*, announces the down-to-earth style that was to characterize so much of his successful poetry years later. Like *Brother to Dragons* (1953; revised 1979), it is a narrative based on a story from Kentucky's past, in particular from the western region of the state to which Warren would later return in much of the poetry considered here—though the latter would be based not on historical legend but on his childhood in Guthrie, a rural community just north of the Tennessee border, and in the surrounding fields and woods.

At the same time, in the 1930s and early 1940s, Warren was developing as a novelist. Two unpublished novels and several published short stories preceded the astonishing (to my eyes) *Night Rider* (1939), a novel based on the Tobacco Wars in Warren's native region at about the time of his birth in 1905 and one whose tightly woven and haunting imagery could perhaps have been achieved only by a poet. The somewhat less compelling *At Heaven's Gate* (1943) followed, set in the present in a town very much like Nashville or Memphis. It could hardly have led a reader to expect the miracle of *All the King's Men* (1946), the combined popular and critical success for which Warren is still remembered today by most Americans who know his name. *World Enough and Time* (1950), perhaps his second-best novel, was based on an incident in early nineteenth-century Kentucky history. It was followed by six more novels between 1955 and 1977, none of which has—I think unjustly—enjoyed much critical or popular acclaim.

Yet as the appreciation of his novels has declined since the mid-1950s, his reputation as a poet has undeniably soared. Warren stopped writing poetry entirely in 1944, so that his period of greatest glory as a writer of fiction was one in which he gave himself completely to that aspect of his talent. When he returned to poetry with the publication of the book-length *Brother to Dragons* in 1953 and then *Promises: Poems 1954-1956*, a second phase of his poetic career began; certainly his poetry acquired a new lease on life. Gone were the archaisms and "subterranean ledges" of *Thirty-Six Poems* and *Eleven Poems on the Same Theme*. There was now a directness, both of style and of connection to a personal, unborrowed, past, that was most appealing; these poems read as well today as they did thirty years ago, and as movingly. William S. Ward pinpoints the change thus: "It was in the summer of 1954 that he regained his talent for lyric verse and a 'new sense of poetry,' following his divorce from his first wife in 1951, his marriage to Eleanor Clark in 1952, and the birth of his two children. The renewal came while he was living with his family in a ruined fortress on the Italian coast about one hundred miles north of Rome. From this renewal three years later was to come *Promises: Poems 1954-1956*, and the beginning of the most distinguished stage of Warren's career" (178). The first sequence within the volume, the five poems of "To a Little Girl, One Year Old, in a Ruined Fortress," is set on that Italian coast; at least as many are lullabies to his sleeping infant son; most of the rest are set in Guthrie or close by. James Justus still considered *Promises* "the greatest single volume of his career" in 1981 (49).

Victor Strandberg has recently wondered whether his next collection, *You, Emperors, and Others: Poems 1957-1960* was not perhaps "Robert Penn Warren's Worst Book" (title of a paper given 16 October 1987 at "Robert Penn Warren: A Hometown Symposium," Austin Peay State University). *Promises* won the 1957 Pulitzer Prize, but *You, Emperors, and Others* reaped much critical scorn. Warren himself may not think much of it now either, for his most recent *Selected Poems* (1985) includes only three of its poems, making it the least represented of any collection. Yet it contains the wonderful "Mortmain" sequence about his father's death, recently reprinted (at greater length than in 1985) in his *Portrait of a Father*.

From *Promises* and *You, Emperors* through *Incarnations: Poems 1966-1968* and *Or Else—Poem/Poems 1968-1974* up to the four sequences that are the subject of this book—*Now and Then: Poems 1976-1978*, *Being Here: Poetry 1977-1980*, *Rumor Verified: Poems 1979-1980*, and *Altitudes and Extensions 1980-1984*—Warren's poetic collections are characterized, I believe, by increasing integration. By that term I mean that in his later collections Warren appears more and more to be writing in each instance a poetic sequence that is itself a poem in addition to being composed of poems. The subtitle of *Or Else*, with its double assertion *Poem/Poems*, seems especially to point in this direction. The fact, too, that the years *Rumor Verified* subtends are wholly included within those indicated in *Being Here*'s subtitle (together with the fact that the latter's years overlap with those of *Now and Then*) suggests that, in contrast with what he published in the 1950s and 1960s, these more recent sequences have evolved into something more than collections defined by the years in which they were written—that they cohere for other reasons.

Even as far back as *Promises* and *You, Emperors* one can detect a progressive tightening of sequence. As Daniel Hoffman has observed, "In *Promises* and thereafter Warren excels in sequences, series of lyrics on a common theme in which we are compelled from one poem to another by unpredictable loopings of thought and slipknots of feeling" (463). *Promises* was divided into two parts: "To a Little Girl, One Year Old, in a Ruined Fortress," with five poems designated by roman numerals, and "Promises," with nineteen. Of the latter, five ("Dark Woods," "Infant Boy at Midcentury," "Man in Moonlight," "Ballad of a Sweet Dream of Peace," and "Boy's Will") were themselves sequences, comprising between three and seven arabic-numbered poems. It is hard to regard the section "Promises" as being a sequence in the same way that "To a Little Girl" is one, since the real sequences appear to be those five sequences within it (though Warren did apparently want each of its nineteen parts to be considered some kind of "Promise"). The result is that the volume encompasses a mixture of sequences and individual poems. Of the forty-six poems in *You, Emperors*, however, all but four are part of some particular sequence (there are nine). Sequence has become, three years later, a more pervasive characteristic of the Warrenian poetic collection.

Even more is this true of *Incarnations: Poems 1966-1968*, all of whose poems belong to one of the volume's five sequences. Though the penultimate sequence, "The True Nature of Time," (as well as the last) contains but two poems, these are closely linked in the same way poems in the later four collections to be studied here will be, by echoing phrases. "The Faring" (57) tells how "the sea-cliffs, / Eastward, swung in that blue wind"; in "The Enclave" (59) "the sea-cliffs, / Far in that blue wind, swing." Both poems speak of the "brightness" or "brightening" of hair. And "The Faring" speaks of yellow roses, of which "One / Petal, yellow, fell, slow. // At the foot of the gray stone, like light, it lay," while in "The Enclave" the cry of the first cock "In the dark, like gold blood flung, is scattered." Upon reflection, we may realize that "gold" is to "blood" (normally red) as "yellow" is to "rose" (likewise more likely to be at least roseate).

If *Promises* clearly marks the beginning of the second phase of Warren's poetic career, it is more difficult to date the third with precision. That there is a third is evidenced by the extraordinary attention being paid to his poetry now. Greatness set in but when? Calvin Bedient says it happened during the late sixties: "Nothing in Robert Penn Warren's long career as a man of letters has so distinguished it as has the final act. . . . His greatness as a writer began with his determination to concentrate on poetry as the extreme resource of language-knowledge, language-being— began with *Audubon: A Vision* (1969)" (3). David Perkins puts it a little earlier, for somewhat different reasons:

> Around 1966 Warren's poetry entered another phase, and to most readers he seemed a greater poet in his sixties and seventies than ever before. It is not easy to say how his poetry was now different, however, for his themes and technical resources remained what they had been. Yet whatever had been rhetorical, mannered, and forced in his poetry gradually disappeared or diminished. . . . And while creat-

ing a more relaxed and natural way of speaking, he re-
tained undiminished his narrative and constructive power,
his psychological alertness and reflective tenacity. Perhaps
the major change was simply the extent to which his poems
now interrelated with one another. [360]

Now although Perkins is speaking of two different kinds of in-
terrelatedness—"the cross-connections within particular sequences" as well as "Warren's lifelong preoccupation with the
same or closely similar themes"—he nevertheless anticipates
much of what I wish to express here: that Warren's most recent
poetic sequences are extraordinarily accessible and that they
remarkably interrelated.

I insist on the term "sequence" for a very good reason, one
having to do with the whole purpose of the present work. It is my
contention that *Now and Then, Being Here, Rumor Verified,* and
Altitudes and Extensions: 1980-1984 (the first eighty pages of *New
and Selected Poems: 1923-1985*)[2]—the objects of my study here—
are arranged (perhaps unconsciously: indeed the unconscious
will be very much at issue here) to be read sequentially. That is,
that each poem in these collections is best read with an eye to
what is going on in the one just before and the one just after it.
This may seem like an extremely simple idea, and it is, but it is
not trivial—and neither are the results if it is followed rigor-
ously, to the letter. Each poem alludes to something in the poem
before by repeating it—a word, quite often; a turn of phrase; an
image; a situation. In each instance, to paraphrase a poem in
Now and Then, what happened "*there* is—just now / In its new ectoplasmic context— / Happening again" (67; Warren's italics).[3]
At this moment Warren is talking about something else, or appears to: a smile that he sees again even though the person who
smiled it is dead. But this discussion of a recurring smile happens
in a poem in the midst of other poems in which another smile
keeps returning, from poem to poem, each time in a new context.
The result is that it is an example of precisely what it is talking
about but only in the wider context of the sequence of poems in
which it appears.

These poems often speak of what they are doing at the moment they are doing it—particularly when what they are doing is
echoing the poem just before or anticipating the one to come. J.

Hillis Miller calls such poetic self-referentiality (the more general phenomenon, of which the sequential self-reference so evident here is a subset) "the linguistic moment": "moments of suspension within the texts of poems . . . when they reflect or comment on their own medium. . . . It is a form of parabasis, a breaking of the illusion that language is a transparent medium of meaning" (xiv). Many of Wallace Stevens's poems, for example, "are poems about poetry. They contain within themselves discussion of what they are and of what they mean. They enact or embody in themselves that function of poetry about which they explicitly talk. This self-labelling opens an abyss of interpretation . . . through the effacement of extra-linguistic reference initiated by the apparent act of self-reference. The language of the poem both performs its function and defines that function, in a self-mirroring that seems to make the poem a self-sufficient entity" (4). In Warren's poetry this takes the form of such moments as the "crackling spread" in the ice in "Small Eternity" that spreads to the next poem's "crackling rush of youthful flare" or "the / Horizon's blue ambiguity" in "Looking Northward" that immediately reappears in "Blessèd Accident" as "The slow bulge of earth purged blue / To join the heavenly blue, no certain // Horizon to be defined." The merging in blue ambiguity of sky and earth metaphorizes the merging of these two passages, just as crackling—both as something that spreads and something that can be heard (as the word "crackling" can be heard spreading from one poem to the next, like a crack in the ice)—names what it is that crackling is actually doing here (not without irony, as it reappears as the opposite of what it had been: then ice, now fire).

Among such instances of self-reference in Warren's poems, some seem to speak directly to the reader who is trying to account in a more global way for what these poems appear to be doing. Thus there are hints at the possibility of catching "a glimpse of the form through interstices" ("The Place") and a certain insistence on what can happen in "the distance between" ("The Distance Between: Picnic of Old Friends") and when "SEQUENCE AND SIMULTANEITY" are combined ("New Dawn"), as if to suggest that there were some glimpses of underlying form to be found in the interstices between the poems, or some explosion of meaning likely to result from mixing simultaneity with sequence. There is the difficulty of distinguishing between logic and accident ("Blessèd Accident") or between the sea's "Arabic scrawl" and a decipherable message ("Aspen Leaf in Windless World"). There is the sequential logic of "sorites" (also in "Aspen Leaf"), a series of premises in which each subject is the predicate of the preceding, an analogue both of the structure of Warren's linked poetic series and of the way he sees his life lived, with events following each other in a kind of plotless yet sequential narrative until the final one appears—one that may promise, but cannot guarantee, some ultimate revelation about all those that preceded it, as the sea's scrawl makes a promise of meaning it too cannot necessarily keep.

Any sustained reading of Warren will at some point have to concern itself with his lifelong meditation on the nature of time. To read these most recent poetic sequences is to come to grips with a number of ways he has found of stating the problem. Thus the presence of *there* in *here*, of *then* in *now*'s new context, and the sequential nature of life's long sorites are not just instances of poetic self-reference, of what Miller calls "the linguistic moment," but also moments when Warren tries himself to draw some conclusions about the mystery of temporality (as one of the inscriptions to *Being Here* puts it: "I thirst to know the power and nature of time").[4] In addition to soritic linkage and *then* happening again *now*, there is time as a snake that swallows its tail ("Identity and Argument for Prayer," "Paradigm of Seasons"), implying not only the eternal return of the same but also the devouring of self to produce "A nobler dimension of that Self" ("Milton: A Sonnet")—as the poems devour each other ("Orphanage Boy," for example, with its snake-bit dog and "Red-Tail Hawk" with its stuffed hawk "fit only / For dog tooth").

Time also works to bring things to fruition, since it sometimes happens that expression precedes substance, "for," as Warren found as far back as *The Circus in the Attic*, "no one knows the meaning of the cry of passion he utters until the flesh of the passion is long since withered away to show the austere, logical articulation of fact with fact in the skeleton of Time" (28). Thus does the boy in "Boyhood in Tobacco Country" yearn for a grief to be worthy of the whip-o-will's sound and find it when his mother dies; thus do the young singers in "Youthful Picnic" sing a sweet sadness their young hearts had no right to, though one day would, "As Time unveiled, / In its own dancing parody of grace, / The bony essence of each joke on joke"—the jokes being bones themselves (the "cheekbones in earth" in the immediately preceding poem, now reappearing in yet another self-referential moment), as these poems reveal what was meant decades before when Warren spoke of the "skeleton of Time."

To read these poems without regard to their sequential echoes, that is, would be to miss out on a significant part of what Warren has to say here about the nature of time, for his poems make use, in their self-referential way, of sequential recurrence to reveal a certain logic of articulation, of fact with fact (of word with word, phrase with phrase), that is also a logic of parody. They enact the parody that time inflicts.

Considerations of time and self-reference seem to grow in an intimate way out of the poems. The former is a constant element of Warren's vocabulary, the latter perhaps an essential feature of all poetry and subject to some particularly striking, and undeniable, manifestations here. But to speak of Freud (whose name is invoked in "Inevitable Frontier" precisely as a name that "must not be spoken") smacks of something like foreign influence. Yet dream, and particularly Freud's notion of "dreamwork," is almost as pervasive in Warren's poetic vocabulary as time, and several of his poems are in fact essays in dream interpretation. In *Now and Then*, for example, "Dream" is immediately followed by "Dream of a Dream," where "the moonlight's bright heel has splashed the stream; / But this, of course, belongs to the dream of another dream." Clearly that other dream is the immediately preceding "Dream," where "Heels slashed" at Jacob's dreamed struggle with the angel is recounted. Now "Dream of a Dream" grants us a glimpse of what dreams are made of, shows us something of the nature of their "texture": "gone / Into the braiding texture of dream." Here, as one dream—and poem—intertwines with its predecessor, it emerges that what the poet says of dreams is true of his poems, of the braiding texture of their sequence. Dreams are thematic as well in "Literal Dream," "The Mission," and, in *Or Else*, "I Am Dreaming of a White Christmas: The Natural History of a Vision." Nor can one forget that most haunting of moments when Warren leaves "Freud on dreams" behind for his father to read, in *Or Else*'s "Reading Late at Night, Thermometer Falling"[5]: "I / Cannot see what book is propped there under that forever / Marching gaze—[works of history, a Greek reader, a college text book] or Freud on dreams, abandoned / By one of the children."[6]

It is a text his readers, too, might read with profit if they want a fuller understanding of his poems. For as certain sequentially linked poems enact the logic of time's parody, so do all the poems in the four sequences read here appear to enact a certain logic of dream—that is, the one Freud outlined in *The Interpretation of Dreams*. For these poems appear, as if they had an unconscious, to dream. And to dream in a remarkably Freudian way: by recycling what Warren himself once called (in the 1925 poem "Images on the Tomb") "Poor fragments of the day," out of "the dark wherein you [= those fragments] all are piled"— the day residue from the events of the immediately preceding day—in order to use them as raw material for the construction of the dream (of "Dreams to release from the troubled heart and deep / The pageantry of thoughts unreconciled"). What happens in the sequences is that fragments of the immediately preceding poem reappear in a new poem, in a "new ectoplasmic context," surviving only as fragments, divorced from their former context, with a new meaning necessitated by the demands of the new poem.

Though I am constrained by my thesis about the consistently sequential structure of these books of poetry to have to demonstrate it more than once (about 180 times, all told), the presence of these self-interpreting self-references, together with the tantalizing possibility of finding another story or stories concealed between the ones the poems individually tell, not to speak of the richness of the examples and the resourcefulness with which Warren elaborates his sequential texture, will, I hope, make monotony no real danger here.

But I must ask the reader of this book to read the poetry first. For this book can in no way stand by itself, and it certainly cannot pretend to take the place of a reading of the poems it seeks to discuss. More than most works of criticism, this one is bound to the text it talks about; it is a companion to the work, a commentary in a perhaps old-fashioned sense. It does not deal with the broad themes of Warren's work, except through the discipline it imposes (and which I believe the work imposes, ultimately) of reading the poetry as something other than the compendium of philosophic statements it quite often appears to make. For this reading strategy reveals that just as often those statements cannot be taken at face value, since they appear in poetic contexts steeped in irony; in particular, the practice Warren observes of saying similar things in radically different contexts may in the end undermine what we may at first have thought those things meant.

An example from a rather different context will show what I mean. In "Blackberry Winter," Warren's most celebrated short story, the young protagonist wanders out to look at a flooded creek and recognizes his father on a horse. "The first thing that happened was, I remember, the warm feeling I always had when I saw him up on a horse. . . . I heard his voice calling, 'Seth!' . . . I did not look up at my father until I was almost within touching distance of his heel. Then I looked up and tried to read his face, to see if he was angry about my being barefoot. Before I could decide anything from that impassive, high-boned face, he had leaned over and reached a hand to me. 'Grab on,' he commanded" (73-74). It is a tender moment, full of "warm feeling." And nothing happens in "Blackberry Winter" to change that warmth. The father will not, for example, be angry that his son is going barefoot. But there is a wider context for this event than just the story, and that is the book—*The Circus in the Attic*—in which the story, together with thirteen others, appears.

It is the second story in that collection, and, remarkably, in the first story something strangely like this episode has already occurred. In that story, also called "The Circus in the Attic," someone approaches a man on a horse and grabs his left leg (recall that the other Seth saw his nearness to his father in terms of being within touching distance of his heel), at which point the man on the horse "leaned over and" (the very same words that will describe the father's gesture when "he leaned over and" reached out his hand to his son) "struck him about the head with his gauntleted fist." The man on the horse is a Union officer; the other man is a Tennessean defending his corn, and in another instant his brains will be blown out by the pistol of a soldier under the officer's command. This similarity would not, perhaps, be so remarkable were it not for the fact that the name of the victim, like the name of the beloved boy in the next story, is Seth— and indeed the name appears in "Blackberry Winter" only at the moment when he walks up to his father on the horse (no other characters bear the name in the short story collection). It is also worth noting that when "The Circus in the Attic" appeared separately in a magazine (*Cosmopolitan*, September 1947), the episode of Seth's death, which is not part of the main plot, was not included.

I think it is fair to say that the warm feeling which Seth said he always felt when he saw his father on a horse can be chilled by the memory of what had just happened in the earlier story to another Seth at the hands of a man on a horse.[7] There seems to be another story, just beneath the surface—a "buried narrative," to borrow words Warren applies in his poem "History During Nocturnal Snowfall" to the story that the protagonist of that poem hopes to be able to guess by making his heartbeat synchronize with that of the woman asleep by his side. His "finger touches a pulse to intuit its truth." Yet there seems to be another narrative buried here too, one to which this man's attention to a pulse is a clue, for in the poem just before, "Youthful Picnic Long Ago: Sad Ballad on Box," our attention is drawn to the "pulse in wrist, and wrist, and wrist" of the rhythm a woman is playing on her "box"—her guitar. I will save a fuller discussion of the relationship of these two adjacent poems in *Altitudes and Extensions* for the first chapter except to observe that the first line of "History During Nocturnal Snowfall" places both the protagonist of that poem and the woman whose pulse he is trying to synchronize with his own in a kind of *box*—"Dark in the cubicle *boxed* from snow-darkness of night"—thereby alluding to the poem before (and even to its subtitle, "Sad Ballad on *Box*").

It is also noteworthy that, like the episode of the unfortunate Seth in "The Circus in the Attic," this key word was not present when this poem first appeared. Under the title "Personal History" in the fall 1983 number of the *Sewanee Review*, the first line originally read: "Dark in the cubicle *curtained* from the snow-dark night." In the end the two hidden narratives may prove to be part of the same story, for as the reading here of *Now and Then* will indicate, the connection in Warren between father and horse is a persistent one.

It has been hard to keep pace with Robert Penn Warren, who in his long career as a poet saved the best for last. Of the four poetic sequences I study here, none had appeared when Victor

Strandberg published *The Poetic Vision of Robert Penn Warren* in 1977, and two had not yet seen the light of day when James Justus's *The Achievement of Robert Penn Warren* appeared in 1981. Since the most recent book-length study at this writing—Calvin Bedient's *In the Heart's Last Kingdom: Robert Penn Warren's Major Poetry*—Warren has already published a new collection, *New and Selected Poems: 1923-1985*, that contains within it a sequence (*Altitudes and Extensions 1980-1984*) in length and significance equal to *Rumor Verified*, *Being Here*, and *Now and Then*.

Though there is much to gain from Bedient's readings, I cannot agree with his contention that Warren's "intimations that certain of his partial collections might be thought single poems are wishful thinking" (127). What Bedient calls partial collections I call sequences and consider, as Warren does, to be single works of art. Bedient and I are looking at much the same body of work (though he discusses *Audubon* and *Or Else*, and I do not; while *Altitudes and Extensions*, which appeared too late for inclusion in his study, takes up a fourth of mine) in quite different ways. Bedient deals with the poetry in bits and pieces, passing from a poem in one sequence to one in another, according to the logic of what he is looking for, and even devoting one of his four chapters to the analysis of isolated single lines. I have no quarrel with his approach, which yields insight into the details of Warren's poetic practice—his omission of articles, his love of hyphenated words, the internal echoes, the rhythm of his line, the poignant ambivalence of his imagery. And Bedient is strongly attuned to the philosophic questing and psychoanalytic resonance constantly present in Warren.

But I believe that by focusing on Warren's exploitation of the possibilities inherent in the poetic sequence, I may in the present study bring light to bear on certain aspects of his poetry that have until now gone unnoticed. Justus, like Bedient, sees not unity in Warren's sequences but rather "unrelated images juxtaposed rather than integrated, in sequences of poems that are themselves only loosely related" (111).[8] More recently, Katherine Snipes has declared that "most poems in *Being Here* are not closely connected" (171).

Well, they are closely connected—both in *Being Here*, as chapter 3 will show, and elsewhere. Perhaps the problem is that there are more possible kinds of connection between the poems than the sort that Snipes, Justus, and other Warren interpreters have had in mind. Snipes, for example, does find that the "Mortmain" poems in *You, Emperors, and Others* form a "closely related series" (91), and they do, but their connections are of a considerably more obvious nature than the ones I will be describing here. The five poems, by the very fact that they share the title "Mortmain," advertise at the outset that they are about the same thing: the poet's father and the occasion of his death (the dying gesture of his spasmodically lifted hand, the dead hand of the past, the inheritance thus passed). The poems in the four sequences to be analyzed here do not so advertise their connections (which makes those connections rather more interesting to discover); indeed, when they are at times grouped under such a larger title, their unity does not flow from that grouping or that title, but, if anything, works at cross-purposes to it.

Actually, Justus is not far from the truth of the matter, for it is in fact a question of "images juxtaposed"—images that have something in common (a situation, a word, a phrase, a name— such as "Seth") but appear in contrasting contexts (the love of a father for his son, the casual violence of civil war) in poems juxtaposed by the sequence the poet has given them. They clash, but at the same time they echo strangely; the result is not, at least not at first, the sensation of being in the presence of an integrated collection of images but rather an awareness of the challenge to figure out the rest of what it is that draws them together.

I should add that among previous critics of Warren's poetry A.L. Clements has been particularly sensitive to the echoes that resonate from poem to poem. In his essay "Sacramental Vision: The Poetry of Robert Penn Warren," he argues that "not only grouping and repeated subjects and thematic concerns but also full sequences with the recurrence of certain words and images conduce to the sense of continuity of integration." He points out that *Or Else* is constructed according to a pattern that progresses through the seasons and from death to rebirth and that certain words (such as "dream" and "see") keep reappearing (226). Clements goes on to state more broadly of Warren's poetic corpus: "each poem is itself an organic system of relationships, and each poem, as each creature, object, and event in the world, has full meaning, value, and being not separately in isolation from but interdependently in relation to all others" (227). Similarly,

William Harmon has suggested that all of Warren's works are "cognate and concentric" and that "any one work—early or late, prose or verse—is a variation of any other" (277).

More recently John Burt, commenting on *Audubon*, finds "Warren's characteristic form" to be "the sequence of lyrics connected by an unwritten story that allows each poem's insistence on the fixity of the moment it presents to be conditioned by the necessity of turning to the next part of the sequence, another moment of fixity whose relations with the last one are not always obvious" (111). This "unwritten story" comes close to sounding like the "buried narrative" that will concern us in these pages. I understand Burt to be saying that, even though the relations with the preceding poem are not always obvious, they are nevertheless present, hidden beneath the surface. "Often enough," he will go on to say, "in later sequences like *Or Else* or *Being Here*, the next poem in a sequence of near-collisions with fatal signifi-cance takes us back to where we were at the beginning of the last poem" (116)—and we will certainly see evidence of that here.

In his reading of *Altitudes and Extensions*, Victor Strandberg speaks intriguingly of its structure: "Always a poet of dialectical impulse, Warren arranges the poems between the beginning and the end of this collection in a loosely contrapuntal pattern. The sunset hawk in 'Mortal Limit' . . . for example . . . is played off against the airplane in the next poem, 'Immortality Over the Dakotas' . . . , where the passenger rides securely distant from the doomed farmer looking up in the night" ("Poet of Youth," 96). Though Strandberg devotes his attention for the most part to somewhat looser contrapuntal patterns than this one, he notes in these two contiguous poems precisely the kind of sequential echo that, I will argue, permeates the sequence.

Recently M.L. Rosenthal and Sally M. Gall have focused critical attention on "the modern poetic sequence," which they credit with being "the crucial genre of modern poetic art . . . , *the* modern poetic form within which all the tendencies of more than a century of experiment define themselves" (vii), and which they define as the "grouping of mainly lyric poems and passages, rarely uniform in pattern, which tend to interact as an organic whole" (9). At first glance, this definition would appear to encompass what I believe occurs in Warren's later poetic sequences. Yet in fact it does not, for nowhere in their long study, ranging from

Whitman and Dickinson to Pound and Plath, do they consider the kind of immediate recurrence of word and image that is so characteristic of the later Warren. Their concern is less with such elements of structure than with "the dynamic interplay among poems and fragments conceived under the same ultimate psychological pressure or creative impulse" (vii)—which is to say not with the way the sequence is put together but with what was on the mind of the poet when he or she wrote it. Thus the sequences they study "exemplify a compelling process, the result of sheer, psychically powerful need on each poet's part to mobilize and give direction to otherwise scattered energies" (9). They are surely right, however, to make the claims they do for the importance of sequence as a modern phenomenon (though they seem to make them at the expense of ignoring all poetic sequences written before Whitman's *Song of Myself*), and the emphasis here on the significance of Warren as a poet of sequences should serve to confirm the importance of the genre.

More relevant to the present study is the work of Neil Fraistat, who insists, as I do, on reading "poems in their place"—on the necessity of making "the poetry book itself—as both idea and material fact—an object of interpretation. A fundamental assumption of such an approach is that the decisions poets make about the presentation of their works play a meaningful role in the poetic process and, hence, ought to figure in the reading process. Studied within the context of their original volumes, poems reveal a fuller textuality, which is to say, an *inter*textuality" ("Introduction," 3). Fraistat finds, for example, in Keats's 1820 *Lamia* collection, "a complex system of verbal echoes, transitional links, and thematic progressions through which each poem revises the meaning of its predecessor" (*The Poem and the Book*, 99). This is, for the most part—with the possible exception of his argument for thematic progression—a remarkably accurate description of what happens in the four Warren sequences we will read here.

In a study of fifteenth-century (and older) Japanese poetic collections called *renga*, in which each poem repeats images and sometimes entire lines from its immediate predecessor, Earl Miner, in a collection of essays edited by Fraistat, proposes the term "plotless narrative" to describe the "sequentiality and continuousness" characteristic of such linked series. These collections consist of poems by different poets and arranged by compilers other than the poets who wrote them, yet the structural parallels with Warren's late sequences are striking despite the unlikelihood (and irrelevance) of influence. In the third chapter I will show how the last two words of *Rumor Verified*— "caverned enchainment"—aptly though not necessarily intentionally describe the linking structure that unites the elements of this and Warren's other recent poetic sequences. Miner's investigation of Japanese linked collections brings to light a similar structure: "like a link of a chain touching only the one before and the one after," he says of renga, "a given stanza has continuous semantic connection only with its predecessor, which is also to say by definition a connection with its successor" (37). Miner's "plotless narrative" comes very close to expressing with I mean by the "buried" variety; because the links of the poetic chain he analyzes (like Warren's) have connections only with those immediately before and after, plot in renga "is utterly unfeasible." Yet, given their sequential linkage, they are nevertheless narrative.

Narrative, Miner writes, can do without plot: "If I am close to being right, then we may posit that, although plot is usual in narrative, it is not necessary to it, and integrated collections are plotless narratives. Sequential continuousness (that is not redundant) is in any event a radical prior to plot in narrative. And the principles of that continuousness are beginnings and endings (in addition to *the* beginning and ending) that are separated-joined by continuances (as opposed to *the* continuousness)" (39-40). What Miner calls "*the* continuousness" is what Rosenthal and Gall focus upon—"the same ultimate psychological pressure or creative impulse" (in their words) under which the "dynamic interplay among poems and fragments" that interests them in their study of modern poetic sequence is "conceived." But the "continuances" Miner opposes to that continuousness will be my focus here—the short-lived recurrences that link poem to poem, that advance, and are survived by, the narrative.

If each work is, as William Harmon proposes, a variation of any other (or as Warren himself puts it in "A Way to Love God": "Everything seems an echo of something else"), is there an original? Not necessarily, though the kind of reading I propose does at times allow one to see connections, to piece together what appear to be parts of some original story. Though such archaeology is not my primary aim, some progress in that direction is bound to accrue to an attempt to follow the poems' mutual allusions. The allusions to which greatest attention will be paid here are those by which each poem shows its continuity with the next, those linkages that go into the making of what may be hinted at in such a phrase (and last word, in a sense) as "caverned enchainment." If there is a buried narrative it may well be buried in such a cave.

ONE

Altitudes and Extensions
"Some Logic Here to Trace"

> There is some logic here to trace, and I
> Will try hard to find it.

To begin at a beginning, what Robert Penn Warren says before
he says anything else in the first line of his most recent poetic sequence—*Altitudes and Extensions 1980-1984*, the new collection
that opens his *New and Selected Poems: 1923-1985*—is to issue
what looks like a challenge to the reader to find the hidden logic
of these poems: "There is some logic here to trace...." Of
course what immediately follows nearly cancels out the effect of
that challenge, plunging us into the poem itself, in which it is the
poet and not the reader who is trying to trace a certain logic. Yet
something still remains of that hint of an invitation: what follows
here is an attempt to respond to it.

Warren has elsewhere said that the order in which his poems
appear reflects his authorship as much as do the poems themselves. In an "Afterthought" to the sequence *Being Here*, he
writes: "The order of the poems is not the order of composition
(and certain poems composed during the general period are not
included). The order and selection are determined thematically,
but with echoes, repetitions, and variations in feeling and tonality." What he had in mind in that instance was that *Being Here*, as
has generally been noted, moves from recollections of childhood
through youth to maturity and old age. "The thematic order," he
then remarks, "—or better, structure—is played against, or with,
a shadowy narrative, a shadowy autobiography." Now what I
want to trace in *Being Here*, as in *Altitudes and Extensions*, *Rumor
Verified*, and *Now and Then*, is something less obvious than that
and something not thus endowed with the author's imprimatur.

It is in fact something that I am quite willing to admit is not the result of any conscious intent on Warren's part. It is nevertheless there.

To be quite frank, the text I am interpreting here is one whose existence is nearly as difficult to establish as the wink Willie Stark may or may not have given Jack Burden in *All the King's Men*. "Did you or didn't you?" Jack asked, twelve years after that encounter in Slade's back room. " 'Boy,' he said, and smiled at me paternally over his glass, 'that is a mystery.' " Paternal (note the nature of the smile) individuals in Warren love to give their sons a mystery to puzzle over, a gesture to decipher. And the mystery is precisely whether or not the gesture—the wink, the text to decipher—was intended. Stark deepens the mystery by suggesting that maybe he just had something in his eye. Is that it then? asks Jack. Stark refuses to say: "Suppose I didn't have anything in my eye?" Exasperated, Jack asks once more. " 'Boy,' he said, 'if I was to tell you, then you wouldn't have anything to think about' " (16).

At a time when Warren was playing the role of critic—which in his literary universe is rather like being a son to a mysterious father—he found himself in a predicament not unlike that of Jack Burden: how can he interpret a poem without knowing the poet's intent? According to the theory of poetic creation he outlined when he wrote about Coleridge's "Rime of the Ancient Mariner" in "A Poem of Pure Imagination: An Experiment in Reading," however, that is a false question, for the poet "cannot do otherwise than 'intend' what his poem says, any more than he can change his own past as past, but he does not fully know what he 'intends' until the poem is fully composed." From this it follows that it would be wrong to speak of the poet having a preconceived (or as Warren puts it, quoting Wordsworth, " 'formally conceived' ") intention; it would even be wrong, it appears, to say that the poet has much choice in the matter at all. The poem comes close to writing itself, working its purpose out through the poet—yet we could not say it does without presupposing the existence of the poem. What it is really like, Warren is evidently saying, is the living of a life. The poet cannot do otherwise than intend what the poem says "any more than he can change his own past as past."

The final word in the matter is this: the intention cannot even be known anyway until the poem is finished ("he does not fully know what he 'intends' until the poem is fully composed"). There is no "blueprint of intention." Given that, he asks, "on what basis may a poem be interpreted? What kind of evidence is to be admitted? The first piece of evidence is the poem itself. And here, as I have suggested earlier, the criterion is that of internal consistency. If the elements of a poem operate together toward one end, we are entitled to interpret the poem according to that end. Even if the poet himself should rise to contradict us, we could reply that the words of the poem speak louder than his actions" (397). The criterion, precisely, of the interpretation of Warren's last four poetic sequences that I will propose in these pages is their internal consistency. The consistency, that is, with which the poems within them continue to behave as if their placement mattered, as if the process through which they arrived at their final, published order of appearance, which was not at all their order of composition, was as much a part of the process by which they were created as the manner in which each one assumed its own final form as a particular poem.

But if the poems were composed at different times, how could they possibly bear any relation to each other according to the sequence of their appearance? How could they read one way when considered individually—as they were, we might presume, created—and another (though it does not necessarily follow that this second reading would have to differ from the first) when read together, and in a particular order? That, as Willie Stark would say, is a mystery. And it also gives us something to think about.

If, to begin again, placement matters, then the first lines of the first poem in *Altitudes and Extensions* could mean something rather special by virtue of their placement, something more than what they mean in their immediate context. "There is some logic here to trace. . . . " They could mean, that is, there is some traceable logic *here*—in the poem, perhaps even in the sequence, that is just now beginning. There is, I think, such a logic, and in the sequence *Being Here*, written of course before this sequence but to be read later here, it acquires a name—that of sorites, the kind of logical argument which *Being Here* tells us life is like, a series of propositions of which each subject is the predicate of the one that went before. Sorites is a logic of *enchaînement* in the French sense of being linked rather than fettered, a sense that may still be active, at least as a secondary meaning, in its appearance at the end of another of the four sequences considered here—in the last words, as it happens, of *Rumor Verified*: "caverned enchainment."

And if placement matters, then the location of "Three Darknesses" (3) the poem whose first lines I have been quoting and consequently the first poem in *Altitudes and Extensions*, could be informative as well. For like the sequence it begins, it too is a sequence, a poem of three (untitled, but numbered) parts. In its three darknesses there is, as it happens, some logic to trace. In part I, the poet remembers a bear in a zoo pounding on the iron door of a cave, vainly "trying to enter into the darkness of wisdom"; in part II, he recalls witnessing the more successful attempt of a friend to penetrate the "Darkness of a lagoon"; in part III, the poet is himself in the dark, the "sudden darkness" of a hospital room when the departing nurse has turned out the light. The progression is clear: from a failed effort (part I) to a successful one (part II), and from witness (parts I and II) to participant (part III). The time of day progresses too, from morning (part I: "one Sunday morning, festal with springtime") to sunset (part II: half light, half dark—a cormorant is seen "black against carmine of sunset," yet the jungle into which the poet's friend disappears is "the lagoon of midnight. / Though it is far from midnight") to night (part III: the night before his operation, scheduled for 5 A.M., doubled by the "dream-night" of a televised western).

There are other sequential connections. Though darkness pervades the poem, only in parts I and II is it something one can enter—"The entrance to a dark enclosure, a cave, / Natural or artificial" in the case of the bear; the jungle defined by "the darkness of trunks rising" and "the darkness of moss suspended" in the case of the poet's friend "As he paddles a white skiff *into* the tangled / Darkness of a lagoon" (as the bear in part I "Was trying to enter *into* the darkness of wisdom"). In part III the darkness is not something one enters, and certainly not something one could intend to enter, but something that unexpectedly descends as the nurse extinguished the light on her way out (the man in the boat in part II had likewise created a sudden darkness by doing to himself what the nurse does to the poet: after drifting in something less than absolute darkness because he had a "powerful light" whose "occasional stabs" are visible to the poet, he then "cuts the light and drifts on the lagoon of midnight"): "The nurse is still here. Then / she is not here. You / Are here but are not sure / It is you in the sudden darkness."

These are the opening lines of part III, and they form a curious echo to the closing, and therefore proximate, ones of part II, which concern another woman's departure (and, in this case, return): "Your hostess / Had gone into the cabin. You hear / The pop of a wine cork. She comes back. The wine / Is breathing in darkness." A hospital nurse is, of course, a kind of hostess, too; in these circumstances, perhaps, a distressing parody of one. The connotations are quite opposed—the ease of being waited on and waiting for wine to breathe versus the dis-ease of being a patient and having to spend a sleepless night waiting for 5 A.M. surgery—but that may be precisely the point. For there to be opposition there must first be sameness, and that recurring sameness will be our most helpful clue should we attempt to find, and trace, the logic that the first lines of this poem, and sequence, tell us is here. This will not be the first time a poem in Warren's sequences takes an event—a situation, a turn of phrase, a word—and gives it a meaning at variance with the one it seemed to have had just a moment before.

That difference of meaning is sometimes, however, less at variance than a variation—continuing, and deepening, the meditation already begun. Thus in part II as well as in part I, acquaintance with darkness appears to impart some secret knowledge. The bear sought "wisdom" in his inaccessible cave; in part II "You / Wonder what your host thinks about / When he cuts the light and drifts on the lagoon of midnight"—but that voyager gives no clue to what he has learned: "Upon his return, / He will, you know / Lie on the deck-teak with no word." You have to go yourself to know, as the poet will come close to doing in part III—though with the realization that the kind of darkness that really has anything to tell us is the one from which no voyager returns, and that this night's darkness is only "A dress rehearsal . . . for / The real thing."

The bear in part I pounded his fist against the entrance to his darkness—"Slugged at an iron door" like a "pile-driver." And "near, far, / Wheresoever we wandered" that morning, the poet tells us, he and those with him could not help hearing that insistent beating. In part II, similarly, "we" (the poet and other guests) from time to time perceive what almost looks like violence performed by the friend upon the darkness in which he is engulfed: "we see the occasional stab of his powerful / Light back in the darkness." That stab is altogether natural in its context (a cliché, in fact), but as a gesture the arm performs, and a "powerful" one at that, it is equally fitting in the larger context formed by its proximity to the "indestructible, / Unforgiving" bear's slugging, "Great paws like iron on iron."

The poet in his hospital bed extends his hand to perform another variation of this gesture—in which, ultimately, light will again burst out with violence: "Your hand reached out in darkness / To the TV button. It is an old-fashioned western. / Winchester fire flicks white in the dream-night." The rifle fire seconds the poet's act of piercing the room's darkness with electric light (the light of the video tube), for it, too, stabs the night with light—as the violence with which darkness is assaulted in this miniature poetic sequence moves from slugging to stabbing to shooting. And the dream-night of the televised desert comes more and more to resemble the lagoon of midnight: in one we see "the darkness of trunks rising / From the side lagoon"; in the other, "Black / Stalks of cacti, like remnants of forgotten nightmares, loom." In one "We think of the sound a snake makes / As it slides off a bough—the slop, the slight swish, / The blackness of water"; in the other we hear that sound, those repeated *sl*'s, again, when "A stallion, white and flashing, slips, / Like spilled quicksilver, across / The vastness of moonlight" (one "slides," the other "slips": compare as well "slop" with "slips," "The blackness of water" with "The vastness of moonlight"; and consider the prominent *s* and *l*'s of "stallion" itself—as if, perhaps, it were generated from the sound the snake made). Dry as it is, the desert of this dream-night can nevertheless evoke even the liquidity that so pervaded the black lagoon, for what we see when the stallion flashes across its moonlit landscape is, strangely, wet—metallic yet fluid: spilled quicksilver.

It comes, of course, as no surprise that the three parts of "Three Darknesses" should so echo each other, given what that title proposes. I have suggested, however, that its position as first in the sequence—and the fact that *its* first line mentions "some logic here to trace"—could be a clue, not necessarily intentional, to a certain logic of reading in the poems that will follow. Whether my assertion is well founded or not will depend, of course, on whether that continuity so evident in the three parts of this poem does not end with its last line but can be found as well in "Mortal Limit," the next poem in the sequence of *Altitudes and Extensions*.

"Mortal Limit" (6) is in fact about—and its title is defined as—darkness, a fourth darkness that, like the other three, is really the same: death, the mortality of the title. A hawk rises "from coniferous darkness" at sunset and hangs motionless in the fading light "before / It knows it will accept the mortal limit" and swing back to earth, to "the darkness of whatever dream we clutch." That fading twilight is, like the televised dream-night, a hyphenated dream: "dream-spectral light." In both, snow peaks mark the farthest imaginable distance: on the television screen, "Far beyond / All the world, the mountains lift. The snow peaks / Float into moonlight. They float / In that unnamable altitude of white light"; in the sky the hawk surveys "There—west—were the Tetons. Snow-peaks would soon be / In dark profile to break constellations." As the departing hospital nurse sufficiently resembled the hostess who left to open the wine to bear an opposing connotation, so here the snow peaks of part III of "Three Darknesses" return in "Mortal Limit" in a quite different light. There they floated in white light; here they are visible only in their darkness, in the way their profile blots out stars.

"Mortal Limit" repeats an image from the second part of "Three Darknesses" as well, again with a precisely opposite connotation. The hawk riding the updraft to gaze at the last light in the west was anticipated in part II by another sunset bird: "we see / The cormorant rise"—compare the similar phrasing of the first words in "Mortal Limit": "I saw the hawk ride" (and note as well that the verb "rise" attaches equally to the latter: "It *rose* from coniferous darkness"). The hawk was a "black speck" against the light of the sun; the cormorant was "black against carmine of sunset." The hawk, though motionless, gazes to the west, as does the poet, absorbing the last light; the cormorant "beats seaward," which is westward in this instance, for "The river gleams blackly west, and thus / The jungle divides on a milk-pale path of sky toward the sea." Yet for all these similarities, the inherent nobility of the hawk who, hanging motionless, tests his mortal limit poses a sharp contrast to the qualities his precursor's sunset flight embodied: "we see / The cormorant rise—cranky, graceless, / Ungeared, unhinged, one of God's more cynical / Improvisations." The hawk found his "Mortal Limit" in the sky over Wyoming. In the next poem, the poet finds, to quote its title, "Immortality Over the Dakotas" (7). Surely the pairing of mortality and its opposite in these two titles—titles that appear in sequence, and not, as might have been the case, widely separated in the collection—should prompt a reading that takes care to trace the logic that unites them. It appears to be a logic, as we are beginning to see, of sameness and difference—or more precisely, of delicately balanced opposition.

"Immortality Over the Dakotas" introduces yet another darkness, after the three detailed in the first poem and the earthbound darkness of which "Mortal Limit" spoke (the "coniferous darkness" from which the hawk rose, which is also "the darkness of whatever dream we clutch," to which it returns in the end). It is a rushing darkness: "It is not you that moves. It is the dark / . . . Dark hurtles past. Now at the two-inch-thick plane-window glass, / You . . . see the furious / Futility of darkness." The hawk experienced mortality in his flight; the poet, in his, precisely the opposite: the darkness "can't get in. / It is as though you were at last immortal." Darkness is still what it was, particularly in "Three Darknesses": death. But something has radically changed, if only for an illusory moment, from the time the poet was plunged into the sudden hospital darkness that he saw as the dress rehearsal for the real thing; for now, he asserts, "You laugh into manic darkness." The perspective is reversed, in more ways than one. In "Mortal Limit" the poet was on the ground, looking up at the sky to witness the testing and acceptance of a mortal limit; here he's in the sky and will soon direct his gaze downward to witness yet another struggle with the limits of mortality.

First he notices something rather uncannily like the dark profile of the mountains that were in fact invisible yet seeable because their black opacity broke the constellations: "an unseeable stone" beside which a little Dakota town "Shines like a glowworm." The dark profile of the invisible mountains is to the stars as the unseeable stone is to the glowworm (whose glow, as it happens, is composed of individual points of light not unlike stars), for the glowworm is the sign of the stone's presence as the missing pieces of constellations tell the observer that mountains must be there. (Why the glowworm is such a sign is not at all clear: is it because glowworms always frequent stones? or because the glowworm that the poet has in mind, the one that the town's lights remind him of, was seen beside a stone? or is this in some way an unacknowledged memory of the poem before?)

Then "suddenly through glass, through dark fury, you see / Who must be down there": a farmer whose doctor has just told him he has but months to live and who "can't bring himself to go in" to the house where his wife sits knitting. "He knows that if he did he might let something slip. / He couldn't stand that. So stares at the blackness of sky. / Stares at lights, green and red, that tread the dark of your immortality." In the progression from "Mortal Limit" to "Immortality Over the Dakotas," metaphor precedes the reality of what it figures. The hawk, staying aloft as long as he can (which also happens to be as long as light remains in the sky), is said to have discovered his mortal limit, but we discover the real meaning of that phrase through the farmer's case. The parallel is all the more strongly drawn in that both must, though they may postpone it, return. And that to return—to earth for the hawk, to home for the farmer—would in either instance be to accept mortality. The man in the Dakota landscape, that is, has not fully accepted it until he can bring himself to tell his wife.

In "Caribou" (8) the poet is again looking down from the air, this time at caribou that "grow clear, / As binoculars find the hairline adjustment." The binoculars were anticipated by two separate elements of the preceding poem, "the two-inch-thick plane-window glass" of the airplane through which the poet stared down at the Dakota town and the bifocals he imagined the wife wearing ("Squinting studiously down through bifocals at what she's knitting") in the farmhouse where he imagined the husband, freshly notified of his mortality, reluctant to go in. Already within "Immortality Over the Dakotas" the *two* inches of glass through which the poet peered and the *bi*focals through which the wife squinted respond to each other, prompting one to ask perhaps what it is they have in common, and upon reflection it becomes clear (like the caribou, when the poet focuses his binoculars): mortality is kept at bay on the other side of those two inches of glass ("It can't get it"), and intimations of (her husband's) mortality are kept from the woman behind the bifocals (expressed in the strongly echoing line "he can't go in"). "Caribou" lends support to this interpretation by having the poet again look down from an airplane not through two inches of glass but through *bi*noculars, and another salient attribute of the woman, her hair—"She's sitting inside, white bun of hair neat as ever, / Squinting studiously down through bifocals"—finds its way into this line, too: "As binoculars find the *hairline* adjustment."

The poet, that is, at the beginning of "Immortality Over the Dakotas" presses his brow against his two inches of glass to peer at the darkness and then below at "Who must be *down* there"— among whom is someone who at the end of the poem parallels his intent gazing by "Squinting studiously *down* through bifocals." And then in the immediately following poem the poet repeats this downward gaze with an instrument that not only seems to echo the two kinds of glass that mediated the two earlier acts of downward peering but that at the same time could almost be taken to allude to the very act of thinking—as we have been doing—of those first two downward gazes at the same time. To allude, that is, to the act of seeing whatever there is in "Immortality" to see through the binocular vision those two moments afford. It is as if "Caribou" were telling us how to read "Immortality" (as well as the sequence the two poems produce). What comes into focus with the binoculars in "Caribou" is a function, of course, not of their stereoscopic but of their telescopic power. And furthermore it could be objected that Robert Penn Warren, who was blind in one eye, was not likely to have seen the caribou in three dimensions. Yet that does not prevent him from playing upon the kind of double vision that distinguishes binoculars from a telescope.[1]

"The First Time" (10)—the next poem—is not the first time the poet gazes at some species of deer. He has been doing just that in "Caribou." Here they are elk, but he pays attention to the same anatomical features in both poems: "dark bull-cape / Of *shoulders* now seeming much darker, architecture of *antlers*" ("The First Time"); "The *shoulders* / Lumber on forward, as though only the bones could, inwardly, / Guess destination. The *antlers*, / Blunted and awkward, are carved by some primitive craftsman" ("Caribou"). So easy is it to see what these two poems have in common, so close is their similarity to the surface, that one wonders what is the point of even remarking on it; if some thought went into the sequence's arrangement (which is by no means provable—it might have just happened, yet nevertheless be there, a constituent part of the text), then surely little would have been required to prompt placing two poems about observing deer side by side.

There is, however, a difference between these two poems, and it is the same difference we found between the two that precede them. In "Mortal Limit" the poet beheld a hawk soaring against the sunset, finding its mortal limit before falling back to earth, while in "Immortality Over the Dakotas" it was the poet who was in the sky and mortality that was visible on earth. In "Caribou" the deer are seen from the air (from an airplane, as the poet imagined he saw the Dakota farmer from a jetliner), while in "The First Time" they are seen from the ground. Still, so far, there is little resemblance, since the hawk in "Mortal Limit" was in the air and these elk surely cannot fly. Yet, upon closer examination, it becomes apparent not only that the poet is on the ground in "The First Time" as he was two poems back but also that pains have been taken to show that he is looking upward at those elk, as he had at the hawk: the poet and his guide Old Jack are going *down* a trail ("downward / The trail") when Old Jack tells him to look back ("Backward / Pointed"), which would be *up* the trail, to see evidence of the presence of elk (" 'Hot elk-turd,' " the guide said). The elk, he says, "come *down*/ For water at sunset." When they first see the elk, poet and guide are looking in an upward direction: "We . . . soon see *upstream* the sandbar, / Each elk." One in particular holds their attention, the great bull, "The pisser" (" 'Now ain't he a pisser!' " Old Jack had exclaimed).

As the hawk in "Mortal Limit" had been seen against the fading light of sunset (a "black speck," as the cormorant in the poem before had been "black against carmine of sunset"), so now this elk's antlers are "sharp against sky, / Balanced and noble, with prongs / Thrust into the bronze-red sky as though, / . . . to sustain . . . the massive / Sun-ball." The point of the story in the poem of the hawk was that he remained aloft as long as possible, until his mortal limit, a moment defined by sunset—or by the final extinction of lingering light; here, similarly, the elk remains backlit against the sky until after the sun touches the horizon: "The sun / Has touched snow before he turns." My point, of course, is not so much to underline the similarity between "Mortal Limit" and "The First Time," though there is one, as to show that "Caribou" and "The First Time," despite their resemblance, are mutually opposed on precisely the same basis (one, that is, of the same bases) as are the two poems that came before them.

Just such a contrasting opposition is evident in "Immortality Over the Dakotas" and "Caribou," despite the strong similarity of their airborne point of view. The poet in "Immortality" is convinced he knows precisely what is going on down below, even though he has no way of knowing it: "you see / Who must be down there," he tells us, and then says not only who it is but what he is doing and even thinking—where, that is, he is not, at least not yet, going: inside. He pleads ignorance, however, in the next poem: "We do not know on what errand they are bent, to / What mission committed. It is a world that / They live in, and it is their life" (an ignorance twice more asserted: "The shoulders / Lumber on forward, as though only the bones could, inwardly, / Guess destination." "But / They must have been going somewhere"). It is their life, of course, as it was the farmer's whose doctor has just told him how long he has left to live. But why could the poet not have drawn the same conclusion about the latter? That it is entirely reasonable to ask such a question is a measure of a certain situational sameness.

"The First Time" is a meditation on the "pisser" of a bull elk that, like the hawk in "Mortal Limit," remains motionless against the sky. Later that night, the poet awakens and still sees, remembering, "the / Great head lifted in philosophic / Arrogance against / God's own sky." "God's own sky" becomes "God's own world" in the next poem, "Minnesota Recollection" (12), in which "Old Grammy" (recalling the "Old Jack" of the poem before) might, and does, "Just step outside to the call of nature, and once out, / See snowflakes falling, falling, and ponder on it a half-hour, / Making no move, sunk deep in the world, like a part / Of *God's own world*, a post, a bare tree, dung heap, or stone." He was in the habit, that is, of doing this, except that on this occasion he never came back. He found, unfortunately, his mortal limit, for he froze to death—becoming, literally, a part of God's own world, something like a post, a tree, or a stone. What is really remarkable is the reason he went out in the first place. Warren has a marvelous way of uniting the trivial and the profound, the homely and the sublime, and this is precisely what "the call of nature" does here. For the man who froze to death was responding both to nature's invitation to become a part of her, to sink deep into her and become like a post or a stone, and to the need to take a leak. The latter call was the reason he first ventured out; the former the reason he stayed. Like the great bull elk, who stands out against "God's own sky," the man who froze to death confronts "God's own world"—though, almost paradoxically, unlike the elk, who, though a part of that world, stands out "in philosophic / Arrogance against" it, Old Grammy, by pondering, becomes a part of it.

I say "almost paradoxically" because they go in opposite directions: the elk, from a human perspective already a part of nature, becomes a philosopher and leaves it; the man, from that same perspective not so much at first a part of it, gives up his separate status (by a kind of philosophizing, too: by pondering too much: "a half-hour, / Making no move") and, by dying, becomes part of the landscape in a Lucretian sense. But the homeliness of his situation is truly *unheimlich*, in Freud's sense (who points out, in his essay on "The Uncanny," that what is *heimlich* [familiar] is sometimes, in fact, *unheimlich* [28, uncanny]). For just at this moment "Minnesota Recollection" reveals its most striking connection to "The First Time," a connection that is uncanny in its homeliness, and in its apparent irrelevance (that is, the uncanny is that which is unreasonably, irrelevantly—frighteningly—accurate, able to shock us out of our normal expectations): in responding to this doubly meant call of nature, Old Grammy becomes precisely what Old Jack said the great bull elk was, the concrete embodiment of what had only been metaphorical in the homely term that was the highest expression of praise the wilderness guide could muster for such a phenomenon of nature: " 'Now ain't he a pisser!' "

When the family back in the snowbound Minnesota farmhouse suddenly realized that Grammy had been gone too long and that he probably had no light (they found his flashlight,

dead), they went out to look for him with lanterns, but one was
dropped and the other went dry. In the darkness "They tried to
make a chain of calls, a rope / To hold the human hope together," but with no success. Before they gave up for good
"voices again picked up / The gnarled, untwisting length of
rope / Of human hope." When it was clear there was nothing
more they could do, they went back inside. "By first flame of the
prairie dawn they found him. / Snagged on a barbed-wire fence
that he'd / Followed the wrong way."

Let us cut now to the next poem, "Arizona Midnight" (15),
where we are truly in a different place and yet where some
things are strangely the same. The poet recalls lying in the desert
in a "sleeping-bag, / Protected by the looped rampart of anti-rattler horsehair rope." "Anti-rattler rope in 'Arizona Midnight,' "
Warren explains in a letter (RPW to RPR, 22 November 1986),
"simply came from the fact that an old, old man long ago told me
how, on hunting trips in the west, you used a rope around your
sleeping bag—rattlers didn't crawl over a really prickly rope."
There could be no connection between this rope and the one in
"Minnesota Recollection" (or between this anti-rattler rope and
the rattlesnake that will appear in "Far West Once," the next
poem after "Arizona Midnight"), Warren insists, because they
were written at different times. The sequence of their appearance is not the sequence of their composition.

> It is difficult to argue about the sequence of poems in actual
> composition. Even in the first section of a "Selected" poems
> there is no certainty of sequence of actual composition. All
> I mean to say here is that contiguity of poems may violate
> times of composition. Of course, this fact would not neces-
> sarily impair an argument about continuity of images or
> themes in the body of the work. But it would destroy any
> necessary value of placement in a book.
>
> In the work of a writer, I should guess, there are con-
> tinuous developments of an idea (conscious or not) or im-
> ages, even phrases. I simply mean that contiguity here
> could not be used as an argument. [RPW to RPR, 22 No-
> vember 1986]

Obviously I must disagree. Contiguity *can* be used as an argument, as long as it is understood that such an argument is not

based on the time of composition. Warren, it should be noted, does not deny that he is responsible for the placement of the poems in his sequences; indeed, in the "Afterthought" to *Being Here* he tells us that "the order and selection are determined thematically, but with echoes, repetitions, and variations"—their placement, that is, is *determined*. Simply put, what connections do arise from one poem to the next are more likely the product of the unconscious than of a conscious decision. They may, and probably do, leave no trace of conscious memory in the mind from which they emerged; but they do leave traces in the text that results. These traces are, in fact, part of what there is to read in the text.

Warren's own account of how poems are made leaves a wide avenue for the unconscious: "It is undoubtedly true that a large part of poetic composition is below the level of immediate consciousness, and very often below the level of any consciousness. It seems to me that in one sense the writer has to give his mind or feelings as fully as possible to the basic—I almost said conception—'feel' " (RPW to RPR, 7 December 1986). To reject the term "conception" in favor of "feel," as he does here, is itself to acknowledge the preeminent role of the unconscious. A poem is less something of which one (consciously) conceives than something one (partly unconsciously) feels, in a realm in which one must feel one's way. There is no accounting for what in a poem feels right to the poet when he is still writing it, when he is still in the process of accepting and rejecting possibilities—or, I would add, in the sequencing of a group of poems—and even the decisions that seem to have been consciously made are quite likely to have been made for unknown, unrealized, unconscious reasons.

Warren goes even further in denying the authority of conscious authorial intent: the conscious must hand over control not only to the unconscious but to the text itself—for what has already been written will have an influence on what is subsequently written: "Very early, of course, whatever is already composed begins to have a governing influence—but certainly in early and middle stages [an] influence more and more important. Important not only in the abstract sense of idea but even in terms of basic physical response of the writer. When it comes to tracing certain patterns of feeling or idea through the work of a single poet, the student, the reader, is really dealing, as you say, with many subconscious factors" (RPW to RPR, 7 December 1986). If I understand him correctly, the implication is that a poem such as "Arizona Midnight," if it were composed before "Minnesota Recollection," could have influenced his choice of words in the latter poem—could have led him to conceive of (or rather to feel) a chain of calls as "a rope." And this influence, which translates into something more of a "physical response" than a conscious (and hence acknowledgeable) memory, a track engraved on the body of the text (and the author) and waiting to be traced by the reader, could have had something to do with the fact that it evidently felt right to place these two poems side by side.

It is not just that the word "rope" appears in both. It is that these two ropes serve such similar purposes. The anti-rattler rope saves the sleeper from death by snakebite; the rope of calls was meant to save the wanderer's life. Within the imagic structure of "Minnesota Recollection" the rope finds an echo in the barbed-wire fence that Grammy followed in the hope it would lead him back to safety (as the two-inch-thick glass of the airplane window in "Immortality Over the Dakotas" finds one in the bifocals). It is part of what makes that poem an aesthetically pleasing whole that the image of the failing rope of calls should double back on itself in the form of the barbed wire that likewise failed to save the man's life—that actually hastened his death. It is therefore of the greatest interest to learn that anti-rattler rope, like this particular fence (when the fence serves the purpose for which it was put up, which is not to save the lost but to prevent animals from crossing over it), is *barbed*: "rattlers didn't crawl over a really prickly rope."

In "Arizona Midnight" the poet, surrounded by that prickly rope, looks eastward and sees "No indication of dawn, not yet ready for the scream / Of inflamed distance, / Which is the significance of day." Now a scream has some prominence in "Minnesota Recollection" as the first acknowledgment of Grammy's disappearance. When Gertie came back with his flashlight "dead / As a monstrous catfish eye. . . . No word she said, just screamed. . . . The scream / Ran out the open door, darker / Than Death." She would scream again when, the search given up, they go back inside. In the Arizona desert the scream that does not yet come is "the scream / Of . . . *distance*." In snowbound Minnesota, Gertie's scream is, likewise, expressed in terms of distance—both because it immediately "Ran out the open door" and because it prefigures the "chain of calls," the "untwisting length of rope / Of human hope" of cries that served both to link the searchers together (so that they, too, would not lose their way) and to reach out to Grammy across a distance that in the end proved unbridgeable.

Though dawn, in Arizona, is not yet ready to utter its scream, "dimly I do see / Against that darkness, lifting in blunt agony, / The single great cactus. . . . I strain to make out the cactus. It has / Its own necessary beauty." Within "Arizona Midnight" the prickliness of the horsehair rope is echoed by the prickliness of the cactus, as the chain and rope of calls and hope that would have led Grammy back was echoed within "Minnesota Recollection" by the barbed-wire fence that led him in the wrong direction. And part of the necessary beauty (necessary because it seems, independent of the poet's conscious will, to be the fulfillment of some logical necessity) of the text before us is the beauty of the way in which the cactus's agony recalls that of the man who was "Snagged on a barbed-wire fence."

Like the cactus ("I strain to make out the cactus"), this beauty can be seen if one stares at it long enough. One agony recalls another as the barbs on the fence are transformed into those on the cactus. (In "Afterward," in *Rumor Verified*, Warren had already anthropomorphized cacti: "Sit down by a great cactus, / While other cacti . . . life up // Their arms, thorny and black, in ritual unresting . . . to that great orb" [that is, the moon].) The fence's victim was found "By first *flame* of . . . *dawn*"; the cactus's agony is what the poet can see in the place of *dawn*'s "scream / Of *inflamed* distance." These conjunctions of solar flame with fence barbs and cactus prickles were anticipated in "The First Time," the poem before "Minnesota Recollection," by the way the setting sun's flame appeared suspended on the prongs of the elk's antlers: "now sharp against sky, / . . . with prongs / Thrust into the bronze-red sky as though, / On prong-tangs, to sustain . . . the massive / Sun-ball of *flame*."

In "Far West Once" (16), as I have noted, a rattlesnake appears: "I . . . knew / That I'd never again . . . see / The old rattler's fat belly twist." Not only the snake appears but the twisting as well, which is even more long-lived than the rattler, persisting through three contiguous poems: "Far West Once," where the rattler's belly twists; "Arizona Midnight," where, protected by the anti-rattler rope, "I take a careful *twist*" in the sleeping bag; and "Minnesota Recollection," where the voices "again picked up / The gnarled, *untwisting* length of rope."

In "Arizona Midnight" the poet waits for dawn's scream of inflamed distance, while "Far West Once" closes with "a dawn / Of dew-bright Edenic promise, with, / Far off, far off, in verdurous shade, first birdsong." That first bird finds a peculiar reply near the close of the next poem, "Rumor at Twilight" (18), when the "*first bat* / Mathematically zigzags the stars." The rumor of the title—"Rumor at twilight of whisper, crepuscular / Agitation"— was anticipated by a soft twilight noise in "Far West Once," the "musical murmur / Of waters" first perceived "in the gloaming" (that is, in the evening dusk) as the poet, walking up a trail, was "lulled by the stone-song of waters." The stream's murmur returns in "Old Dog Dead" (19), the poem after "Rumor at Twilight," when the poet, having had to take the family dog to the vet to have it put to sleep, goes out at night to sit on a mossy stone and "Stare, intent / On the *stream's* now messageless *murmur* of motion."

These three poems are in fact linked by several strands. The "first birdsong" of "Far West Once" becomes, as I have noted, the "first bat / [that] Mathematically zigzags the stars" in "Rumor at Twilight"—while in "Old Dog Dead" it's a star (actually a planet) that behaves mathematically: "Now Jupiter . . . in the implacable / Mathematics of a planet, / Has set." The connection between bat and heavenly body, and between these neighboring poems, is evident as well in the verb that attaches to each: "In a dark cave, / Dark fruit, bats *hang*" in "Rumor at Twilight," while in "Old Dog Dead" "The stars are high-*hung*." In "Rumor at Twilight," after the first bat comes out to zigzag the stars, "You fling down / The cigarette butt. Set heel on it"—a gesture that echoes the moment in "Far West Once" when the poet felt his "boots / Crush gravel, or press the soundlessness / Of detritus of pine or fir." That gravel returns in "Rumor at Twilight" when the poet thinks of how, in a cave, generations of bat droppings, "soft underfoot, would carpet the *gravel*," while the detritus of pine reappears, dispersed, in "Old Dog Dead," in two moments that are in fact connected; the earth, red clay streaked with / Black of humus under / The tall *pine*, anonymous in / The vet's woodlot" has, that is, a real but perhaps not immediately evident relation to "The unlabeled *detritus* and trash of Time" in the poem's last line that the poet imagines his daughter (whose puppy the dog had once been), when she will have become an old woman, "Now alone, waking before dawn to fumble for" in the dark. For when the poet dies, she will be "the last to remember tonight" (a similar concern is voiced later in the collection in "Re-interment: Recollection of a Grandfather" [49], when the poet remarks that when he dies there will be no one to remember his grandfather's face; there, too, there are "fingers fumbling" in the dark—they belong to the grandfather's ghost in the poet's skull). The connection between this unlabeled detritus and trash of Time and the dog is thus already explicit, but it is heightened by the way *unlabeled* echoes *anonymous*. So when the poet in "Far West Once" feels his "boots / Crush gravel, or press the soundlessness / Of detritus of pine," he is almost already stepping on the "unlabeled detritus" of that anonymous grave under the pine.

One more echo deserves mention. In "Rumor at Twilight" the poet speaks of what happens "when, *in darkness*, your head first / Dents the dark pillow, *eyes wide*, ceilingward. / Can you really reconstruct your mother's smile?" In "Old Dog Dead" the smile reappears in the eyes of his daughter, in his memory of how they were "Dancing with joy-light" when she first saw the puppy. "That was what my *eyes, open in darkness*, / Had now just seen."

The immediately following "Hope" (22) adds another link to the chain of flying creatures (in "Far West Once" the "first birdsong") and bats (in "Rumor at Twilight" the "first bat"), except that now they are no longer first but last: "Soon, / While not even a last bird twitters, the last bat goes." But it is in these lines that "Hope" seems to express the most intriguing reminiscence of what has gone before: "The first star petals timidly in what / Is not yet darkness." As "detritus of pine" in "Far West Once" anticipated the identity within the poem that would follow, uniting the "unlabeled detritus and trash of Time" with the dog's unlabeled grave beneath the "pine, anonymous in / The vet's woodlot," so here this subject and this verb bring together once more the elements of what in fact belongs together in "Old Dog Dead." But to show that it belongs together it may be necessary to take a detour through another poem, one not by Warren, but one that his poem here seems convincingly to evoke. The passage in "Old Dog Dead" is:

Now Jupiter, southwest, beyond the sagging black spur
Of the mountain, in the implacable
Mathematics of a planet,
Has set. Tell me,
Is there a garden where
The petal, dew-kissed, withereth not?

The question about the possibility of a petal untouched by decay
follows immediately upon the heels of Jupiter's disappearance—
and it is apparent that the petal's withering parallels Jupiter's
disappearing—while in the poem that immediately follows these
two events are conflated (though reversed, from disappearance
to first appearance, from death to birth) in the form of a petaling
star.

Now Jupiter disappears too, seeming to die, and a daughter
weeps, in that other poem, Whitman's "On the Beach at Night."

On the beach at night,
Stands a child with her father,
Watching the east, the autumn sky.

Up through the darkness,
While ravening clouds, the burial clouds, in black masses
    spreading,
Lower sullen and fast athwart and down the sky,
Amid a transparent clear belt of ether yet left in the east,
Ascends large and calm the lord-star Jupiter,
And nigh at hand, only a very little above,
Swim the delicate sisters the Pleiades.

From the beach the child holding the hand of her father,
Those burial-clouds that lower victorious soon to devour all,
Watching, silently weeps.

We can hear her weeping, too, it seems, in "Old Dog Dead": "Far
off, a little girl, little no longer, would, / If yet she knew, / Lie in
her bed and weep / For what life is." In both poems a father con-
soles, or would console, a daughter in the face of death, figured
in the disappearance of stars (in particular, Jupiter). The father
in Warren's poem is alone; he would comfort his daughter if she
were there, if she knew. He goes out, at night, not to a beach but

to the edge of a stream to contemplate the stars. In Whitman's poem, the stars are seen as if through water: "And nigh at hand . . . / *Swim* the delicate sisters the Pleiades"; in Warren, they are seen, some of the time, reflected in the stream: "The stars are high-hung, clearly / Defined in night's cloudlessness, / But here, below, identity blurred / In the earth-bound waver of water. // Upward again I look. See Jupiter, contemptuous, / Noble, firmly defined." Warren's Jupiter is noble, Whitman's is "the lord-star." Whitman's Jupiter is devoured by "*black* masses" of "burial-clouds," while Warren's disappears "beyond the sagging *black* spur / Of the mountain."

"On the Beach at Night" does not simply reappear (as Whitman's father promised his daughter that "Jupiter shall emerge . . . again another night"), resurrected, in "Old Dog Dead." For there is a significant difference between the poems, one announced by what the father in Warren's poem, remembering the anonymous grave in the vet's woodlot, thinks of doing: "Absurdly, / I think I might go and put, stuck in the clay, / A stone—any stone large enough. No word, just something / To make a change, however minute, / In the structure of the universe." Now Warren disclaims all memory of Whitman's poem: "Perhaps I had read [it], but that had been so long back that I did not think of it again until you mention the title and quote from the poem. . . . Certainly, it was not one of the many poems or passages [from Whitman] that I could remember. I must say, however, that your argument here would sound totally convincing" (RPW to RPR, 22 November 1986). Were it possible, however, to imagine that he had intentionally set out to rewrite it, the gesture contemplated here would have come uncannily close to describing such a rewriting. For what Warren would have done (had he done it) would have been to add the stone—that is, to add the dog for which the stone is, as it happens, the convenient symbol—to the story of Jupiter's disappearance, a daughter's grief, and a father's consolation. Significantly, perhaps, Warren's personal denial itself finds a parallel of sorts in the poem, in the father's disavowal of literary ambition. I will not, he declares, actually write anything on that grave. I will simply make the slightest possible change that is still a change—the very limit case of a change: "No word, just something / To make a change, however minute." I have not really been influenced by Whitman's poem (much less wanted to inscribe my poem on his), since I haven't the slightest recollection of it.

In "Hope," a certain echo intrudes: the evening sun's "gold *intrusive* through the blackening spruce boughs" and the "*intrusion* of truth or lie" that has been afflicting the poet's soul all day. "Let your soul // Be still," the poet advises himself, for soon "the moon // Will dominate the sky, the world, the heart, / In white forgiveness." In "Why You Climbed Up" (23) it is the poet who intrudes: "where the rusty needle / Falls from the pine to pad earth's silence / Against what *intrusive* foot may come, you come." The poet's self-advice in "Hope" to let his soul be still, to "Lay . . . aside" the intrusive "truth or lie" and to find peace in "The promise / Of moonrise" bears a strong resemblance to the reason why he will have climbed up the mountain in "Why You Climbed Up." It was "As though to forget and leave / All things . . . you call / The past" and "The Self." And it was also because he could remember the same kind of event that in "Hope" he was promising his troubled soul, a moonlit experience: in "Hope," we recall, "The promise / Of moonrise will dawn, and . . . the moon // Will dominate the sky . . . / In white forgiveness." In "Why You Climbed Up" "you . . . remember . . . how once / In the moonlit Pacific you swam west hypnotized / By stroke on stroke."

Hypnosis recurs in "Literal Dream" (24), whose subtitle explains how it is, in fact, a literary dream: "(Twenty Years After Reading *Tess* and Without Ever Having Seen Movie)." In his dream, the poet is present, like a ghostly spectator, in Hardy's novel, in the downstairs room where the old woman's eyes "widen in *hypnotic* slowness" as she becomes aware of a stain growing on her ceiling. The liquid spot "gathered to a / Point. / Which hung forever"—strangely like the afternoon's silence in the poem before, which "Like substance hangs"—before it dropped. What happens next had also happened before: In "Why You Climbed Up," the "rusty needle / Falls," while in "Literal Dream," the "knitting needles . . . dropped."

In the last stanza the poet gives what appears to be an explanation of the physiological stimulus that could have given rise to the dream:

I woke at the call of nature. It was near day.
Patient I sat, staring through the

Wet pane at sparse drops that struck
The last red dogwood leaves. It was as though
I could hear the plop there. See the leaf quiver.

He dreamed this dream for the same reason that Old Grammy in "Minnesota Recollection" went outside and froze to death, to answer the call of nature. He dreamed, that is, of a drop on the ceiling that hung forever before it fell because he had a great need to micturate. It was this bodily demand that caused him to awaken ("I woke at the call of nature").

But nature cooperates, accompanying this dream and the dreamer's awakening with falling drops of its own, whose sound, if it could be heard during sleep, could just as easily have provoked such a dream. Later in this sequence, "Whatever You Now Are" (76) will explore what can happen when one falls asleep to the sound of water: "Are the stream and the Self conjunct all night long . . . ? What elements, shadowy, in that dream interlace . . . ?" The drop that fell from the ceiling was red in *Tess* and hence also in the dream: "I could not make out the color. . . . / But knew. I knew because I'd read the book." The drops outside his window are not, of course, red, but they come remarkably close: "sparse drops that struck / The last *red* dogwood leaves." Their redness, Freud would have said, was displaced onto the surface where they fell.

Yet nature, viewed through the wet windowpane, also seconds the dream in a way that is less easily connected to its cause: "It was as though / I could hear the plop there. See the leaf quiver." For this quiver appears in the dream, or is conspicuous by its absence, when, having dropped her needles, the old lady gathers her courage to touch the drop that had fallen to the floor: "then, / The finger, sharpening in massive will, / Suddenly no quivering, / Touched." If the poet gives the appearance of interpreting his own dream by allowing one to draw the conclusion that it had been prompted by the call of nature that woke him up (Freud contended, by the way, that dreams "serve the purpose of prolonging sleep instead of waking up. Dreams are the guardians of sleep and not its disturbers" [267]; hence such a dream as this was meant not to alert the sleeper to his need but to disguise it, to translate it into something else—namely the drop that hung forever before falling), then how could one interpret this quivering echo after the fact?

Dreams, of course, have more than one cause, as the poem it-self seems to be telling us. For it appears to suggest two different causes, both somatic: the call of nature, and the sleeper's hearing the sound of the rain outside—as, in "Whatever You Now Are," the poet will wonder what effect the sound of a murmuring stream can have on his dreams. "Dream of a Dream" (30), in the earlier sequence *Now and Then*, gave an even fuller account of the multiple causality of dreams when it spoke of "the braiding texture of dream"—in which the braids are Time and water: "In my dream Time and water interflow, / And bubbles of con-sciousness glimmer ghostly as they go." "Dream of a Dream" presents, in fact, a theory of dreaming wholly consistent with Freud's account in *The Interpretation of Dreams*. For somatic stim-uli (such as hearing the murmur of water outside one's window or feeling the call of nature) are not in themselves sufficient to prompt a dream, according to either Freud or these poems. Such physiological promptings must be combined with something else before a dream is born. Warren calls it Time; for Freud, too, it is the past: the more immediate past of the "day's residues," what is remembered from the day that has just passed as well as more ancient memories. Warren speaks much the same language in an early *Fugitive* poem:

> . . . sleep, the dark wherein you all are piled,
> Poor fragments of the day, until there come
> Dreams to release from the troubled heart and deep
> The pageantry of thoughts unreconciled.
>   ["Images on the Tomb."]

Here Freud's "day's residues" become the "Poor fragments of the day" and dreams are said to be what Freud argued they were, a pageant of unreconciled thoughts from deep within a troubled heart.

As Freud put it: "stimuli arising during sleep are worked up into a wish-fulfilment the other constituents of which are the fa-miliar psychical 'day's residues'" (262). And in greater detail: "The dream-work is under the necessity of combining into a unity all instigations to dreaming which are active simultane-ously. . . . when two or more experiences capable of creating an impression are left over from the previous day, the wishes derived from them are combined in a single dream, and simi-larly . . . the psychically significant impression and the in-different experiences from the previous day are brought to-gether in the dream-material, provided always that it is pos-sible to set up communicating ideas between them" (261).

I have quoted Freud at such length for good reason. It is not just that some of Warren's poems—"Literal Dream," "Whatever You Now Are," "Dream of a Dream," and others—speak a dis-course on dreaming so consonant with his but that they appear as well to enact, literally, the very dreamwork of which Freud speaks. These insistent echoes, repetitions, and variations from one poem to the next can be described, that is, in the same way that Freud described how a dream picks up those poor frag-ments of the day, both "psychically significant" and "indifferent experiences," and combines them in a single dream by setting up communicating ideas between them. Thus the needles that fell from the tree in "Why You Climbed Up" fall again in "Literal Dream" and are connected (by what Freud would have called a communicating idea) with the "hypnotic" slowness with which the lady who dropped them widened her eyes—even though the "hypnotized" state of the swimmer in the poem before was not so clearly connected to that poem's falling pine needles (in this in-stance, they are actually more connected in the second poem, where they are elements in the same episode, than they were in the first, where they belonged to two separate incidents—though in the latter they were of course, ultimately related, since they were part of the same aesthetic whole, the poem). It is one way to account for the facts, a form of analysis that may be particularly useful because it explicitly seeks to account for the workings of the unconscious—and the unconscious seems after all to be in charge. The unconscious in charge, of course, is that of the poet, which, as I have suggested, is quite capable of remembering more than his conscious realizes. The result, however, whatever its mysterious origins, is a text that gives the striking appearance of having an unconscious of its own—a text, that is, that dreams.

The hypnosis that was first apparent in "Why You Climbed Up," when the poet "swam west, hypnotized" in the moonlit Pa-cific, and that immediately returned in "Literal Dream," when the old lady's eyes "widened in hypnotic slowness," makes a third sequential appearance in "After the Dinner Party" (26), when one of two people seated at the table after their guests have left "Moves soundless, as in hypnotic certainty" to the other end of the table, so that hands might touch. "How long it seems till a hand finds that hand there laid." The situations recounted in this poem and in "Literal Dream" are as different as can be, but with what uncanny certainty does the latter's residue reappear, recycled, here. Four fragments, at least, have returned: (1) the hypnotic state (and the repeated words in "*in hypnotic* slowness" and "*in hypnotic* certainty"), (2) the drawn-out slowness (3) until a finger touched something or hands touched each other (and, again, a repeated phrase: "*How long* would it now take for the tremble / Of finger to sharpen into the instrument / To touch / The spot . . . ?" and "*How long* it seems till a hand finds that hand there laid"), and (4) a falling red liquid: the drop of blood on the ceiling "Which hung forever" before it "Dropped" and the red wine that is suspended, gravity-less, before it, too, inevitably falls, in the opening lines:

> You two sit at the table late, each now and then,
> Twirling a near-empty wine glass to watch the last red
> Liquid climb up the crystalline spin to the last moment when
> Centrifugality fails.

In addition, for the third time, a precisely repeated phrase—"*the last red* / Liquid"—here recalls "*The last red* dogwood leaves" that received the drops of rain.

The "now and then" that concludes the first line of "After the Dinner Party" will reappear, with new meaning, and new emphasis (in italics that are Warren's own), in the opening lines of "Doubleness in Time" (27).

> Doubleness coils in Time like
> The bull-snake in fall's yet-leafed growth. *Then*
> Uncoils like *Now. Now*
> Like *Then.*

The "now and then" of "After the Dinner Party" is, to all appearances, the most insignificant of expressions, not far from being the most insignificant part of the poem, almost nothing more than a formulaic turn of phrase. But like the stone the builders rejected, it becomes the cornerstone of "Doubleness in Time," which breaks that turn of phrase apart to begin a meditation on how alike, and how different, its constituent elements are. Each is the double of the other, as in fact the two appearances of "now and then" are: *Then* is to *Now* as the "now and then" of "After the Dinner Party" is to the *Then* and *Now* of "Doubleness in Time." The meditation in "Doubleness in Time" on *Then* and *Now* could be taken, that is, as a self-referential meditation on the relation of this "now and then" to the one that preceded it.

Warren's poems provide more than one metaphor to talk about what it is they do—and, of particular concern in this instance, about what their sequences do. Their analogy to the dreamwork of the unconscious is one; "Doubleness in Time" (both in itself and in its relation to "After the Dinner Party") suggests another: that the poems in sequence unfold like Time, which itself coils and uncoils like a snake (coiling like a snake hiding in the underbrush, ready to stage a surprise; uncoiling to reveal the return of the same, *Then* uncoiling like *Now*, as well as the other way around). In "Identity and Argument for Prayer" (66), a poem in the collection appropriately titled *Now and Then* (which, as it happens, is the first sequence in which these sequential echoes seem to appear), Time is serpentine in yet another way: "Have you ever / Seen serpentine Time at the instant it swallowed its tail?" And in that poem, what happened before happens again, as it does in "Doubleness in Time"—doubly so: (1) in the narrative "Doubleness in Time" recounts, in which the poet experiences his mother's death fifty years earlier as if "now at last it truly / Happens. Only *Now*"; and (2) in the way the "now and then" of the poem before returns, like a meaningless fragment of the day before, to become a constituent part of the dream of the poem. In "Identity and Argument for Prayer," the poet, walking on a beach, treads his old footprints of years before, "making new the old tracks / . . . As though I had dreamed all the years / This dream of return." And finds that "what did happen *there* is—just now / In its new ectoplasmic context— / Happening again!" (Warren's italics). There and here, then and now, the mystery of identity ("that old *I* is not I any more . . . the *I* here now / Is not dead, only what / I have now turned into. This / Is the joke you must live with" (Warren's italics): a constant concern in Warren's poetry, all the more pervasive in that it is reenacted in the poems themselves, as these returning nows and thens reveal.

"Doubleness in Time," perhaps more than most poems in this collection, finds so obvious an origin in the poet's personal experience—the death of his mother fifty years before—that any connection with other poems in the sequence, including those that just happen to be in the same part of the sequence, seems highly unlikely. As Warren says of "After the Dinner Party" and "Literal Dream": "I happen to remember the process of writing those two poems and I can promise you, insofar as such a promise can be made, that I remember the emotional quality that went into the two moments of composition" (RPW to RPR, 7 December 1986). That is, he can remember their respective emotional origins and can assure me that they were not the same and that neither poem was written with any (conscious) thought of the other. I am not, of course, arguing that the emotions or the origins were the same (a distinction that was not as clear as it might have been in the version of this chapter to which Warren was responding) but just that the words ("in hypnotic . . . in hypnotic"; "How long . . . How long"; "the last red . . . The last red") and some situational elements *are* (the drawn-out slowness of a finger touching the spot on the floor and of a hand reaching out to find another hand; a suspended red liquid that finally falls). And I am trying to make sense—with Freud's help and that of Warren himself—of why they are.

It is, as it happens, at the most private of moments for the poet, the moment of his mother's death in "Doubleness in Time," at the very moment she gives her son and the rest of the family her last smile, and after each of these farewells stares up at the ceiling that something happens in the poem to deny the particularity of that moment:

> The face fixes on each face, and for
> Each face constructs
> A smile.
> . . . .
> Her eyes, after each effort, fix
> On the ceiling of white plaster above them. The pink
> Of sunset tints the ceiling. I stare
> At the ceiling. It is Infinity.

The event in the most uncanny and perhaps even upsetting way wrenches that moment out of its uniqueness to remind us that this is not just a poem but part of a larger work of art, the larger text of the sequence that includes anticipatory echoes of this very moment. We have, that is, already seen a woman staring up at a white ceiling: "it was / On paint, on whitewash, on paper, whatever / The ceiling was. I can't remember." It is tempting to say that he *can* remember now: it was white plaster. And it is more than tempting, but surely quite reasonable, to say that "Literal Dream" is really about—was prompted by the memory of—the death of the mother as "Doubleness in Time" recounts it and that at this moment, assisted by a careful attention to the sequential echoes and anticipations these poems display, we have begun to get a glimpse of the "buried narrative"—which is, after all, a family plot—that lies here.

For not only do both the woman in the dream of *Tess* and the poet's mother stare up at a white ceiling, but what they see there is—as certain subtle and sequential transformations in these poems suggest—strikingly similar. Specifically, what the woman in "Literal Dream" saw on the ceiling was red, although much is made in the poem of the refusal to say that it was. In fact it is precisely because the poet "could not make out the color" yet "knew . . . knew because I'd read the book" that it is all the more likely that the memory—repressed, in this instance—of the scene of his mother's death is at work in the dream. It should be noted that the other detail of the dream of which he said he wasn't sure—what it was the white ceiling was made of—is part of this very cluster of remembered yet acknowledged images (it's in the account of her death, as I have noted, that he declares it was plaster rather than paint or whitewash).

Within "Literal Dream" the named (by the reference to the book) yet unnamed color is in fact named by the manner in which it is displaced onto "The last red" leaves that the drops of rain struck as their fall and splash paralleled those of what was on the ceiling. And what happened then—for these sequential changes behave like a narrative themselves, a chain of events, of things that *happen*—was that "The last red" immediately reappeared in the next poem ("After the Dinner Party"), still a liquid, but changed into wine. It would appear, at this juncture, that the pink of sunset tinting the white plaster ceiling that was the very last thing the poet's mother saw on this earth has more in common with its incarnation in "Literal Dream," where it appeared on a white ceiling, than with the "last red / Liquid" in the dinner party wineglass in the poem that more immediately precedes it. Nevertheless, like the wine, this pink has something last about it, for it is, coming as it does from the sunset, both the last light of day and the last light she will see. Lest I be accused of going too far, let me quote yet another sequential—and therefore, it must surely be granted by now, significant—echo, in this instance from the poem that immediately *follows* "Doubleness in Time" ("Snowfall" [30]): "Over my western hill the white cavalry comes / To blot the last dying crimson that outlines the slope." Here the light of sunset is precisely described as last and as red—and, perhaps even more to the point, as dying.

One more transformation: the smile that, dying, the mother gives each mourner—that most personal and private of communications—does not, perhaps, belong to the mother alone. For when it appears, it is already the echo of another smile, namely the one the couple at the dinner table in the poem just before remember on the face of a loved one long gone: "tonight one guest has quoted a killing phrase we owe / To a lost one whose grin, in eternal atrophy, / Now in dark celebrates some last unworded jest none can know." That echo is strengthened by the circumstance that both the smile and the grin are seen in death. And it is even further strengthened in its quality of being an echo—of being an apparent, if unwitting, quotation—by the fact that the grin in "After the Dinner Party" is itself evoked through quotation (the living guest's quotation of the grinner's jest).

The sun's "last dying crimson" that snow's white cavalry blots out in "Snowfall" is not only, as I have pointed out, an echo of the pink of sunset tinting the white plaster ceiling about the dying mother in "Doubleness in Time"—both, that is, being a last red, and dying, light—but also its reversal: instead of white becoming pink, crimson is replaced by white. At the end of the poem, white's conquest of red is celebrated once more: "cottony hooves, the wheeling of squadrons, / That tramp out last embers of day." But in the meantime the seasons pass, the white giving way to green: "Years pass, and always so much to remember, forget: the first / Green to spring in green turf advertising / Earth's old immortality." In "Snowfall" the insistent military imagery is the central framing metaphor of the poem, apparent at its opening and close. "Squadrons" of airborne (that is, snowy) "cavalry" with "no creaking of stirrup, no steel-flash," invade the landscape to accomplish the strategic objective of blotting out the dying crimson ("Was there a bugle?" the poet asks, continuing the militarization of the landscape, "Or only wind in the spruces?").

This sudden appearance of military imagery in *Altitudes and Extensions* (not quite the first: recall "the enemy fleet below the horizon, in / Its radio blackout, unobserved" in "Rumor at Twilight") heralds more than a change in the weather; it announces the poem to follow, Warren's sustained meditation on the bombing of Hiroshima (a major work in its own right, originally written for another context, having been commissioned to serve as preface to a new deluxe edition of John Hersey's *Hiroshima* [New York: Limited Editions Club, 1983]). This is a poem whose title answers the transformation in "Snowfall" of meteorology into military metaphor by making a meteorological metaphor from what had been a military operation: "New Dawn" (32). "There, / The apocalyptic blaze of / New dawn // Bursts. // Temperature at heart of fireball: / 50,000,000 degrees centigrade." The connections between the two poems are even more intricate than that; and are in each instance a reversal: in "Snowfall" the sun's light is blotted out by the military force of what falls from the sky; in "New Dawn" a new sun is created by what falls from the sky. The abolished sunset in "Snowfall" is followed by an artificial sunrise in "New Dawn."

"New Dawn" is an extraordinary poem not only in its subject but also in its treatment of that subject. The bombing run of the *Enola Gay* is recounted in so bare bones a way that it seems at times to be a poem only because one has faith that it is one—particularly at the outset, where the first of its fifteen sections is nothing more than a table telling what time it was in seven different places when it happened:

I. EXPLOSION: SEQUENCE AND SIMULTANEITY

Greenwich Time	11:16 PM	August 5	1945
New York Time	6:16 PM	August 5	1945
Chicago Time	5:16 PM	August 5	1945
.			
.			
.			
Hiroshima Time	8:16 AM	August 6	1945

Or in part 5, a great deal of which is nothing more than the technical manual for assembling the bomb: "1. Plugs, identified by the color green, / Are installed in waiting sockets / 2. Rear plate is removed / 3. Armor plate is removed / 4. Breech wrench frees breech plug / 5. Breech plug is placed on rubber mat / 6. Explosive charge is reinserted, / Four units, red ends to breech." The atomic bomb dropped on Hiroshima, it would seem, is a reality so compelling that all a poet can do is cite the facts of what happened. It is not to be embroidered.

The facts speak for themselves, in their own context. But in a somewhat larger context, they speak for more than just that truth, important and horrible as it is. In the context of the sequence that "New Dawn" and "Snowfall" together form, the very idea itself—central to the poem—of a militarily induced "new dawn" turns out to be part of a larger embroidery. And the homely and even dreary details of the breech plugs so matter-of-factly (and seemingly unpoetically) reproduced in part 5 are not without their irrelevant (to the poem's ostensible subject) relevance either. The bomb could not be activated if a certain final, precise instruction were not followed: "Later, 6:30 A.M. Japanese Time, last lap to target, green plugs / On the log, with loving care, tenderly, quietly / As a thief, will be replaced by plugs marked / Lethally red." This substitution of red for green has its own reason for being, since "New Dawn" was based on the facts of what happened, but it was anticipated (not in time but in the sequence of events in *Altitudes and Extensions*) by what happens in the poem just before: there white replaces red as the snow blots out the light of sunset (itself the reversal of the white ceiling's rubescence in the poem before that); but winter's white will give way to green ("the first / Green to spring in green turf advertising / Earth's old immortality")—while the color that disappeared with the sunset will come back, too, when "autumn bends with weight glossy and red." White has the last word in "Snowfall," for the green and red of the changing seasons are recalled only in memory, while the present overwhelming reality is the "silence of cottony hooves, the wheeling of squadrons, / That tramp out last embers of day"—in the last words of the poem, "the darkness of whiteness / Which is the perfection of Being." And in "New Dawn" the change from greed to red also leads to a certain perfection in whiteness: the "plume . . . / Of pure whiteness" that mounts from the center of the mushroom cloud. In the end, we will be where we were two poems earlier, in "Doubleness in Time," when this conflict of colors began (when white first turned to red on the ceiling that bore his mother's final gaze), staring at the ceiling:

15. SLEEP

Some men, no doubt, will, before sleep, consider
One thought: I am alone. But some,
In the mercy of God, or booze, do not

Long stare at the dark ceiling.

That the bombers of Hiroshima should in the end assume what had been, two poems earlier, the final pose of the poet's mother is, to say the least, shocking. One might want to say as well that the fact that they do is pure coincidence and that mothers could have nothing to do with what happened on August 6, 1945. On the other hand, thanks to the name he gave his bomber ("the plane, which he / Has named for his mother, Enola Gay"), Colonel Tibbets's cargo—infantlike, as if in a maternal interior, "So quiet, so gentle as it rocks / In its dark cradle, in nameless- ness. . . . / It sleeps, with its secret name / And nature"—was borne in his mother's belly ("The air-slick belly where death sleeps").

In "Doubleness of Time," the account of his mother's death, the poet too found himself staring at the ceiling that had caught his mother's gaze: "Her eyes . . . fix / On the ceiling. . . . I stare / At the ceiling. It is Infinity. // It roofs all Time." At the close of that poem he would stare again upward: "It is autumn, *Now* as *Then* (Warren's italics), for it was in October that she died.

The moon is full, white, but
Westering above black roofs
Of the little city.
People live there.

I stare at the moon,
And wonder why it has never moved all these years.

I do not know why, nor know
Why my grief has not been understood, nor why
It has not understood its own being.

It takes a long time for it to learn
Its many names: like
Selfishness and *Precious Guilt.*[Warren's italics]

That the men who bombed Hiroshima should in the end assume the same ceiling-staring posture that the poet's mother did in death is not, then, so difficult to understand or to accept. First, the proper comparison may be less with the poet's mother than with the poet himself, who likewise stared at that ceiling (though not, like his mother and the *Enola Gay* captain and crew, from a supine position). Second, both poems are about guilt, particularly at their close. Had Colonel Tibbets ever felt a twinge of guilt for naming his instrument of death for his mother? Neither that guilt nor any for the bombing itself is recorded here, only the possibility that "some men" (that is, among Tibbets and his crew) might consider, just before they fall asleep, that they are alone and that others, thanks to the great quantity of alcohol they consumed in their congratulatory feasting, might not have stared long at that ceiling. Yet the way that all things fit together is perhaps instructive: the booze that curtailed such ceiling staring can recall, for the reader, if not for the crew of the *Enola Gay*, the maternal womb imagery used in "New Dawn" in connection with the way the bomb was transported "In its dark cradle," in the "*belly* where death sleeps," for the drink with the power to make them forget, and not long stare, has taken over the bomb's ventral space: "the slosh / Of expensive alcohol / In *bellies* expensively swollen."

If it is fitting to pay some attention to the words that are repeated in a poem and to where they are repeated, it is likewise legitimate to do so for entire phrases in a poetic sequence, especially for poems as close together as "Doubleness in Time" and "New Dawn." A case in point appears at this juncture, when the westering moon—"The moon is full, white, but / *Westering* above black roofs / Of the little city. / People live there"—at which the poet stared at the end of "Doubleness in Time" (which gains in significance for having replaced the white plaster ceiling that bore his upward gaze at the beginning: those "black roofs" recall how the white ceiling "roofs all Time") should reappear in, of all places, "New Dawn": "Over Iwo Jima, the moon, now *westering*, sinks." The land- and skyscape in "New Dawn" thus bears a troubling resemblance to the one that captured the poet's attention two poems back when he meditated on his maternal grief and guilt. In "Doubleness in Time" the westering moon was visible above the roofs of "the little city. / People live there"— words that come back to haunt us now, in "New Dawn," when we realize that we know that city's name: "Movement begins / In the city below. People / May even copulate. Pray. Eat." It is Hiroshima.

If there is something vaguely unsettling about the discovery that despite the importance of its subject "New Dawn" is just as likely as any other poem in the sequence to be haunted by echoes from other poems, that it does not function poetically only on its own terms but also in ways that seem unrelated to its apparent subject (that somehow its chosen subject of Hiroshima is subordinate to, or coexists with, other concerns), then we should welcome the opportunity to examine more closely the essence of this troubling doubleness that the very first words of the poem, already quoted, provide:

I. EXPLOSION: SEQUENCE AND SIMULTANEITY

This heading, it will be recalled, introduces the coordination of "Hiroshima Time, 8:16 A.M., August 6, 1945," with the time in Greenwich, New York, and Chicago (and San Francisco, Pearl Harbor, and Tinian Island). Like the lines in part 5 that are nothing more than the instruction manual for assembling the bomb, this first section of the poem is itself a little scandalous. Is it poetry? Is this all there is? Is it simply there to make the reader face up to the banality of reality (and evil), or could it—as poetry, particularly Warren's, normally does—mean something else at the same time? As for part 5, we have seen that the replacement of green breech plugs by red is not without some larger resonance. Here the heading that Warren has given this section, requoted above, makes it possible to see that this is not in fact all there is. *Sequence and simultaneity* is in fact the name of the game, the precise description of the kind of reading it seems to me that these poems encourage and in which I have been engaging here. That is, I have been reading the poems in sequence, thereby discovering the persistence of one poem in the next, and thus the simultaneity, the copresence, of squadrons that blot out the last light of the sunset and a bombing crew whose mission was to create a new dawn.

If "New Dawn" is, among other things, an attempt to determine exactly how such a thing as Hiroshima could happen, with consequently an almost scientific attention to the detail of the historical record, it serves at the same time as another kind of record for the reader, for the closer the poem comes to the facts of the matter, the more nearly, perhaps paradoxically, it lays bare the machinery of sequence and simultaneity that so pervades the text in which it appears. We have seen, in the case of the red and green plugs, that the more we learn about how the bomb is assembled, the more we also learn about how these poems are put together. Indeed, while we cannot necessarily credit Warren with the design on the front cover of his book—*New and Selected* and *1923-1985* on a green background, *Poems* on red and *Robert Penn Warren* on white—it does anticipate the bomb's own construction: red and green components that, when properly combined, eventuate in a plume of white.

"New Dawn" is remarkably specific about its construction. We are told the bomb's dimensions—"The cargo, / Inert as a sawed-off tree trunk ten feet long"—and more than we probably already knew about how it works. There are two parts to the bomb, one at either end of that ten-foot length, with a nonatomic explosive device in between that causes them to come together for the atomic explosion:

Like the dumb length of tree trunk, but literally
A great rifle barrel packed with uranium,
Two sections, forward one large, to rear one small, the two
Divided by a "tamper" of neutron-resistant alloy.
All harmless until, backed by vulgar explosive, the small will
Crash through to
The large mass
To wake it from its timeless drowse. And that

Will be that. Whatever
That may be. [Warren's italics]

EXPLOSION: From SEQUENCE (one at either end) to SIMUL-
TANEITY (their explosive encounter). Now, what happens
next, in the sequence of this book's construction, is a poem whose
subject is precisely about the distance between two dangerously
unstable entities, about how that distance is overcome, and about
the resulting catastrophe. In "The Distance Between: Picnic of
Old Friends" (41), a man and a woman, each married to someone
else, meet again at a picnic after many years. Innocently recalling
the past, they drift away from their spouses and children, wander up the hillside to a

> glen, where moss-streaked and noble, great cliffs
> From ferns rose, and no bird sang. Ten feet
> Apart they stopped. Stood. Each fearing
> The sudden silence too much to lift eyes.
>
> Of a sudden, she stared. Watched that face, start and strange,
>   moving,
> Through distance, at her.
>
> No resistance: seizure, penetration.

The distance between this episode and what "New Dawn" recounts is immense—not only in subject matter but in time as
well: Warren writes that " 'Picnic' was written well before the
other poem, probably years." And that the reason he gave the
bomb's length as ten feet was that that was in fact its actual length
(RPW to RPR, 7 December 1986). Yet earlier manuscript versions
do not show such a concern for historical accuracy, as they give it
variously as "fifteen," "near-fifteen," and "some fourteen feet
long.") Despite its improbability, the parallel is striking. Though
to consider these two sequential poems simultaneously in this
manner is clearly unauthorized by the author (which does not
mean it is not authorized by the text), the possibility is not exactly ruled out either: "When you come to the poem 'Picnic of
Old Friends' in relation to 'New Dawn,' I was surprised at the
connection. But my surprise would not necessarily work against
your being right about a subconscious connection in writing.

That simply lies beyond my awareness. But the actual awareness cannot be, as such, a decisive fact in this kind of reasoning. It is quite clear, in general, that patterns may exist, patterns of this kind, without the writer's awareness" (RPW to RPR, 22 November 1986).

Something of this pattern can even be detected within "New Dawn" itself. The number ten that is so remarkable a factor in the parallel between the two parts of the bomb and the two participants in adultery (so much so that the title itself of the second poem—"The Distance Between"—may already seem an echo of the specific circumstances detailed in that earlier account) functions elsewhere in "New Dawn" to stand for the very thing that I may be guilty of here. There is a place, that is, in "New Dawn" for me—a place where my role as bringer of excess baggage (when I read too much into the poem) is at the same time acknowledged and rejected—and that place is defined, precisely, by a factor of ten. The very first line in the poem after the chart of sequential and simultaneous time zones (the first line of the narrative that will make up all the rest of "New Dawn") alludes to this very problem, which is not an insignificant one for a bombing run with an abnormally heavy load:

> Now that all the "unauthorized items" are cleared from the
>   bomber, including
> The optimistic irrelevance of six packs
> Of condoms, and three pairs of
> Pink silk panties.

What is irrelevant here is precisely what I am claiming *is* relevant. What one does with condoms, an item with which the couple in the next poem no doubt dispense, given the unpredictable suddenness of their encounter, is here defined as that which does not belong on board the plane. And that which does not belong on the plane could be defined as well as that which does not belong in a reading of the poem, though it does, as it happens, in this instance. And all the more does it deserve to belong there, now that we realize that its irrelevant relevance is announced from the start. It is "unauthorized," it does not have the author's sanction, but the very act of naming and removing it reveals that it has been there all along. Chief among the unauthorized items in my reading of the poem is my insistence on the number ten, which resurfaces in "The Distance Between" as that which in both poems defines the distance between. And it happens that, despite the removal of those unauthorized items, the plane is still overweight, and it is overweight by a factor of *ten* (percent):

> Wheels,
> Under the weight of 150,000 pounds,
> Overweight 15,000, crunch
> Off the apron, bound for the runway.

"True Love" (42), the following poem, is about love *at ten* (as "The Distance Between" was about lust at ten feet): "In silence the heart raves. It utters words / Meaningless, that never had / A meaning. I was ten" and in love with a girl who sat with an older boy in a Buick in front of the drugstore.

> There is nothing like
> Beauty. It stops your heart. It
> Thickens your blood. It stops your breath. It
>
> Makes you feel dirty. You need a hot bath.
> I leaned against a telephone pole, and watched.
> I thought I would die if she saw me.

Guilty in love, the way the poet finds support in the pole recalls the guilty stance of the lover in the poem before who afterward "stood by a beech, some twenty feet off, head down." While he was doing that, his partner in this brief encounter "sat in the rich, sap-bleeding, wild tangle of fern, *and wept*." In "True Love" the girl the poet loved marries the boy in the Buick; the poet had so strong an imagination that he can see her on her wedding night doing in effect what the woman was doing in the poem before: "I lay in bed that night / And wondered if she would *cry* when something was done to her." "True Love" closes as "The Distance Between" began, with families *drifting* apart: the latter begins with the man and woman leaving "All others behind them, friends, husband, wife, / And small children" as they wandered off from the picnic "*Drifting* like breath." At the end of the other poem the girl who got married "never came back. The family [her mother, her drunkard father, her slick-faced brothers] / Sort of *drifted* off."

If beauty as the poet experienced it at age ten makes one feel dirty ("It // Makes you feel dirty. You need a hot bath"), beauty in old age—as we learn in the next poem, "Last Walk of Season" (44)—can be what comes after, not before (as the result of, not the reason for), bathing: "Now / No cloud in the *washed* evening hours . . . / The season's first rain had done duty . . . How bright, / Rain-*washed*, the pebbles shine!" Though it's not a girl's beauty but nature's, its effect on the beholder is very much the same: in "True Love" "the heart raves," while here "the heart leaps / That soon all earth will be of gold." Struck by such beauty at age ten, the heart "utters *words* / Meaningless, that never had / A *meaning*"; in the season's last walk (that, at this late date, may as well be "the last time, for this or perhaps / any year to come in unpredictable life") the heart-stopping perception of beauty gives rise to a rephrasing of the connection between such words and such meaning: "Can it be that the world is but the great *word* / That speaks the *meaning* of our joy?"

It is rephrased once more in "Old-Time Childhood in Kentucky" (45). Though no longer a question about beauty, it is still one about the *world* and about a certain great *word* and its meaning. Right away, in the very first line, the world (for which "Last Walk of Season" had proposed a working definition: "is but the great word / That speaks the meaning of our joy") and what it may mean occupies center stage: "When I was a boy I saw the *world* I was in. / I saw it for what it was. Canebrakes with / Track beaten down by bear paw." The bathing rain that brought such beauty in "Last Walk of Season" had made tracks, and the music they consequently make, precisely the only thing the poet could at first perceive: "The season's first rain had done duty. Dams and traps, / Where the old logging trucks had once made tracks, now gurgle. That / Is the only voice we hear. We do not ask / What burden that music bears. // Our wish is to think of nothing but happiness. Of only / The *world's* great emptiness." "Old-Time Childhood" is a reminiscence of the poet's grandfather, who used to tell him stories of the Civil War, but more importantly of a great *word*: "This for honor. I longed / To understand. I said the magic word. / I longed to say it aloud, to be heard." The word "honor" was the proper response to the world "for what it was." The world runs the risk of meaninglessness, given the crinoid stems and fishy fossils his grandfather showed him at the mouth of a cave—for all was once under water, " 'no saying the millions / Of years.' " Nothing remains the same forever; the world, seen in this geological perspective, is inherently unstable, has no certain form, perhaps no reality. The boy knows this and asks: " 'Grandpa, . . . what do you do, things being like this?' " The answer is an exegesis of the magic word to which one clings in response to this realization of what the world really is, honor (as opposed to the discovery in "Last Walk of Season," where it is the world itself that is a great, magical word): " 'Love / Your wife, love your get, keep your word, and / If need arises die for what men die for.' "

Having said these words, his grandfather departed, leaving the boy at the mouth of the cave to imagine what it must be like to be under water: "I stretched out the arm on each side, and, waterlike, / Wavered. . . . as though / In eons back I grew there in that submarine / Depth and lightlessness, waiting to discover / What I would be, might be, after ages—how many?—had rolled over." The cave, the water, and the desire to discover one's identity in darkness are recombined in the next poem, "Covered Bridge" (47). There the poet, again as a boy, is once more in a kind of cave, "the *caverning* dark beneath that roof " (the roof of the covered bridge). In the poem before, he had been in a cave and imagined himself *under* water; here the cave is *above* the water of the stream it bridges. There, he had stretched out his *arms*, waiting to discover what he would be; here, "to prove identity you now lift up / Your own *hand*—scarcely visible in that gloom."

Those arms and hands may stretch as far as the next poem, "Re-interment: Recollection of a Grandfather" (49), where they reappear as the grandfather's: "His lips move without sound, his hands stretch out to me there." But the identity of those hands or arms—which in the two poems before could prove identity in the very act of being stretched out—is itself in question now, for though they belong to the grandfather, it is to the grandfather within the poet, the one he carries in his skull in the "re-interment" to which the title alludes, a burial that is at the same time a pregnancy: "What a strange feeling all the years to carry / It in your head! Once . . . a young woman carried it / In her belly."

He hears "strange noises / All night in my skull," noises "That sometimes fill the great dome my shoulders bear." As extraordinary an image as this is, it was already anticipated by the immediately preceding poem, wherein there was also a sound that could *fill* the dome one's shoulders bore and which could only be heard at *night*: "only at night might you find / That echo filling the vastness of your mind" (the echo of hoof or wheel striking the loose boards of the covered bridge).

Unlikely as it would seem, certain central moments of "Re-interment: Recollection of a Grandfather" reappear in the account in "Last Meeting" (51) of the poet's running into an old black woman in his hometown who had known him as a child. The grandfather's "fingers fumbling to get out . . . , fingernails clawing to get out" that the poet felt within his skull in "Re-interment" and would feel even more intensely as he got older and his hair got thinner—"Each year more clawlike—as I watch hair go thin"—are now *her* fingers: " 'Ro-Penn, Ro-Penn, my little tadpole, / . . . Git off yore hat so I'll see your haid.' / And I did. She ran her hands through thinning hair. / 'Not fahr-red, like it used to be.' / And ran her fingers some more. 'And thinner.' " "Re-interment" had closed with the regret that the time would come when "there'll be nobody left" to remember his grandfather, "To love him—or *recognize* his kind. Certainly not his face." "Last Meeting" is precisely about recognition, too: the woman "Comes peering at me, not sure yet, / For I'm in my city clothes and hat"—it's the hat that makes it particularly difficult for her to recognize him, as it conceals his red hair; all the more reason for her to have to do what his grandfather did, touch her fingers to his skull, only from the outside this time—"But in the same instant we *recognize* / Each other."

Though the characters change, the story is the same. Indeed, the story is more important than the characters, though we don't really know what the story is until we have read all the versions of it there are; only then will we be in a position to understand that the story is not the one about dropping the atomic bomb or a picnic adultery but is about something else that those stories only begin to tell us. Yet another indication of this is the fact that "Last Meeting" strongly recalls a poem we have already read a little earlier in this tightly enchained sequence, "True Love." For there too the poet sees a woman on the street of his hometown, and there too the color of his hair—the color "Last Meeting" tells us he had more intensely as a boy—is significant enough to be mentioned: "I was ten, skinny, red-headed." Perhaps most significantly, "True Love" anticipates the extraordinary event that will occur in "Last Meeting" when the old black woman says "Ro-Penn, Ro-Penn, my little tadpole." It is extraordinary because it is the only place in any of Warren's poems where his name appears. It doesn't appear in "True Love" either, but the event of its being spoken has a profound effect on the poet: "She / Named my name. I thought I would wake up dead." (He will return to muse upon her pronouncing his name in the last line of the poem: "She called my name once. I didn't even know she knew it.")

Paying honor to the dead is what the poet does in a most haunting way in "Re-interment: Recollection of a Grandfather," by carrying his aged parent, Anchises-like, around with him in "the jail of my head" from which his grandfather sometimes emerges to stretch out his hands to the poet in the darkness. "Last Meeting" gets its title from the poet's awareness that his encounter with the old woman, forty years before, was the last. She had asked him, " 'but 'member me!' / I tried to say 'I couldn't forget,' / But the words wouldn't come." He tries to make amends by visiting her grave but can't, on the first try, find it. "Next time I'll promise adequate time. / . . . It's nigh half a lifetime I haven't managed, / But there must be enough time left for that." These last words of "Last Meeting," with their hint of the poet's own mortality and the realization that when he's gone the possibility of the woman's being remembered will have gone, too, echo the conclusion of "Re-interment," where "there'll be nobody left, in that after-while, / To love him—or recognize . . . his face."

The poet's skull is again at issue in "Muted Music" (53) (as it will also be in "The Whole Question" [54]). Here an analogy is drawn between "the cruising hum / Of a single fly lost in the barn's huge, black / Interior" and the "muted music" humming in the poet's brain that "was all the past was, after all." Does the past, in other words, "now cruise your empty skull like / That blundering buzz at barn-height?" But other analogies suggest themselves too. Is the analogy itself between the poet's empty skull and the empty black space of the barn analogous to the one between the "vastness of your mind" filled by the echo heard at

night in the darkness of the covered bridge and the enclosure itself of that bridge three poems back (for the echo resounds in
both)?

Or does not the fly's "hum," the "muted music" of the poem's
title, have something to do with the sound the old black woman
made in "Last Meeting" when she traced her fingers through his
thinning hair, "rocked her arms like cuddling a child, / And
crooned" ("Croon: To sing or *hum* in a low, gentle tone")? The
black space within the barn is not entirely black—it "is dark / Except for the window at one gable, where / Daylight is netted *gray*
with cobwebs"—and neither is the woman, who has "yellow-*gray*
skin." By a constant process of reversal from poem to poem, the
woman who in "Last Meeting" was in some manner the grandfather in "Re-interment" who was inside the poet's skull is now
the great black humming inner space of the barn within which
the poet lies, a black space that is like the emptiness in his skull
where the past with its muted music now cruises like the fly in
that barn. No wonder the poet is lying there, trying "of all the
past, to remember / *Which* was *what, what, which*" (Warren's italics).

"You'll have to rethink the whole question," the next poem—
"The Whole Question" (54)—begins. As if jiggled in a kaleido-
scope, the elements of "Muted Music" reappear in a different
formation here. Instead of a fly cruising the barn like the past
cruising his skull, "Metaphysical midges . . . plunged at the single flame / That centered the infinite dark of your skull." It's a
poem about the whole question of getting born: "a hand slapped
blazing breath / Into you, snatched your dream's lulling noth-
ing- / ness into what Paul called the body of this death"—
wherein the blazing and the lulling are newly rearranged from
their appearance in "Muted Music": "lost in the barn's huge,
black / Interior, on a Sunday afternoon, with all the sky / *Ablaze*
outside . . . while you, here, *lulled*, lie." Even the fly's "cruising
hum" reemerges "when underneath / The curtain dawn seeps,
and on wet asphalt wet tires *hum*." The hum, in other words, is
once again something the poet hears while lying awake in the
dark ("You woke in the dark of real night to hear"). And that
blazing and lulling now accompany the process of birth suggests
that the poet in the dark of the barn in "Muted Music" might
have been remembering precisely that or trying to.

"Old Photograph of the Future" (55) rethinks the whole question of being born and growing up in terms of a snapshot of the poet as infant viewed seventy-five years later. But more interesting is the way "Old Photograph" repeats a key phrase ("key" because it was itself a phrase that embodied a multiple allusion to "Muted Music")—"Metaphysical midges that plunged at the single flame / *That centered* the infinite dark of your skull"—of "The Whole Question" in its very first line: "*That center* of attention—an infantile face" (repeated, too, in the first line of the second stanza: "*That center* of attention, swathed"). Surely this repeated center should be the center of our attention in reading these poems. It has been, in any event, already, since what is the "infantile face" in "Old Photograph" is the same recurring character as "your skull" in "The Whole Question," "your empty skull" in "Muted Music," the pate with thinning hair that the old black woman in "Last Meeting" fingered, "my skull" and "the great dome my shoulders bear" in "Re-interment," and "the vastness of your mind" through which an echo resounded in "Covered Bridge."

That character appears in "Why Boy Came to Lonely Place" (56) in pretty nearly the same disguise it assumed in "Old Photograph," where he was "That center of attention—an infantile *face*": "You move your fingers down your *face*, / And wonder how many years you'll be what you are." The poet was only thirteen then, but he did the same thing—"You count the years you have been in the world"—he was to do in "Old Photograph": "Most things show wear around seventy-five, / And that's the age this picture has got."

It seems fair to say that the seven poems from "Covered Bridge" to "Why Boy Came" have a common thread, their attention centered on the poet's head, skull, or face. The next half dozen, from "Platonic Lassitude" to "If Snakes Were Blue," share at least a common landscape, that of the natural world. Though "Platonic Lassitude" (57) could also be read as a counter to "Muted Music," in which everything is just the opposite of the way it was in the dark barn with that single fly buzzing overhead. For now, precisely, "No fly, no gnat, / Stirs through the bright unreality of air." No longer enclosed in the dark, we're in the fresh air; though, as before, we are "lulled." Yet "Platonic Lassitude" nevertheless does not fail to pick up echoes of the immediately preceding "Why Boy Came to Lonely Place": "The *sky* is flaw*lessly blue*" in the latter, while the former speaks of "the *sky's* depth*less blue.*" "No bird" sings in one, and "no bird sings" in the other. More curious, as always, is the manner in which a homely detail is lifted out of its apparent insignificance: the boy in "Why Boy Came to Lonely Place" came with a "cheese sandwich crumbling, and lettuce brown-curled," a curling that returns (as a spiral returns, curling back) in "Platonic Lassitude" in the form of "the smoke that is curled / From a chimney" that "may never uncurl in greater or lesser distance." There it stands for what cannot be taken back, time that cannot return, words that cannot be recalled: "No utterance / May come again." Yet precisely this utterance comes again, and so soon as to suggest an answer to the question that accompanied its first appearance: of what worth is stale, curled lettuce? "Canteen now dry and of what worth / With the cheese sandwich crumbling, and lettuce brown-curled?" (the question was asked of the canteen, but one can easily imagine its being asked of the rest of the boy's provisions). Its worth is that it can serve, in Warren's larger context, as a homely metaphor for curling itself—what the lettuce does, what smoke does, and what the verb itself does as it returns, with a twist, so soon after its first appearance.

"Seasons" (58) is a poem in two parts, each with its own title: "I. Downwardness" and "II. Interlude of Summer." Since it is the general title, "Seasons," and not the titles of the two sections that is printed in the same typeface as the titles of the other poems in the collection, its two parts ought perhaps to be considered one poem with regard to the sequential structure of the collection that concerns us here. In any event, there are connections both between the two of them and between them and "Platonic Lassitude" and "The Place." "Platonic Lassitude" speaks of "the world's ontological collapse," an image that returns in the allusion in "Interlude of Summer" to "the world's disaster"—and, in a more concrete incarnation, in the collapse of melting snow in "Downwardness": "Downstream, a high out-thrust of snow groans, loses structure, / Falls."

In "Platonic Lassitude" the sun hangs "like the collage of a child to blue paper glued," while in "Downwardness" "daylight [will] glitter in the highest leaf like green foil," and in "The Place" (60) "The stars would not be astonished / To catch a glimpse of the form through interstices / Of leaves now black as enameled tin." The form thus tantalizingly and interstitially glimpsed is that of the poet, who is thinking "of the possibility of lying on stone, / . . . and waiting / For the shadow"—and later the stars—to find him. The kind of reading we are practicing here allows us to do something very similar, for it is an interstitial reading, one that narrows its focus to what lies between the poems, as the stars' field of vision was limited, by the poet's own choice, to what lay between those enameled tin leaves.

In this particular instance, the tin leaves that define the interstice for the stars are themselves what constitute the interstice for us, for they are the latest avatar of a recurring character. By a gradual transformation, little by little the sun that in one poem ("Platonic Lassitude") was flattened out into paper glued to paper becomes in the next poem ("Seasons") foil (which is by dictionary definition flat: "a very thin sheet or leaf of metal") at the same time that it becomes a leaf. Now this union of sunlight to leaf was anticipated in "Platonic Lassitude" when "a high few [leaves], / As they *hang* without motion, shine *translucently* green" and when, a few lines later, the sun too, "like the collage of a child to blue paper glued . . . / *Hangs*). While in "The Place" what had been the bright sun is now "black as enameled tin," losing its brightness and no longer a sun, though remaining both leaf and metallic: changing from paper to foil to tin, as it changed as well from sun to sun-drenched leaf to leaves devoid of light.

The brook in "Platonic Lassitude" "meditates in serene / Silence." There is a watery silence, too, in "Seasons I. Downwardness" or what seemed to have been one: "What seemed such silence is only the singing / Of a thousand driblets and streamlets." A heaved boulder is an element common to "Downwardness" and "Interlude of Summer": "*Boulders* go grudging and grinding in rupture, / And one, *heaved* in air, chimes"; "rising waters *heave* to shoulder a *boulder* past." And "Platonic Lassitude" and "Interlude of Summer" combine fruit with absence or loss of definition in parallel utterances: "To remind you / That nothing *defines* itself in joy or sorrow, / The crow calls from the black cliff forgotten but beckoning behind you. / Had you forgotten that history is only the fruit of tomorrow?" ("Platonic Lassitude"); "Your own life seems to lose *definition,* as it did last

year. / But garden and grape-arbor have fulfilled your ambition, / And gullet has sucked juice from the golden and tooth-
gored pear" ("Interlude of Summer").

In both, fruit appears as compensation for that loss of definition: the "But" signifying in the latter passage that garden,
grape-arbor, and thoroughly enjoyed pear mitigate somewhat
the loss of life's definition, while because history is only the fruit
of tomorrow—that is, the future creates the past—nothing defines itself in joy or sorrow in the other passage, for only time has
the power to define. Thus no event is in itself joyful or sorrowful;
only time will tell, and what once seemed sorrowful may become
something quite different in the fullness of time's fruition. This
reversal constitutes Warren's eternal return, evident for example
in "The Leaf" (from *Incarnations*), where again a grape is the
agent of such change: "The world // Is fruitful, and I, too, / In
that I am the father / Of my father's father's father. I, / Of my
father, have set the teeth on edge. But / By what grape?" (*N&SP*,
238).

The mysterious connection between time and the crow that
called from the black cliff in "Platonic Lassitude" is evoked, if not
explained, in "The Place" when "You hear, distantly, a bird-call
you cannot identify. / Is the shadow of the cliff creeping upon
you? / You are afraid to look at your watch." In the more immediately proximate "Interlude of Summer," time creeps, too, in
the march of the seasons and in the way the sun's shadow advances with daily precision: "Green will soon creep back in
white's absence. // Each day, at mathematically accelerated
pace, / The yet unseen sun will flood the eastern notch / With
crimson. . . . // Evening by evening, the climactic melodrama of /
Day flares from behind the blackening [remember that the crow
called "from the *black* cliff"] silhouette / Of the mountain for the
last and majestic pyre of / What of today you can remember, or
forget." That uncertainty of whether one is forgetting or remembering is picked up in "The Place" at the "hour when what is
remembered is / Forgotten. When / What is forgotten is remembered, and / You are not certain which is which."

"The Place," we recall, suggests the possibility of catching (of
the stars' catching) "a glimpse of the form through interstices /
Of leaves now black as enameled tin." The immediately following "First Moment of Autumn Recognized" (62) likewise focuses

on what is between, the first moment of autumn which is really not a moment precisely because it has that interstitial quality: "We know / This to be no mere moment, however brief, / However blessèd, for / Moment means time, and this is no time, / Only the dream, untimed, between / Season and season."

The question of the relation of time and seasonal change is the subject as well of the next poem, "Paradigm of Seasons" (63). "Each year is like a snake that swallows its tail," we are reminded in the opening line. "How long since we have learned, of seasons, the paradigm?" We have long known that the cycle repeats itself, but through forgetfulness we perceive sameness as if it were difference. And so, awed by seasonal change and the beauty of spring, we fall victim to irony: "We know, too, how the heart, forgetting irony, stares at / The first apple bough to offer blossom, / Parody of snow. We know / The sweetness of the first secret / Tear, not brushed away." Those who forget irony are condemned to repeat it; and we do, every spring, so enraptured by white blossoms that we forget that we have seen this whiteness before, as snow, and thus fail to see the apple blossoms for what they really are, the parody—the second, the later, ironic, version—of that snow. Like the tin leaves' interstices, so too this blossoming parody of an earlier occurrence appears to speak as well to what the poems in sequence do, for the reading I am promoting in these pages seeks to make those earlier occurrences remembered, to make the parody visible. Perhaps, that is, what each poem does in returning to fragments of the one that precedes it is in fact as much a parody of what went before as the apple blossoms are of the snow so soon forgotten (and perhaps as well the beauty of each poem and its own apparent reasons for being—like the blossoms'—blind us to the reality of the parody).

One of these fragments is the verb in "Can you feel breath *brush* your damp / Lips? How can you know?" in "First Moment of Autumn Recognized" that reappears in "Paradigm of Seasons" in the sentence that immediately follows the blossom's parody of snow in the form of a damp fragment that is allowed to persist (and thus name its own fragmentary persistence from one poem to the next): "We know / The sweetness of the first secret / Tear, not *brushed* away."

"If Snakes Were Blue" (65) takes the model of serpentine time in "Paradigm" ("Each year is like a snake that swallows its tail") and transforms it back into something closer to the timeless moment that was the subject of "First Moment of Autumn Recognized":

> If snakes were blue, it was the kind of day
> That would uncoil in a luxurious ease
> As each mica-bright scale exposed a flange of gold,
> And slowly, slowly, the golden eyes blinked.
>
> It was the kind of day that takes forever.

By something resembling a Hegelian progression of thesis, antithesis, and synthesis, "If Snakes Were Blue" unites elements from two contrasting accounts of time, the timelessness of "First Moment of Autumn Recognized" and the notion in "Paradigm of Seasons" of time as a snake. The timelessness evident in the earlier poem's account of an autumnal stillness—

> We know
> This to be no mere moment, however brief,
> However blessèd, for
> Moment means time, and this is no time,
> Only the dream, untimed, between
> Season and season.

—is evoked here again in "the kind of day that takes forever— / As though minutes, minutes, could never be counted—to slide / Among the clouds like pink lily-pads floating / In a crystal liquid pure enough to drink." That atmospheric crystal we recall from "First Moment": "Perfection of crystal, purer / Than air," and the sliding from the observation in "Paradigm" that "Summer slides / Over night-nakedness like a wave." "First Moment" and "Paradigm" both spoke of seasons but in contrasting ways—the former focuses on the timeless moment "between / Season and season" (the seasons being summer and autumn), while the latter, as intent on their relentless sequence as "First Moment" was on making it stop, speaks of the paradigm of each's parody of the one before. "If Snakes Were Blue," however, does not speak of seasons (it is in fact impossible to tell to what season this timeless

afternoon belongs) but does recreate the kind of timeless moment experienced in "First Moment" and makes it uncoil like the
snake that in "Paradigm" was the model for the very opposite of
stasis, the seasons' unstoppable, though circular (and hence serpentine), movement. The serpentine orientation of both "Paradigm" and "If Snakes" is all the stronger for the fact that it is in
the first line of both that the snakes appear.

"Little Girl Wakes Early" (66) begins a new series, after the
one from "Platonic Lassitude" to "If Snakes Were Blue" that was
composed of meditations on the natural land- and skyscape and
the passage of time, distinguished among other things by the
fact that these will be narrative poems. The little girl in what
could have been a short story had it not become a poem was "the
first one awake, the first / To stir in the dawn-curdled house."
Though the meditation on time that characterized the preceding
poems ceases with "Little Girl Wakes Early," the linkage of childhood and dawn in its opening lines had nevertheless already occurred in "If Snakes Were Blue" when the poet spoke of "the
kind of promise / We give ourselves in *childhood* when first
dawn / Makes curtains go gold, and all night's dreams flood
back." The child in "Little Girl Wakes Early" who was up alone at
dawn had the nightmarish daydream that everyone else was
dead: "behind shut doors no breath perhaps drew, no heart
beat." She ran outside to her playmate's house and was unable to
call her name, paralyzed with the thought that maybe "there was
no breath there / For answer"; then ran back home and cried to
her mother but couldn't explain why. And now that the little girl
has grown up, her "mother's long dead. And you've learned that
when loneliness takes you / there's nobody ever to explain to—
though you try again and again."

The daydream, in the fullness of time, unfortunately comes
true—and thereby forms a dark counterpart to the conclusion of
"If Snakes Were Blue." For there, childhood's dreams, and
dawn's promise, of happiness were promised fulfillment: "They
["the kind of promise / We give ourselves in childhood when first
dawn / Makes curtains go gold, and all night's dreams flood
back"] had guaranteed our happiness forever. // And in a way
such promises may come true."

"Winter Wheat: Oklahoma" (67) tells another version of the
story the girl imagined. A farmer approaches his house after a

long day in the fields yet "hates to go home." At first we don't know why. Reasons are given that are not the real reason: "It's rough to the lane, / And tough on sciatica. The lane ain't no broadway, nohow." He recognizes the lawn, the barn, the maples. And then he begins to reveal why he's so slow to go in: "But she's not sitting / To wave when he gets close. Now no smoke in the chimney, / These nights"—though it is only with those last two words that we begin to grasp the actual reason for his reluctance: his wife's not just not there, she's dead. Our slow realization as he approaches the house matches what the girl in "Little Girl Wakes Early" imagined as she approached a house whose inhabitant she imagined dead, as she "climbed the fence to the house of [her] dearest friend" and "thought how awful, if there was no breath there / For answer." Her tears—"Tears start . . . but tears aren't over / And won't get over"—are answered by his—"a man oughtn't sit and see tears ruin his booze." (If, incidentally, dawn is "curdled" and therefore milky in "Little Girl Wakes Early," dusk in the opening lines of "Winter Wheat: Oklahoma" has a similarly culinary look: "The omelet of sunset vibrates in the great flat pan. / A certain amount of golden grease will splatter.")

When the farmer in "Winter Wheat: Oklahoma" thought about his wife dead and buried, he would "wonder / How flesh would peel off cheekbones in earth"—an image haunting enough to persist in the next poem, "Youthful Picnic Long Ago: Sad Ballad on Box" (69), where the grave reappears as an adjective but the cheek is still revealed: "and let / Flame reveal the grave cheek-curve." The poems in their sequence here work like Time itself, which—like the white apple blossom on "Paradigm of Seasons" that parodies winter's snow—ultimately reveals, by parody, the bony essence. The young woman whose grave cheek-curve is revealed by the flame sings in such a way in "Youthful Picnic" as to express a future she could not have known.

> The voice confirmed the sweet sadness
> Young hearts gave us no right to.
>
> No right to, yet. Though some day would,
> As Time unveiled,

In its own dancing *parody* of grace,
The bony essence of each joke on joke.

Here the poem speaks of itself and its place in the poetic sequence in a way one could almost think it had no right to, for it is
precisely the *bony* essence of peeled-off "cheekbones in earth"
and "grave cheek-curve" that is revealed when we read these two
poems in light of each other. To read them together, as we are
reading all the poems in *Altitudes and Extensions*, is to perform
on the text what Time does to song, memory, and the human
body, "for"—to recall Warren's words in "The Circus in the Attic," written about four decades earlier—"no one knows the
meaning of the cry of passion he utters until the flesh of the passion is long since withered away to show the austere, logical
articulation of fact with fact in the skeleton of Time" (28). Time
eventually reveals what these poems will one day mean, and their
eventual meaning is not necessarily the same as the meaning
they had when they were first composed. They will, for one
thing, come to mean more than the "emotional quality that went
into the two moments of composition" (RPW to RPR, 7 December 1986) by virtue of their appearing together in sequence.

The uncanny ability of such repeated fragments to refer to
themselves is remarkable. In "Youthful Picnic" the self-referentiality is apparent in two ways: (1) it is the "bony essence" that is
"unveiled" when the sequencing of this poem and "Winter
Wheat" makes "Flame reveal the grave cheek-curve" of the girl
singing at the campfire just after the Oklahoma farmer had
thought "How flesh would peel off cheek bones" in his wife's
grave, since it is a bony essence that persists in these two poems;
(2) the poet's observation in "Youthful Picnic" that the girl's
"voice confirmed the sweet sadness / Young hearts gave us no
right to" and that her "dancing fingers enacted / A truth far past
the pain declared / By that voice that somehow made pain sweet"
is an observation that could equally be made about the ability of
these poems and their repeated fragments to say more than they
could have intended to say. It is a self-referential statement about
self-referentiality.

In the next poem, "History During Nocturnal Snowfall" (71)
another finger provides yet another model of self-reference. In

that poem, the poet tries to "devise the clever trick / Of making heartbeat with heartbeat synchronize" so that he might "guess the . . . buried narrative" of his wife asleep beside him: "my finger touches a pulse to intuit its truth." But we can do the same, in the hope of intuiting a similarly hidden story, by putting our finger on what is quite literally the "pulse" of the poem, on the word that would allow us to realize the synchronization of one poem with its neighbor. For in this instance the pulse just happens to be a pulse—and the wrist a wrist, the heart a heart—for in the immediately preceding poem these elements had all already appeared and had done so in a meaningful configuration: "delicate / Was the melancholy that swelled each heart, and timed / The pulse in wrist, and wrist, and wrist." The pulse is in the wrist in a different way than the pulse in "History During Nocturnal Snowfall," for in "Youthful Picnic" the repeated strokes of the wrist on the strings of the "box" (the guitar) constitute the pulse, the rhythm of the song that the heart's melancholy times. But in a self-allusive way this pulsing rhythm looks ahead to the scene the next poem will recount, without of course realizing that it is doing so; we are in fact told that it cannot be aware of the meaning it contains: it was a "sweet sadness / Young hearts gave us no right to. / . . . the dancing fingers enacted / A truth far past the pain declared."

What we learn by reading the poems together is that the first speaks not only of the story it tells but of another, larger story—one the collection tells about itself, an adventure in reading in which the reader plays a necessary role. That role involves reading the poems for the ways they refer to how they can be read in this larger context, and in that regard the "clever trick" of synchronizing two pulses is likewise a self-referential clue for the reader who does not mind being told that he or she is reading too cleverly. In this story, the first words of "History During Nocturnal Snowfall"—"*Dark* in the *cubicle boxed* from the snow-darkness of night"—look both backward to the box from which the unjustifiably prophetic pulse of music came in "Youthful Picnic Long Ago: Sad Ballad on *Box*" (repeated in "their delicate dance / On the strings of the *box*" and "The face leaned over the *box*") and ahead to the next poem, where the poet will be in a different kind of "*dark cubicle.*"

Time may sometimes need, however, a little help if it is com-

pletely to reveal the skeletal articulation and inner rhythm of
these poems—and such help is precisely what Warren provided
(whether knowingly or not I do not know) when he revised "History During Nocturnal Snowfall" for its appearance alongside
"Youthful Picnic" in *Altitudes and Extensions*. When it was first
published in the fall 1983 number of the *Sewanee Review* under
the title "Personal History," its first line read: "Dark in the cubicle *curtained* from the snow-dark night"—a line since changed in
Altitudes and Extensions to "Dark in the cubicle *boxed* from snow-
darkness of night," thus making possible an even richer reference to the preceding "Youthful Picnic Long Ago: Sad Ballad on
Box," where fingers delicately dance "On the strings of the *box*."

Those first words of "History," as I have mentioned—"*Dark* in
the *cubicle* boxed"—give the impression of alluding to the poem
that follows, "Whistle of the 3 A.M." (72), where the poet remembers hearing that train blow nightly for the crossing and awakening "With the thought that some night in your own *dark
cubicle*, // You would whirl" past some such town as the one in
which he used to hear that train. The dark cubicle that persists[2]
from one poem to the next changes its referent but keeps its
wording—a bedroom in one, a train compartment in the other.

The train persists, too, into the next poem, "Last Night Train"
(73), the last commuter train of the evening out of New York.
"Whistle of the 3 A.M." had combined a night train and the
quality of being last in another way, for there the poet had asked
"Am I the boy // Who *last* remembers the 3 A.M.?" Is everyone
else who could have remembered this defunct train dead? "What
if some hold real estate nearby, / A good six feet long, but not one
of them / Would wake, I guess, to listen, and wonder why // The
schedule's gone dead of the 3 A.M." Awakened by its whistle, the
boy thought of the day when he would be in such a train, in his
"own dark cubicle" whirling "*Past* some straggle of town with
scarcely a street*light*." The dream comes true in the next poem,
when the poet, now an adult, in that last night train goes "slam-
banging / . . . *past* caterpillar- / Green flash of last *light* on deserted platforms." The dead, of whom "not one of them / Would
wake" to listen for the 3 A.M. nor realize what has happened to its
schedule, find a counterpart in the middle-aged black woman
who is the only other passenger on the "Last Night Train." For
she does not wake either, and the poet worries, as his stop ap-

proaches, that she may, like the dead in the poem before, be sleeping in ignorance of the schedule: "My station at last. I look back once. / Is she missing hers? I hesitate to ask, and the snore / Is suddenly snatched into eternity." In "Whistle of the 3 A.M.," after the train's "magisterial headlight swept" the landscape and it receded into the distance, "There was nothing but marmoreal moonlight" and the poet asks, "Did you *stare* at the sheet's trancelike white- / ness, which held no hint of the world's far fury and heat?" A similar moment occurs in "Last Night Train" when the poet stands alone on the platform after having gotten off the train and *stares* at the quiet sky:

> The last red light fades into distance and darkness like
> A wandering star. Where that brief roar just now was,
> A last cricket is audible.
> ....
> I *stare* upward at uncountable years beyond
> My own little aura.

That "last red light" of the train that disappears from our poet's sight like a wandering star returns in the following "Milton: A Sonnet" (75) in the form of the "Late carmine" (that is, again "last" and "red") of the setting sun (literally a star, too) that another poet—Milton—could once see but no longer can. "No doubt he could remember how in the past / Last carmine had bathed the horizon with wide kindness. / Not now." And in his private darkness, he could hear something like the last audible cricket the poet in "Last Night Train" could discern as that last red light faded: "In darkness he prayed, and at the last / Moved through the faithful brilliance they called blindness, / Knew burgeoning Space in which old space hummed like a fly."

When for Milton "The past and future are intrinsicate / To form a present in which the *blessèd* heart / May *leap like a* gleaming *fish* from water into / Sunlight" likewise made intrinsicate are two otherwise separate moments in "Last Night Train," one of swimming ("And I think of swimming, naked and seaward, / In starlight forever") and the other of blessing ("I feel / Like blessing the unconscious wallow of flesh-heap" of his fellow passenger in the commuter train). They are, that is—though in

"Last Night Train" they seem to have no particular relation to each other—brought together in "Milton" when the heart that has received blessing swims, or leaps, like a fish. And this happens at precisely the moment when "Milton" is talking about two other otherwise separate entities—the past and the future—that come together "to form a present in which the blessèd heart / May leap like a gleaming fish."

"Whatever You Now Are" (76) continues the discussion "Milton: A Sonnet" began about Time and Space (Milton in his blindness "Knew burgeoning *Space* in which old space hummed like a fly, / And *Time*") by seeking to know what lies beyond those two capitalized categories: "What elements, shadowy, in that dream interlace / In a region past categories of *Time* and *Space*?" If "Milton" was concerned with a certain intrinsication, "Whatever You Now Are" is as well, though now it is called by a different name, intertwining—"Is it you that flows from distance, to distance, / With the tune of time and blood intertwined forever?"—and, in the line just cited, interlacing. The past and future are intrinsicate in "Milton" to form a present which is like water, a stream in which the blessèd heart may leap like a fish; in the "region past categories of Time and Space" explored in "Whatever You Now Are," the self of the dreaming poet is likewise in a stream, or the stream is in him: "You fell asleep to the star-bit and murmurous flow / Of the stream beneath your window, but frontierless / Are the stream and the Self conjunct all night long."

"Wind and Gibbon" (77) continues the meditation that "Whatever You Now Are" began about how what we hear when we sleep influences our thoughts by influencing our dreams. In "Whatever" it was the rustle of the stream; here it is the sound made by the wind:

> All night, over roof, over forest, you hear
> Wind snore, shift, stir, like a dog uncomfortable
> In sleep, or dreaming. . . .
>   . . . You drowse.
> Wake. Decide it is only a spruce bough wind-dragging
> Across the corner of the house.

As the poet marveled in the poem before at the possibility that the murmur of the stream could "Define the pattern of your whole life's endeavor" by exerting an influence on one's dreams—a possibly unwarranted influence, since that natural noise of "log-ripple and stone-chance" was nothing but the product of chance yet an influence nevertheless—here he must remind himself that the wind he hears in sleep "Has no mind / That could rationally dictate change. Its head / Is like a dried gourd rattling / A few dried seeds within."

Awakened by the wind, "You get up. Wander. Gibbon, you see, / Is on the shelf, volume by volume, solid as masonry. At random, / You seize one. . . . // It does not matter where you begin." The most significant feature of Gibbon's text, by this account, is its quality of enabling the reader to pick up the thread of narrative at any point. That quality is named as *sequence* in a parallel passage several poems back, in "Covered Bridge," where the poet said some of the same things about himself that he says here of Gibbon:

> Another land, another age, another self
> Before all had happened that has happened since
> And is now arranged on the shelf
> Of memory in a sequence that I call Myself.

The poet, like Gibbon—and like the book in which these poems appear—exists as a text and as sequence. Like Gibbon's volumes, in which it doesn't really matter where you start, the events of his life are texts on a shelf *in sequence*. If the analogy these parallel passages propose is accurate, then we are invited to read *Altitudes and Extensions* the way the poet reads Gibbon—with an eye to sequence (and, as "Covered Bridge" suggests, to the possibility that these sequential texts—these poems in sequence—are the poet's "self," his buried narrative). To read it, in fact, with the realization that sequence is all there is: no beginning, no end—or no truth: "History is not truth. Truth is in the telling." Gibbon does not tell the truth, but there is truth in his telling.

The reason is that the essence of Gibbon's prose is precisely what we have had reason to identify as the persistent quality of Warren's sequential poetry: *irony*. As "Paradigm of Seasons" expresses it: "how the heart, forgetting irony, stares at / The first apple bough to offer blossom, / Parody of snow" and as "Youthful Picnic Long Ago: Sad Ballad on Box" itself enacts "its own dancing parody of grace, / The bony essence of each joke on joke." For

> Gibbon's hot lava
> Seethes over the conical brim of the world whence
> Lifts flame-tongue. Glowing,
> If flows, like incandescent irony, over
> Vineyard, sheepfold. . . .
> . . . stone hut, villa, the brawny and noble
> Cockmaster about to insert the tool of wizardy, that
> Moan-maker.

Gibbon's irony is like Vesuvius's lava, freezing all human and animal activity in Pompeii into time forever, turning all it touches into statues, into fixed objects for later study—into something like a text.[3]

No matter where one begins in the poetic sequences we will be reading here, one can pick up the thread of their buried narrative, and at any point one can find something like Gibbon's lava-like "incandescent irony"—one can even find it in the very next poem, "Delusion?—No!" (79), where the poet stands on a high place and discovers his own "light of inner darkness burn" like lava, and like lava flow downward over the landscape: "In that divine osmosis I stood / And felt each discrete and distinct stroke / Of the heart as it downward fled— / Cliff, cleft, gorge, chasms, and far off, / Ravine. . . . I knew the / Glorious light of inner darkness burn." Again the repeated term, the hidden inner rhyme, names itself and provides a clue for the interpretation of its function, and that of the metonymic structure of which it is a part, in the landscape of *Altitudes and Extensions*. It is irony, like Gibbon's incandescent variety, irony that flows over the entire collection and gives a different cast to everything, changing (or deepening—depending, perhaps, on whether one is happy with the change) what one thought was the meaning of each poem (what one thought as long as one read only that poem). Such irony puts quotation marks around what it ironizes, changes its register, gives it a new context for the reader to reckon with.

To say, as "Wind and Gibbon" and "Delusion?—No!" certainly

seem to say, that Warren's irony of sequence works like Vesuvius's volcanic lava is to express in just slightly different terms what Warren had earlier said in "The Circus in the Attic" about how "no one knows the meaning of the cry of passion he utters until the flesh of the passion is long since withered away to show the austere, logical articulation of fact with fact in the skeleton of Time" (words that "Youthful Picnic Long Ago," in the present volume, echo when it has Time unveil, in its "parody . . . / The bony essence"). For again it is the flesh of passion—Pompeii's "brawny and noble / Cockmaster about to insert the tool of wizardy," in this instance—that finds itself transformed by the ironic cast that lava can provide.

Confirmation that it was indeed lava that was present but unnamed in "Delusion?—No!" comes in the following "Question at Cliff-Thrust" (80), where, as in "Delusion," the poet stands on a high place looking down and where what he there sees is "Age-rotten pumice and *lava*." The poet's descent in "Question," however, is not, as in "Delusion," the effect of osmosis ("In that divine osmosis I stood") but that of hypnosis, and here the downward strokes ("And felt each discrete and distinct stroke") are not of the heart but of the swimmer's arm:

> You lean forward and stare
> At the shelving green of hypnosis.
>
> . . . bladelike, your fingertips
> Into the green surface slash
> ....
> You take the downward strokes, some two or three.
> Suddenly your lungs, aflame, burn.

The poet had stretched out his arms in "Delusion," too, though not to swim but to fly: "Yes, stretch forth your arms like wings, and from your high stance, / Hawk-eyed, ride forth upon the emptiness of air, survey." One way to read the two poems is to see the second as the literal embodiment of what was in the first a dream—as the one in which the poet takes his own advice, and moves from surveying to flying, which turns out in this instance to be diving into a green ocean: "From the outthrust ledge of sea-

cliff you / Survey, downward. . . . / Who would guess / It would
be as easy as this?"

It is toward the last stanza of "Delusion" that the poet moves
from the feeling of downward osmosis, of flowing over the landscape like lava, to the fantasy of flying hawklike over the earth;
and it is that latter section that most resembles his leap into the
ocean in "Question at Cliff-Thrust." Similarly, it is in the second
half of "Question" that one can find the link between it and the
following poem, "It Is Not Dead" (82). In that descent into the
beckoning hypnotic green, "A pebble companions your white
downward flash. / You do not hear what must be its tiny splash /
As bladelike, your fingertips / Into the green surface slash."
That companionable pebble, now grown huge, is the entire subject of "It Is Not Dead": "It is not dead. It is simply weighty with
wisdom. / A long way and painful, it has come to become / What
it is." "In nameless heat" it was formed deep within the earth,
"seething in depth and darkness," like the poet himself in "Delusion?—No!," who "knew the / Glorious light of inner darkness
burn." Like lava, it was once liquid, "glowed / To change its liquid
mind to hardness." A glacier left it in the brook, where "fingers
of water, weak but uncontrollable, / Worked in their tangle of
multitudinous will" upon it, honing it "to perfection . . . / And,
naked, I lie on it, / Brooding on our common destinies. / . . . I
lie, in brotherhood" with that rock.

"Half in, half out, of my brook it lies"—half in, half out of this
poem (in "my b[r]ook") it lies, the other half in "Question at
Cliff-Thrust," where this stone brother was the "pebble [that]
companions" the poet's downward splash, that shares a common
destiny, falling with him from the cliff to where the poet's "fingertips / In the green surface slash," fingers *in* water reassembled in "It Is Not Dead" to become the "fingers *of* water" that
work their will on the rock "*until* / Half in, half out, of my brook
it lies." That *until* becoming a self-referential statement in the
poem, referring not only to the water of the brook but at the
same time to the hands, the fingers, of the poet of this book that
shape and hone that rock—"Honed to perfection, perfect in
structure"—until it really does become the companion, the double, of the pebble that kept the poet company in the poem before.

Repetition and difference are what *Altitudes and Extensions* is consistently about. They are also what the next poem, "Sunset" (84), will be about—about sunsets that are "Not repetitious / But different each day, for day to day nothing / Is identical to eye or soul," and about stars, "which have no / Originality and know / Nothing but repetition, and which / We call constellations." Sunsets are thus to stars as sunset is to sunset, similar but not the same—similar in that they are similar (sunset to sunset, the stars of one night to the stars of another), dissimilar in that sunsets are dissimilar and constellations are not. But there is something of a paradox here, for what makes sunsets not the same is not something in the sunsets but something in us, something in the eye or the soul that makes nothing ever exactly the same from one day to the next: "for day to day nothing / Is identical to eye or soul." And isn't that same something in us when we view the "Heavenly algebra" of stars?

A contradiction thus lies at the heart of this poem, the penultimate in the collection. It could be resolved by saying what the poet doesn't say, which is that constellations are indeed always the same, whereas sunsets are not, because sunsets, unlike stars, occur in context—the context of clouds or of clear sky and of whatever is on the horizon. Though for Warren even that is not necessarily true, since stars in his poetry are quite often viewed through some context, through a framing device such as the one that subtends all of the sequence published just before this one— the small round aperture through which Dante could catch a glimpse of the heavens at the end of his journey through hell in the epigraph to *Rumor Verified*, which is possibly the context and frame through which that entire sequence might be read. Another example would be the one that concludes "It Is Not Dead": "naked, I lie on it, / . . . All night, it will lie there under the stars, / . . . and I lie, in brotherhood, where I lie, / . . . though a curtain bars / Me in darkness except in one twisted spot where I spy / A fleeting fracture of the immensity of the night sky."

As "Question at Cliff-Thrust" had concluded with the poet *lying* ("Until you lie in lassitude and strengthlessness / On the green bulge of ocean" after the plunge into the ocean's depths), so too does "It Is Not Dead" thus conclude with the poet lying ("I lie, in brotherhood, where I lie"), looking up at the stars that in the immediately following "Sunset" he will interrogate: "At

night, at a late hour, I / Have asked stars the name of my soul. /
'Oh, what shall I call my soul in a dire hour?' " The dire hour is
defined in "Sunset" as the hour of nakedness: "the time when
you must speak / To your naked self "—a nakedness that had already begun in the preceding "It Is Not Dead": "naked, I lie on
it, / Brooding on our common destinies."

"But there is no answer from / Heavenly algebra," "Sunset"
tells us, no reply from the "military squadrons / Of ignorance . . . which / We call constellations." For their *algebra* is ignorant, as *geometry* is equally unknowing in the next and final
poem: "Think of a girl-shape, birch-white sapling" with a "curve,
coign, sway that no geometries know." But more links the last
two poems in the collection than algebra and geometries alike in
their ignorance, as their titles indicate: "*Sunset*" and "Myth of
Mountain *Sunrise*" (85). The difficult paradigm that opposed
sunsets to stars in "Sunset" could be prolonged (is prolonged, if
this reading is accurate) to oppose sunrise to sunset as embodi-
ments of both sameness and difference: absolutely alike at any
photographically frozen moment yet each the precise reversal, in
time, of the other. The echoing symmetry of peaks in the first
and last lines, respectively, of these two poems—

Clouds clamber, turgid, the mountain, peakward . . .
   ["Sunset"]

The sun blazes over the peak. That will be the old tale told.
   ["Myth of Mountain Sunrise"]

—suggests a similar symmetry in the poems themselves, one paralleled in the reverse symmetry of sunrise to sunset. It would be a
pattern to which every other two neighboring poems in the collection have until now conformed, enacting their own paradoxes
of sameness and difference as if it were through this almost end-
lessly repeated spiritual exercise that one could finally get at the
truth of such questions as the one he asks here.

He cries out to the stars in "Sunset" to tell him the name of his
soul—" 'Tell me that name,' I *cried*, 'that I may speak / In a dire
hour' "—but received no answer from the ignorant algebra of
constellations. "Myth of Mountain Sunrise" offers no answer, either, or at least does not appear to; but it does offer another cry:

"Leaf *cries*: 'I feel my deepest filament in dark rejoice. / I know that the density of basalt has a voice.' " By now we can surely place some faith in these poems' repetition of words, having already found so many twice-spoken words that were signs pointing to other, more elaborate repetitions within the two contiguous poems in which they occur. If the poet cries, therefore, in one poem and a leaf does so in the next—and if the poet's cry is an unanswered question and the leaf's a deeply felt assertion of knowledge—does the second cry in some way answer the first?

Something else about that leaf suggests that such may be the case: "The leaf, *whetted* on light, will *cut* / Air like butter." Two poems before "Sunset," the poet himself performed nearly the same gesture: "*bladelike*, your fingertips / Into the green surface *slash*" ("Question at Cliff-Thrust"). The question he asked in "Sunset" was the name of his soul: is this the answer? is he the leaf?

The leaf bears an interesting relation to the mountain; it is the cutting edge of its desire:

> The curdling agony of interred dark strives dayward, in stone
>   strives though
> No light here enters. . . .
>   . . . All mountains want slow-
> ly to bulge outward extremely. The leaf, whetted on light, will
>   cut
> Air like butter. Leaf cries: "I feel my deepest filament in dark
>   rejoice.
> I know that the density of basalt has a voice."

The leaf, in the gesture that reveals its consanguinity with the poet in "Question at Cliff-Thrust," fulfills the mountain's will to bulge outward by doing what that stone cannot. And when it does, it feels its deepest filament in dark rejoice, knowing that the equally dark mountain can now speak, is speaking through the leaf's gesture.

There is something filial about that filament, since other information that we are given about the mountain suggests that *it* is, for the poet, the father. For the attributes of upward movement (or the desire to ascend: "The curdling agony of interred dark strives dayward") and of voice ("I know that the density of basalt has a voice") belong as well to another dark stone, in another last poem, a stone that is clearly paternal. "Myth of Mountain Sunrise," the final poem in *Altitudes and Extensions*, reworks certain elements of the much older "To a Face in a Crowd" (*N & SP*, 322), the last poem in the *New and Selected Poems* of which *Altitudes and Extensions* is the first section. It is the quintessentially last poem in Warren's poetry, the one to which he keeps returning, having placed it at the end of each of the other three *Selected Poems*. That finality is worth special attention; like "Myth of Mountain Sunrise" its subject is stone that almost seems to speak:

> the taciturn tall stone,
> Which is your fathers' monument and mark,
> Repeats the waves' implacable monotone,
> Ascends the night and propagates the dark.

It is not mute but *taciturn*, which is to say "almost always silent" (*Webster's New World Dictionary*), "reserved in speech; saying little; uncommunicative" (*Oxford English Dictionary*). The "taciturn tall stone" of "To a Face in a Crowd" says no more than to repeat "the waves' implacable monotone," but one has the impression, precisely because of the adjective *taciturn*, that it could say more. Now in "Myth of Mountain Sunrise," written some sixty years later—the span of years defined by *New and Selected Poems'* subtitle, *1923-1985*—this father stone, which in the earlier poem had been the very limit case of speech that was just barely speech, has come significantly closer to having something to say.[4] Like the taciturn tall stone that repeated the wave's monotone, these crags make echo as well: "steel-ringing / To dream-hoofs." But the stone of this mountain does more than that, for there is a text inscribed within—"Words stone-incised in language unknowable"—that miraculously speaks: "somehow singing / Their wisdom-song." And the son—the leaf—rejoices now in the knowledge that this father's stone can finally speak: "Leaf cries: 'I feel my deepest filament in dark rejoice. / I know that the density of basalt has a voice.' "[5]

That this father-mountain should echo to dreams of horses ("crags steel-ringing / To dream-hoofs nightlong") is a riddle that will have to await our reading of *Now and Then*, where the poet dreams of horses that are in fact the father.

Interlude: A Forerunner

In 1989, the year I write these words and about four years since I began to read Warren's poetry in this way, I finally discovered the text of Warren's that, had I been sufficiently thorough, I would have read before I even began. This text would have told me what I needed to know, namely, that seventeen years before I began to read his poems with attention to their insistent sequential echoes, he himself had read one of his literary fathers in the same way.

John Crowe Ransom has a peculiar claim to that paternity, for unlike his exact contemporary T.S. Eliot (both were born in 1888), his influence on Warren was personal and direct. Ransom was the man who awakened Warren to poetry as his English professor at Vanderbilt University. The second half of his freshman year he studied "forms of versification" and "poetry writing" with Ransom, Warren told Peter Stitt in a 1977 interview. "He was also the first poet I had ever seen, a real live poet in pants and vest. I read his first book of poems and discovered that he was making poetry out of a world I knew: it came home to me" (*RPW Talking*, 225). And it was Ransom who invited Warren two years later to join the Fugitive meetings (*RPW Talking*, 227).

The text of Warren's that I should have read but didn't until now appeared in the *Kenyon Review* in 1968 and has just been reprinted in his *New and Selected Essays*. Coming upon it now causes me both embarrassment at not having tracked it down before and delight at realizing that I was right all along: that sequential echoes are something of which Warren was acutely aware, at least as a reader, if not as a poet. And that Ransom's role as initiator, as the "first poet I had ever seen," as model, as teacher, made it not improbable that something in Warren's verse would imitate his. Indeed, one can find in Warren's early poetry something very close to Ransom's mixture of archaic and colloquial expression and a less successful attempt at the same pervasive irony. "Notes on the Poetry of John Crowe Ransom at His Eightieth Birthday" begins with Warren's confession that between the ages of nineteen and twenty-five he "rebelled against that power exercised by [Ransom's] poems, and exercised, so unwittingly I may add, by their author. . . . I could never emulate that grace, live by those truths, nor accept such authority. . . . all the harmony and control embodied in the poetry and the man seemed to undercut life-possibility for me and deny life-need. But the rebellion was imperfect" (304). So imperfect that Ransom's poetry, or something it resembled more than anyone else's did, would remain one of the two predominant influences on the young Warren's: "I myself, in trying to write poetry, and in thinking about poetry, was torn between the Pound-Eliot strain and another possibility, shadowy to me and undefined, which, though not like Ransom's poetry, then seemed nearer to it, in some way, than to anything else" (305).

It may be that Warren has still not been able to define what that other, shadowy influence is or was. But his discussion later in this essay suggests that there is something in Ransom's poetry whose influence will become discernible a half-century later in Warren's (I am thinking of the span of years between the publication of Ransom's *Two Gentlemen in Bonds* in 1927 and what I take to be the first clear appearance of the braided poetic sequence in Warren's *Now and Then* in 1978). In 1968, at the time Warren wrote of discovering it in Ransom's poetry, it had not yet appeared in his own (at least as far as I can discern). This long gestation of a paternal text uncannily resembles the bud of the century plant in "Paradox of Time" in *Rumor Verified* that takes decades to bloom and that is itself the metaphor for the last unfinished text, written to his son, penned by Warren's actual father before he lapsed into unconsciousness (of which more later, in chapter 2).

Before getting to what Warren will say in this essay about Ransom's sequential echoes, I'd like to preface it (as does Warren himself) with an anecdote which, in light of a strangely similar anecdote about Warren's real father in the recently published *Portrait of a Father*, gives rise to a remarkable, if unconscious, echo. The present essay is not the first Warren had written about Ransom; in 1935 he published "John Crowe Ransom: A Study in Irony" in the *Virginia Quarterly Review*. When he showed the article to his former teacher "he read it with attention, and then, with charming but (I thought) irrelevant friendliness, asked if he couldn't have his middle name back. The title, by some slip, was

'The Irony of John Ransom'—and so 'Crowe' got put back where it belonged" (305). It is clear that the slip was Warren's, for what he gave Ransom to read was a manuscript ("I walked away with the manuscript in my pocket" [306]), not a galley proof. If it had been a typist's mistake the glaring mutilation of the name of this paternal authority figure had nevertheless escaped young Warren's attention even though it was right there at the top of the page. The slip is surely Freudian, and its significance lies not only in the fact that it happened but that Warren should retell it here, at the moment when he is doing his best to sort out the issues of influence and rebellion in his relationship to John Crowe Ransom.

Now in the recent *Portrait of a Father*, Warren, just after placing Ransom and his father together in the same scene, on a blanket under a maple tree reading Hardy aloud, and after saying that "John and my father had hit it off splendidly, going aside for conversations" (indeed, the two fathers were wonderfully reconciled: "on this occasion, in the presence of John and my father, it really occurred to me why my father had so easily surrendered to me for not accepting the study of law"), tells another story about a father reading a son's manuscript in which part of the father's name is missing. "I had begun to publish what I hoped were poems. . . . one of them, in some sort of reflex against the triple names of many nineteenth-century authors, was signed 'Penn Warren.' My father had read the poem and made a friendly but critical remark. Then, still holding the little magazine . . . , he asked me whether I did not like the name 'Robert.' With an instant of shame—it must have been shame— I remembered that he had once signed his full name" (62-63). (His father had once published poems, signing them Robert Franklin Warren.)

I will have more to say in a later chapter about this denial of the father's name and in particular about which part of the father's name was denied. For the moment it is enough to observe that this event preceded the other by a decade and that it might have had some unconscious influence on the slip made with his mentor's name. The story Warren tells about Ransom's first reaction to his former student's essay about him could be interpreted in two ways: either Warren wanted unconsciously to do to his literary father what he had done to his biological one (who is also, as we will see, a literary father), and perhaps even wanted to get caught doing it, or, in despair at his inability to measure up to Ransom as a poet, Warren wanted to transform Ransom into something like himself, and in particular into what he had been ten years before, when he had most intently felt his inadequacy in the face of Ransom's "power" and "authority": a two-named poet. Or perhaps both statements are true.

Now to the point. In "Notes on the Poetry of John Crowe Ransom," Warren asks, "Is it by accident that in the volume *Two Gentlemen in Bonds* the poem 'Morning,' which is not obviously about man as poet, comes immediately after 'Persistent Explorer'? For the poems are theoretically linked, are complementary" (315). Warren has already established that the persona in "Persistent Explorer" is man as poet because in that poem the "pilgrim" listening to a waterfall refuses to accept the explanation that it is only water; he persists, like the aging man in "Semi-Centennial," in "projecting his poems, his myths, his values upon the blankness of the world." In "Morning," Ralph, not fully awake, experiences, in Warren's words, a "moment of enchantment" in which he imagines proposing to his wife Jane that they go walking and singing in the meadow, but then he fully awoke "and was himself again. / Simply another morning, and simply Jane." Warren finds that in that earlier moment Ralph had been a poet, like the man in the preceding poem. "The other Jane who is not 'simply Jane' must be created by the poet-Ralph—which is not to say that she, the other Jane, is more of a fiction than 'simply Jane' " (316). The difference between the "literal" reading of the waterfall as "nothing but water" and the man's conviction that "That is more than water I hear" is echoed by the difference between "simply Jane" and the "other Jane" Ralph for a brief moment "enchantedly" thought of.

Given Warren's interest in the complementary linkage between these two sequential poems, by the way, it is curious that he should have neglected to observe that both speak of tenantry. In "Persistent Explorer," "the smoke and rattle of water drew // From the deep thickets of his mind the train, // The fierce fauns and the timid *tenants* there" (78).[6] The tenants of the protagonist's mind will soon return in the first lines of "Morning"—return doubly, both in the sequence of these two poems and in the narrative the second tells: "Jane awoke Ralph so gently on one

morning / That first, before the true householder Learning /
Came back to *tenant* in the haunted head . . . " (74). In both
poems the "tenants" of the mind (the "timid tenants" from "the
deep thickets of his mind" in "Persistent Explorer," the tenant-
ing "householder Learning" in "Morning") are momentarily absent, to the advantage of what Warren calls the poetry (of the
waterfall as something more than water, of Jane as more than
Jane).

That Warren was interested in repeated words is apparent from
what he says about the contiguous poems "Two in August" and
"Somewhere Is Such a Kingdom." In the former

> the distraught husband, after a nocturnal quarrel, goes out
> of the house and hears the night birds crying: "Whether
> those bird-cries were of heaven or hell / There is no way to
> tell; / . . . the birds talked / With words too sad and strange
> to syllable." Thus the poem ends with the ambiguous birds,
> to be followed by "Somewhere Is Such a Kingdom," in
> which the speaker of the poem affirms that when the birds
> ("of heaven or hell" in "Two in August") fall out and "croak
> and fleer and swear," he himself must seek "Otherwhere
> another shade / Where the men or beasts or birds / Ex-
> change few words and pleasant words. / And dare I think it
> is absurd / If not such beast were, not such bird?" Can we
> avoid the implication of this sequence? [322-23]

Can we indeed? "Even the placement of the poems is sometimes
of importance" (322). Warren evidently disagrees with Donald
A. Stauffer, who concluded that "Ransom does not do much with
interweaving between poems" (93). For he demonstrates with
masterful skill that all sixteen of the poems of the section "The
Manliness of Men" in *Two Gentlemen in Bonds* are linked by
"cunning interlockings." "Puncture" and "Semi-Centennial," for
example, have "a teasing relationship. . . . The comic poems
'Survey of Literature' and 'Amphibious Crocodile' come together and thematically supplement each other" (323). Like
Warren's own sequential poems, these of Ransom's may appear
at first glance to have nothing to do with each other, but on closer
inspection they yield up their secret: " 'Jack's Letter' is followed
by 'Antique Harvesters,' which seems so different, but is, if our

earlier discussion of it is valid, a repetition, in another range, of
the same theme of the creative power of love" (322).

Warren has had to come to grips with the same question of authorial intent that I had to consider in reading Warren, a matter
of wondering whether these echoes are not somehow unconscious or due to chance: "We have tried to indicate the thematic
coherence of the section called 'The Manliness of Men,' and the
interlocking relations among the poems composing it. This is not
to imply necessarily that the section was planned in this spirit.
The poems may well have been written before the poet made
such a grouping. . . . It would be interesting to have the chronology of composition of the poems in this section, to know to what
degree, if at all, the interlockings come from the fact that one
poem seems to lead, as it were, to another" (324 and 324n).

To stumble across these "Notes on the Poetry of John Crowe
Ransom" now, to discover that Warren had been just as fascinated as I by sequential echoes, is a little like coming across a father's pornography collection and realizing that we have both
shared the same secret vice. It is in fact a moment already inscribed in one of his novels about sons and their fathers' texts—
the moment in *Meet Me in the Green Glen* when Angelo Passetto
opens the big armoire upstairs with the mirror on the door in
which he had at first failed to recognize his own reflection and
discovers the old man's stash of detective and skin magazines,
wherein lay a "tale always empty of meaning" yet "charged" with
a certain obsessive "heavy atmosphere" (122).

TWO

Rumor Verified

"Caverned Enchainment"

Rumor Verified: Poems 1979-1980 bears as its epigraph the last lines of Dante's *Inferno*, which ends, as do *Purgatorio* and *Paradiso*, with a look at the stars.

> . . . io vidi delle cose belle
> Che porta il ciel, per un pertugio tondo,
> E quindi uscimmo a riveder le stelle.

> . . . I saw some of the beautiful things
> That heaven bears, through a round opening,
> And from there we emerged to see the stars again.

Warren will similarly glimpse the stars through a narrow aperture in "It Is Not Dead" (82), the antepenultimate poem of *Altitudes and Extensions*: "a curtain bars / Me in darkness except in one twisted spot where I spy / A fleeting fracture of the immensity of the night sky." If we were to adopt this Dantean inscription on the lintel of *Rumor Verified* as our guide to what lies beyond that doorway, we might find ourselves reading the sequence as Dante viewed heaven's "cose belle" (and as Warren will in "It Is Not Dead"), through the perspective afforded by the admittedly narrow scope of something like that "pertugio tondo": reading, as we have already in *Altitudes and Extensions*, each poem as, starlike, it passes our line of sight; viewing each constellation of word and metaphor in the sequence chosen by the poet, bearing in mind as we scan each poem the still resonant memory of the one that has just left our field of vision. It is not the only way to read Warren, but it is one that his use of sequence, and his Dantean epigraph, encourage. Warren will complain in the next poem after "It Is Not Dead" that the stars, "Heavenly algebra," cannot, or will not, tell him what he needs to know. The constellations "have no / Originality and know / Nothing but repetition" ("Sunset")—yet that very return to the topic of stars reminds us of how his poems, read in sequence, resemble the constellations in that they, too, know a great deal about repetition. Unlike the stars, they know more.

Yet there is much they can teach us even if we pay attention only to what they repeat. Thus "Chthonian Revelation: A Myth" (3), the first part of "Mediterranean Basin" and the first poem in *Rumor Verified*, follows upon the heels of Dante's pertugio tondo with a "dwindling aperture" of its own, the mouth of a sea cave from whose "mystic and chthonian privacy" the eye may stare (as if from the chthonian darkness of inner earth, which is the vantage point from which Dante glimpsed heaven at that moment, as he began his ascent from hell) at "the world of light-tangled detail / Where once life was led that now seems illusion of life." Warren will not therefore be saying the same thing at all as Dante, even if—or, perhaps, because—he is a times rewriting him: Dante glimpsed the future, and a more desirable realm, from his pertugio in hell, while the protagonist here, from his "secret purlieu" (where "*pur*lieu" and "*ape*rture" pun on Dante's "*per*tugio"), in gazing at the sunlit blue of the sea contemplates a past that seems less appealing than his present chthonian darkness.

But at the end of the poem it is, like Dante, with "Eyes starward fixed" that the man and woman emerge from the cave. And it is "with starlight the only light they now know" that they swim home, finding a star glimpse "At arch-height of every stroke" when at each fingertip a drop of water hangs suspended, "each a perfect universe defined / By its single, minuscule, radiant, enshrinèd star." It is not perhaps by accident that it is through the *arch-height* of each stroke that such enshrinèd stars appear, for it was, earlier, "In *arched* dusk from the secret strand" within the cave that the eye had first stared. Then, it saw no star, only "far waters whose tirelessly eye-slashing blue / Commands the wide world beyond that secret purlieu," only the light-tangled detail of past illusions. Then, Dante's epigraph was not fully incorporated into the poem, not entirely rewritten into Warren's text. Only at the end of "Chthonian Revelation," in the very last word, does what Dante saw become what Warren's protagonists see, through the arch (of sea cave and swimming stroke) that is the equivalent here of his pertugio, a framed, glorified, fragment of heaven:

> At arch-height of every stroke, at each fingertip, hangs
> One drop. . . .
> . . . each a perfect universe defined
> By its single, minuscule, radiant, enshrinèd star.

In this poem a man and a woman climb down an island cliff to a beach and the mouth of a cave, into which the woman first goes, the man following; there he finds her standing, naked, "face upward, arms up as in prayer . . . , Eyes closed." He approaches her slowly; their fingertips make contact. Later, they awake "in hermetic wisdom"; one assumes they have made love. They swim back to the headland by starlight, seeing that single enshrinèd star in the drop suspended from the arch-height of every stroke. In the immediately following "Looking Northward, Aegeanward: Nestlings on Seacliff" (6), the second part of "Mediterranean Basin," "you" climb up a sea cliff to find a nest of baby gulls, then make your way down, thinking of an earthquake and volcanic eruption eons ago, of a king's son sacrificed in vain, of unbelieving eyes staring long at the sky—and again of the "blind yearning lifeward" of the infant birds. The stories are not the same, though they both take place in the vicinity of a cliff overlooking a body of water that the larger title these two poems share tells us is the same sea. But then what we found in reading the first is that it did, in the end, recast the scene told in the Dantean fragment that preceded it. Will a similar retelling become visible as our gaze shifts from "Chthonian Revelation" to "Looking Northward"?

What "you" see in gazing at "The unfeathered pitiless weakness of necks that scarcely uphold / The pink corolla of beakgape, the blind yearning lifeward" of gull chicks whose eyes haven't opened yet is in its unfeathered nakedness, its blindness and its upward striving something very much like the woman in the cave, naked ("bare-hided"), closed-eyed ("Eyes closed"), and upward-yearning ("face upward, arms up as in prayer"). Even the woman's "gracility," if taken in its genuine sense of meager,

emaciated slenderness (having nothing to do with grace), anticipates the "pitiless weakness" to be seen in the nest.

The two paths to these parallel visions resemble each other in
their difficulty. Making their way down the cliff to the beach and
the cave, the man and the woman "Painfully picked past lava,
past pumice, past boulders / High-hung and precarious over the
sea-edge" while "you" "inch up" and have "risked neck" to get to
a "rock-shelf outthrust" over the sea. The distant possibility of
an earthquake is hinted at in "Chthonian Revelation" when precariously hung boulders are imagined to be "awaiting / Last gust
or earth-tremor"; while in "Looking Northward" you imagine
what it must have been like when "land heaved, and sky / At
noon darkened" and there was "the gargle of blood on bronze
blade" when the priest sacrificed the royal son to bring back the
sun and calm the waves. "But even / That last sacrifice availed
naught. Ashes / Would bury all. Cities beneath sea sank." Even
that sacrificial instrument made a preliminary appearance in the
preceding poem in a blade that was in fact the sun: "After sun,
how dark! . . . after sun-scimitar."

How can we make sense of these parallels? Is there a single
story beneath these two, or is there only the semblance of a story
in either case—only a semblance of a story in either poem, undercut by the way one story and one poem fade into the others,
only the semblance of a story to be glimpsed between the two
poems and their two stories, as they pass our field of vision like
constellations crossing the narrow aperture that is our only
frame of reference? Despite their mutual allusions, it seems impossible to piece together a single, coherent tale from these two
versions of what may be no original, for the gull chicks with "unfeathered and feeble" necks the woman so strongly resembles
themselves become the king's son whose head the priest drew
back and whose exposed and defenseless "Throat-softness"
awaited the sacrificial blade, while it is the priest whom the
woman now resembles, for he prayed in darkness ("sky / At
noon darkened. . . . That was the hour / When . . . / Priest's grip
drew backward curls of the king's son"), and she does, too:
"there, / In that drizzle of earth's inner darkness, she / Stands,
face upward, arms up as in prayer or / Communion with whispers that wordlessly breathe." She is, perhaps, both sacrifice and
sacrificer, both victim and aggressor. And "Looking Northward,

Aegeanward" would be a poem that devotes itself to interpreting another poem—"Chthonian Revelation: A Myth"—whose revelation, or myth, would be that that is what such a sexual encounter is all about.

Perhaps so. But such an interpretation of an interpretation must subject itself to what the next poem can tell us, and "Blessèd Accident" (11) will refuse to allow us to consider this the final word on the subject because it will return us once more to beach, crag, earthquake, a beloved hand touched in the dark, and even Dante. "Even if you are relatively young," it begins, "— say, / *Nel mezzo del camin*," quoting the first words of the poem whose last words Warren quoted in the passage at the beginning of this series of perpetual echoes, "you have, in fleeting moments of icy / Detachment, looking backward on / The jigsaw puzzle, wondered how you got where you now are, / And have tried to distinguish between logic / And accident." Strangely enough, we are, reading the sequence, doing the same thing; looking back at the puzzle these poems have already begun to pose, trying to piece together the larger picture these tantalizing self-referential fragments (of which this is precisely one) tell us might exist.

We are also trying to distinguish, in attending to these echoes, between logic and accident. Is it by accident or some deeper logic that "Blessèd Accident" should ask "Are you . . . some fragment / Of wreckage *strand*ed on a lost *beach*" when "Chthonian Revelation" found us on a beach that was a "secret *strand*"? Is it by accident that the "fragment of wreckage" should remind us of the "huddle of trash" we found in the nest in "Looking Northward"? Or that the difficulties experienced in climbing up or down in those poems should recur here, when "bare knees scraped and bruised, / One hand somewhat bloody, are you now standing / On the savage crag . . . ?" Or that "the / Horizon's blue ambiguity" in "Looking Northward" should recur with precision: "The slow bulge of earth purged blue / To join the heavenly blue, no certain / Horizon to be defined," as if these two poems had no horizon either, no boundary that one could define with precision, each fading into the other at the very moment they speak of such blue ambiguity?

Yet clearly "Blessèd Accident" is, ostensibly at least, about something else: intimations of mortality, looking back on one's life to determine the ratio of logic to accident, love's need: "But, / In deepest predawn dark, have you / Grasped out and found the hand, clasped it . . . ?" (Though even here one hears an echo of the ritual in the cave: "over immeasurable distance, / Hands out, as though feeling his way in the act, / On the soundless sand he moves in his naked trace. / At last, fingertips make contact.") The blessèd accident in question appears to be death, expressed in a manner that looks both back to the "earth-*tremor*" anticipated in "Chthonian Revelation" and remembered in "Looking Northward" and ahead to the scene about to be depicted of Warren's father's death, whose "unconscious hand had dragged / The pen as he fell."

> Slow tears swell, like bursting buds of April, in
> Your eyes, your heart, and felt breath stop before
>
> The possibility, doomful, of joy, and the awful logic of
> The tremor, the tremble, of God's palsied hand shaking
>
> The dice-cup? Ah, blessèd accident!

Poems later, in "Redwing Blackbirds" (75), third part of "Glimpses of Seasons," Warren will marvel at the redwings' ability to keep their yearly appointment with April, and wonder how long he will be able to do the same: "The globe grinds on, proceeds with the business of Aprils and men. / Next year will redwings see me, or I them, again then?" Happiness at April's return would be inextricably mixed with awareness of death's inevitable arrival for a man whose birthday, like this poet's, is April 24. Hence the tears that swell like bursting buds of April. But those buds at the same time anticipate the memory, in the next poem ("Paradox of Time" [13], a poem of three poems), of how the poet found that his father's death reenacted the slow emergence of "The bud of a century plant / That was straining against the weight / Of years, slow, slow, in silence, / To offer its inwardness." That's because his father died of a cancer whose knowledge he kept to himself—

> the cancer of which
> Only he knew.
> It was his precious secret.

It was as though he leaned
At a large mysterious bud
To watch, hour by hour,
How at last it would divulge
A beauty so long withheld—

as once the poet sat in candlelight with friends, watching the mysterious bud of a century plant finally come to life. "Paradox of Time" begins with an appreciation of what is similarly precious: "Each day now more precious will dawn." I say "similarly," because, in the network of interrelationships shared by these neighboring poems, the preciousness of each new dawn continues what the poet had just been saying in the last lines of the preceding poem ("Blessèd Accident") about his awareness of death. That knowledge makes slow tears swell like bursting buds in April, but it also makes each new day what the private knowledge of the certainty of his death was to his father: precious. What was precious to the father was the secret of his emerging flower, the certain, and singular, knowledge of his death; what is precious to the son is, in light of his knowledge of approaching demise, each new dawn whose arrival staves off death's.

"Gravity of Stone and Ecstasy of Wind," the first part of "Paradox of Time" and whose first line I have just quoted, reassembles once again some of the elements of the poems that precede it. "Blessèd Accident" spoke of "looking backward" on the jigsaw puzzle of one's life, while "Gravity of Stone" looks backward when it speaks of the possibility of atoning for all folly "now left behind." To accomplish this end, it suggests we do something not unlike the expedition in "Looking Northward" to view the nestlings though physically easier: "Sit on the floor with a child. / Hear laugh that creature so young. / See loom its life-arch." (Ought we to see in that life-arch the "arched dusk" and "arch-height of every stroke" of "Chthonian Revelation"?)

The first lines of "Law of Attrition" (14) provide a seamless connection with the last two of "Gravity of Stone" ("Learn the gravity of stone. / Learn the ecstasy of wind"): "Learn the law of attrition, / Learn that the mountain's crag-jut." It is enough to suggest, as the larger title "Paradox of Time" already does, that they are parts of a larger single poem (of which the third part, "One I Knew," tells the father's death). This would account for why the line in "Blessèd Accident" "wreckage *stranded* on a lost *beach*" is so closely echoed here in "an unmapped *strand*, / . . . a *beach* where no foot may come," for "Blessèd Accident" and "Paradox of Time" (of which "Law of Attrition" is part) are contiguous poems. "Blessèd Accident" asks whether "you" are "some fragment / Of wreckage" stranded on that lost beach, while "Law of Attrition" asks us to consider the fate of a single particle of what had been a piece of mountain, that is carried by a river to the sea, passes eons in its depths, and eventually winds up as "A single, self-possessed grain / Of sand on an unmapped strand."

What happens to that grain of sand combines elements of both "Blessèd Accident" and "Gravity of Stone" to tell its story. "Day dawns" in "Law of Attrition" (recalling the opening of "Gravity of Stone": "Each *day* now more precious will *dawn*"),

> and then the sand-grain
> Exposes the glaze of a tiny
> And time-polished facet that now
> Will return from its minimal mirror
> The joy of one ray from above,
> But no more joy for this than
> When tropic constellations,
> Wheeling in brilliant darkness,
> Strike one ray at that same facet.

The comparison implied here is between the poet and the grain of sand, as "Blessèd Accident" makes clear with its suggestion that "you" may become "after storm"—as did the sand particle after "turn and churn of the globe"—"some fragment / Of wreckage stranded on a lost beach. This possibility is all the more likely when we consider that in the later "It Is Not Dead" the poet will "spy / A fleeting fracture" of the stars from his "one twisted spot"—a narrowed perspective already anticipated in the "dwindling aperture" of *Rumor Verified*'s first poem and the "pertugio tondo" of its Dantean epigraph. Here the aperture is defined by the minimal mirror of the tiny and time-polished facet of the crystal of sand, struck by a ray from the wheeling constellations.

As the end of one poem fades into the next, that star-reflect-

ing facet of a grain of sand becomes, in the opening lines of
"One I Knew" (16), the third and last part of "Paradox of
Time," a genuine aperture:

> At the time of sinew dry
> And crank, you may try
> To think of a snow-peak glimpsed
> Through a sudden aperture
> In clouds, and one last sun-shaft
> Flung to incarnadine
> In glory that far, white
> Arrogance before
> Clouds close.

That aperture, in its sense (from *aperire*) of, literally, an opening,
is transformed later in the poem into the image there used for
the father's illness, the opening, the blossoming out of the century plant whose mysterious budding was as much a source of
sorrow for the poet as the "bursting buds of April" (likewise
from *aperire*: when the earth opens) that swell like "Slow tears"
in "Blessèd Accident." When the father fell, unconscious, to the
floor,

> The shimmering
> White petal—the golden stamen—
> Were at last, in triumph,
> Divulged. On the dusty carpet.

Warren makes yet a third flower stand for death in "Small
Eternity" (19), after April's sorrowfully swelling buds and the
century plant whose beauty was so long withheld: the dandelion,
whose seeds scatter in the wind as the memory of someone we
once knew, like him, dies. "The time comes when you count the
names" (he begins, continuing a thought begun in "One I
Knew": "Try to name their names, or try / To think of the nameless ones / You never knew") "—whether / Dim or flaming in
the head's dark" (and here again, an allusion to the poem just
ended, to the scene in which the poet beheld the emergence of
the century plant: "In a room lighted only by / Two candlesticks,

and / Two flames, motionless, rose / In the summer night's
breathlessness."),

                         or whether
In stone cut . . .

But a face remembered may blur, even as you stare
At a headstone. Or sometimes a face, as though from air,
Will stare at you with a boyish smile—but, not
Stone-moored, blows away like dandelion fuzz.

It is very disturbing. It is as though you were
The idiot boy who ventures out on pond-ice
Too thin, and hears here—hears there—the creak
And crackling spread. That is the sound Reality

Makes as it gives beneath your metaphysical
Poundage.

The image of spreading danger in the crackling of the ice is a
beautiful reworking of the spread of his father's cancer, for the
century plant, too, not only grows, blossoms, and spreads like
cancer and like a crack in the ice, but, like the ice, strains against
poundage: "The bud of a century plant / That was straining
against the weight / Of years, slow, slow, in silence, / To offer its
inwardness."

This crackling itself spreads beyond this poem to the next,
"Basic Syllogism" (20), where "Through an eyelid half sleeping,
the eye receives / News that the afternoon blazes bright," a blaze
that is not consumed, from whose "ash resumed / The *crackling*
rush of youthful flare." Phoenixlike, the word itself rises from
the ashes, from extinction to life, from ice—which it had been
in the poem before—to fire. It doubly names its role in the sequence, both as that which spreads ("the crackling spread" of a
crack in the ice) and as that which returns (is "resumed").

The eyelid half sleeping recalls the "some / Small act of careless kindness, *half* unconscious" that "may glow / In some other
mind's dark that's lost your name, but stumbles / Upon that momentary Eternity" in "Small Eternity," which itself recalls the
half-conscious act (half conscious because he lost consciousness
in the middle of performing it), the text, the poet's father left

him in his dying—the unfinished letter: "I saw / The ink-slash from that point / Where the *unconscious* hand had dragged / The pen as he fell." And he could read the salutation: "Dear Son." In "Small Eternity" the poet is hoping for some immortality for himself, for some small half-conscious act of careless kindness that may glow in some other mind's dark. In "One I Knew" this is very close to what his father's death does when it assumes the form of a "large mysterious bud" that the son sees open in candlelight in a dark room.

As the father's secret was "at last, in triumph, / Divulged. *On the* dusty *carpet*," a baby sits "*on its blanket*" and blows a "crystalline / Bubble to float, then burst / Into air's nothingness" in "Sitting on Farm Lawn on Sunday Afternoon" (21)—like "Basic Syllogism," a poem about afternoon. That there is in fact a connection between the carpet and the blanket is borne out by the fact that what arises from it bursts, as do the "bursting buds of April" that announced—in the sequence of events in *Rumor Verified* divulged in the sequence of its poems—the emergence of the father's secret, and deathly, flower. And death bursts again in "Going West" (25) when a pheasant crashes into the windshield of the poet's car: "I do not see, sudden out of / A scrub clump, the wing-*burst*. See only / The bloody explosion, right in my face, / On the windshield . . . in blood, in feathers, in gut-scrawl." (It had already burst in surprisingly similar fashion in "Looking Northward, Aegeanward: Nestlings on Seacliff" when the poet imagined the cataclysm aeons back in which "sky / At noon darkened . . . / And in that black fog gulls screamed as the feathers of gull-wing / From white flash to flame burst.")

The "Nameless Thing" (27) in the poem of that name may be death, but it turns out in the end to be, if only for a mistaken moment, the poet himself. From the sound it makes when it roams the house at night we could perhaps deduce that what it really is is Reality: "usually / Soundless, but sometimes a creak on tiptoed stair," for that creak has been identified in "Small Eternity"—"the creak / And crackling"—as "the sound Reality / Makes." "But sometimes in silence the effluvium / Of its being is enough": a smell like that "left / By funeral flowers"—of which we have seen three already (April buds, the century plant, and dandelion fuzz). He gets up from bed to confront it, standing by the door, poker in hand. "I hold my breath. I am ready. I think of blood"—as he had been equally unbreathing and full of the perception of the blood of the pheasant's impact on the windshield in the poem just before: "I, / With no breath, at the blood stare." There was nothing there. But once he thought he had it trapped in the bathroom: "I snatched the door open, weapon up, and yes, by God!— / But there I stood staring into a mirror. Recognition / Came almost too late. But how could I / Have been expected to recognize what I am?"

"Rumor Verified" (29) is about recognizing one's face, or disguising it: "you sometimes shudder, / Seeing men as old as you who survive the terror / Of knowledge. You watch them slyly. What is their trick? / Do they wear a Halloween face?" A Halloween face is precisely what he saw in the mirror when he saw his own image and thought it was the nameless ghost. It was simply his own image, which is what the rumor verified is, too: "the verification / That you are simply a man, with a man's dead reckoning, nothing more."

But the verification of the rumor could lead a man to drop everything and "secretly sneak / Into El Salvador" to join the guerrillas "and for justification lead / A *ragtag* squad to ambush the uniformed patrol." "Sunset Scrupulously Observed" (31) reenacts such a scene when a cloud, "with / *Ragged* margin" lies in wait for "A jet, military no doubt." When the jet emerges on the other side, there is another "dark cloud now crouching on the horizon, waiting"—as if in ambush posture.

When the jet and its "white trail emerge" from the ragged-edged cloud, "the previously / Invisible fuselage bursts / On vision" as the pheasant emerged from the bush by the side of the road with its "wing-burst" (and as gulls "to flame burst" in "Looking Northward"). That analogy of bird to military aircraft is underscored later in the poem when "five swifts, blunt-bodied like / Five tiny attack planes, zip by in formation."

The plane and accompanying white trail that "emerge" (literally, *e* + *mergere*, "to come out of water") and "burst" upon the poet's vision are transformed in "Minneapolis Story" (33) into an image both for the story in question and for what goes into the making of any poem. On the occasion of the death of a friend, something that happened in Minneapolis years before emerges from the poet's memory: "That old white bubble now arises, bursts / On my dark and secret stream." Indeed,

Whatever pops into your head, and whitely
Breaks surface on the dark stream that is you,

May do to make a poem—for every accident
Yearns to be more than itself, yearns,

In the way you dumbly do, to participate
In the world's blind, groping rage toward meaning.

It may serve to make a poem here, but it's the sixth time something has burst and the second time (after the crystalline bubble that floated from a baby's blanket, "then burst / Into air's nothingness" in "Sitting on Farm Lawn on Sunday Afternoon") that what has burst was a bubble in this sequence of poems. If poems are made from accidents that yearn to be more than accidents, what is made from such accidents within a sequence of poems as these recurring bursts and bubbles? For they also yearn, it seems, to be more than chance occurrences (the same question arises, we noted, apropos of "Blessèd Accident" when the difficulty of distinguishing "between logic / And accident" within one's own life parallels a similar quandary in the reader who notices the accidents of recurring words and wonders what the logic of that might be).

What this bubble brings to the surface is the poet's memory of having, on his way to a bar in Hennepin, stumbled across a drunk on the sidewalk—"half-sprawled, one hand on a hump, / The hump human. Unconscious, but, / With snow scraped off, breath yet." He ran for a policeman, and an ambulance bore the man away. "And I wonder why / That old white bubble now arises, bursts / On my dark and secret stream." What is there, he wants to know, about that relatively trivial incident that makes him remember it now, when a friend has just died? Given all that this poem repeats, I will hazard a guess: he may have been reminded of the unconscious hump on the occasion of that death because both, unconsciously, reminded him of the death of his father, who "Collapsed, and *unconscious*, slid / To the floor" in "One I Knew" (an adjective reiterated later in the poem, when "the unconscious hand had dragged / The pen as he fell"). The other hump in *Rumor Verified* belongs, in fact, to the father: "Ah, menhirs, monoliths, and all / Such frozen thrusts of stone, arms in upward anguish of fantasy, images / By

creatures, hairy and humped, on heath, on hill, in holt /
Raised!" (in "Afterward," penultimate poem in the sequence).
"To a Face in a Crowd" makes it quite clear that such menhirs,
monoliths, and cromlechs are all versions of "the taciturn tall
stone, / Which is your fathers' monument and mark." Those
creatures, pathetically hairy and humped as they may have
been, are our—and his—fathers, for "We are the children of an
ancient band / Broken between the mountains and the sea. / A
cromlech marks for you that utmost strand."

The poet had treated the drunk with reverential care and had
been especially careful with his eyes: "I wonder why / . . . again
waiting alone, I see / The nameless, outraged, upturned face,
where, blessèd / In shadow, domed architecture of snow, with
scrupulous care, / Is minutely erected on each closed eye. / I had
wiped them clear, just a moment before." The "scrupulous care"
with which the snow erects its domed architecture on the eyes
(and, surely, with which the poet wiped them clear) was already
exemplified in the way he observes a sunset in the title: "Sunset
Scrupulously Observed." A scrupulous reading of both poems
would not fail to point out that both end with closed eyes: "Minneapolis Story," in the lines just quoted; "Sunset," with "The
evening slowly, soundlessly, closes. Like / An eyelid."[1]

What had led the poet toward Hennepin in "Minneapolis
Story" was the prospect "of / High-quality high-proof " in that
bar district; what he finds on the mountain trail in "Mountain
Mystery" (35) is "infinite thirst for / The altitude's wine"—another sort of "high"-proof altogether. He is "Alone, but not
alone, for if / You lift your eyes, you see, some forty / Feet off,
her there—unless, of course, / The track now rounds an abutment, and she / Has ceased to exist." Now in "Convergences"
(37) something strangely similar happens: walking alone as a
boy, down a "mountain's near-vertical side / To the V-deep
gorge below," and slaking his thirst in a stream, he discovers
someone staring at him—a tramp with a wolfish, slit-eyed look
who robs him of his sandwich and breaks his thermos because it
contained only milk. What's interesting here is the way the
tramp's disappearance parallels the momentary disappearance
of the woman in "Mountain Mystery": if "The track now rounds
an abutment" then "she / Has ceased to exist"; similarly, the
man follows a railroad *track* whose rails converge at the mouth

of a tunnel at which point he ceases to exist, impaled and sucked into nothingness: "the hidden railroad track. / . . . Where two gleaming rails became one / To impale him in the black throat / Of a tunnel that sucked all to naught." The convergence of the rails parallels, so to speak, the convergence of these two sequentially related episodes.

V is doubly prominent in the topography of "Convergences," appearing vertically in "the V-deep gorge" and horizontally in the "converging gleams of the track." Another letter, the one closest in the alphabet to being the mirror-image of V, is just about as prominent in "Vermont Thaw" (43): the A of "the A-frame" down which there is melting "snow *sliding* / Down the steel roof-pitch"—as the poet in "Convergences" had let himself "*slide* / Down the mountain's near-vertical side / To the V-deep gorge below" in "Convergences." Not only is there sliding in both instances, but there is sliding down the steepness of the letter.

The poet in "Convergences" saw the converging rails and tunnel as a metaphor for his life: "I turned my own way to go / Down a track that I did not yet know / . . . Down the tunnel of year, day, hour, / Where the arch sags lower and lower, / . . . Sometimes you think you can hear / The mathematical drip / Of moisture" in the cave to which those rails and that tunnel opening led. He is at this moment within the V of the rails' convergence. Similarly, in "Vermont Thaw" he is inside the A—"Inside the A-frame"—listening, as he did enclosed in the V in the cave, to an insistent drip: "now / Roof-edges dripped in a rhythm that redefined / Life as blankness." It's precisely because the house is an A-frame that so much dripping is going on, "snow sliding / Down the steep roof-pitch with channels of black." The intensified dripping becomes the whole content of his thoughts: "eaves, / To your heart, say now only one thing. Say: *drip*. / You must try to think of some other answer, by dawn."

"Cycle" (45) is a meditation on the passage of seasons that contrasts the poet's knowledge that change will come to the ignorance of birds, who "do not know / That a time for song will, *again*, come. . . . They know only the *gasping* present, / . . . But I know that snow, like history, will come." The preceding poem, however, insisted on his *not* being able to believe in such change. Using words that would be recycled with a different global meaning in "Cycle," "Vermont Thaw" told us that "Sun sank, and you felt it *gasping* for breath. / You felt it might suffocate, not rise / *Again*." In "Cycle" birds, "*motionless*, gasp"; in "Vermont Thaw" the sound of dripping "hung in *motionless* silence." At the end of "Vermont Thaw": "You *wake in the dark* to the rhythm of eaves. / Can you comfort yourself by thinking of spring? / . . . No." In the last line of "Cycle": "*In the dark* I will *wake*, on the hearth see last coals glow"—the sentence cast in the future tense, spoken in the heat of summer in the secure knowledge that winter will come, that it will again be cold enough to keep a fire going all night.

"Cycle" transforms other elements as well of "Vermont Thaw." In the latter, snow slid "Down the steep roof-pitch with channels of black / Where all winter your eye had loved whiteness," its melting streams doing to the white surface of the roof something similar to what the fat porcupine has done in the next poem to the wall of another structure, "the log backhouse that by his tooth, long back, is well scored." It's so warm in the A-frame that "you found / Yourself sweating, though only one eye of a coal / Yet winked. You built it up only enough / To cook by"; "Cycle" alludes to cooking when it speaks of stones in a stream "of which the tops are hot as stove-lids" and to the last coal on the hearth in its last line ("on the hearth see last coals glow"). It's so warm in the thaw that there's "No need to *bank* fire on a night like this"—a line answered in three ways in "Cycle": (1) in its conclusion, with its knowledge that someday it will again be cold enough to bank a fire, to keep it going all night, (2) in the bear "I see propped, leaning / Back like a fat *banker* in his club window," and (3) the poet's desire "to lie in water, black, deep, under a *bank* of shade."

In "Summer Rain in Mountains" (47)

The edge of the drawn curtain of rain is decisive
Like a knife-edge. Soon it will slice the reddening sun across
    with delicate
Precision. On the yet sunlit half of the mountain miles of
    massed trees,

Glittering in green as they forever climb toward gray ledges,
Renounce their ambition, they shudder and twist, and
The undersides of leaves are grayly exposed to crave mercy.

Here the sun will be sliced with a knife; in "Cycle" it was cut with
scissors: "The sun / Is pasted to the sky, cut crude as a child's collage." What happens when, in the half of the landscape that is
in sunlight, trees glittering in green turn their leaves over under
the force of the rain-announcing wind is precisely what the poet
asked to have happen in "Cycle": "If only one birch, maple, or
high poplar leaf would stir / Even in its sun-glittering green!—
but this air / Is paralyzed."

In "Summer Rain in Mountains" "A dark curtain of rain
sweeps slowly over the sunlit mountain. / It moves with steady
dignity, like the curtain over the / Great window of a stately
drawing room." This window-obscuring rain is transformed
from figurative expression to concrete reality in the opening
lines of "Vermont Ballad: Change of Season" (49), for here it
really does cover a window:

All day the fitful rain
Had wrought new traceries,
New quirks, new love-knots, down the pane.

And what do I see beyond
That fluctuating gray. . . .

In "Summer Rain" the curtain of rain was about to "slice the
reddening sun" in half (likewise, half the mountain is covered
by the curtain of rain, while the other "yet sunlit half" is nevertheless turning gray because the wind is baring the undersides
of leaves—"grayly exposed to crave mercy"). Now, the argument of "Vermont Ballad" is based on the graying of the poet—

. . . I think how the flux,
Three quarters now of a century old,

Has faithfully swollen and ebbed,
In life's brilliantly flashing red
Through all flesh, in vein and artery webbed.

But now it feels viscous and gray.

(Note how the *flux* of his blood echoes the "*fluctuating* gray" of the rain.) It is also based on his transmutation of the rain pouring down the window into the "last flood of vital red— / Not gray—that cataracts down," the last thing he would see if he shot himself in the head. These transmutations of red to gray and gray to red were anticipated, with some precision, by the curtain of rain that was to "slice the reddening sun across with delicate / Precision," turning its red, or half of it, to gray. The sun that was to be divided in half in "Summer Rain in Mountains" would, incidentally, resemble the leaves whose undersides the wind is baring to view, for they, too, are divided, precisely, into two colors—green on one side, gray on the other.

In "Vermont Ballad" the poet stares at the "rain's blurring tracery" on the windowpane and, having already felt his blood turning as gray as that rain, imagines what it would be like to see his blood streaming down in cataracts in front of his eyes as the rain is now. In "Questions You Must Learn to Live Past" (53), he speaks of picking up a snakeskin and staring through its translucence—"Would you hold that frayed translucence up . . . ?"— and then of projecting one's own life, or rather, death, onto it, as he had onto the translucence of the curtain of rain on the window: " . . . Or think that this bright emptiness / Is all your own life may be—or will be—when, / . . . a lithe sinuosity / Slips down to curl in some dark, wintry hole, with no dream?" If in "Vermont Ballad" the poet seemed strangely desirous of blood, to see his own flow down in front of his eyes, in "Questions" that hunger exists, too, though it appears in the "up-lunges of seafoam fanged white, / That howls in its hunger for blood"—a combination of water and teeth that echoes the stream in "Vermont Ballad" that "like a maniac / In sleep . . . grinds its teeth."

"Questions" closes with death figured, Thanatopsis-like, as sleep: dying as curling up "in some dark, wintry hole, with no dream." "After Restless Night" (55) does just the opposite, figuring sleep as death: asleep, "in the trough of Time, as of earth or water, we / Lie—no wind, no wave, / To stir us in that nocturnal grave." In a similar reversal, though this time of the way we usually talk about dreams, we don't decipher our dreams so much as discover that our dreams decipher us: "we . . . see how the dream, anguished or funny, strives / To decode the clutter of our lives." That *anguish* is echoed later in the poem when the

poet imagines his parents in their graves, as he is in his nocturnal one, "sunk in their cogitation. / . . . I advise no distraction
to their frozen *agon*." But the echo is even stronger from the
preceding poem, when one of those parents is in bed, and anguish: "Have you stood by a bed whereon / Your father, unspeakable anguish past, at length / To the syringe succumbs."
Sister, "crazed, . . . cries: / 'But it's worse—oh, it's driving pain
deeper, / Deeper to hide from praying, or dying, or God.' " The
poet in "After Restless Night" reenacts in the act of going back
to bed and to dream what the father is accused of doing, of re-
treating "Deeper to hide": "Then back to bed, / Where warmth
of pillow yet summons your head, / And consciousness for *deeper
concealment* gnaws / Into the fat dark of your skull."

This characterization of consciousness as something that
gnaws in the dark is continued in "What Was the Thought?" (57)
when "The thought creeps along the baseboard of the dark
mind"—a thought that is a mouse whose identification with the
poet to whom the skull in the preceding poem belongs is made
complete when the cat triumphantly awakens the poet to present its kill: "There, blood streaking the counterpane, it lies— /
Skull crushed, partly eviscerated." This blood streaking the
counterpane reminds us of the rain streaking "down the pane"
that would be replaced by a cataract of blood in "Vermont Ballad" (and of the pheasant's "blood streaks" on the poet's windshield in "Going West"). Indeed, the elaborate imagery of
"Summer Rain" and "Vermont Ballad" had never been far away,
for in "After Restless Night" there is yet another curtain on a
window, and behind it is streaked redness: "first dawn-streak,
sallow / Or slow glow from one small cinder of red / Beyond
black trees . . . you may lift a curtain by the bed / To reassure
yourself that the world indeed / Exists."

Thinking of the mouse creeping along the baseboard in
"What Was the Thought?" the poet thinks of its "little heart,
more delicate, more / Intricate, than a Swiss watch." The "Dead
Horse in Field" (59), having been shot with "A 30.06 in *heart*," is
now an "*intricate* piece of / Modern sculpture, . . . *intricate*, now /
Assuming in stasis / New beauty!" Later it will be covered with
love vine, "each leaf / *Heart*-shaped." To assume that intricate
beauty it had to be, like the mouse, eviscerated; this was accom-

plished by "nature's flow and perfection," whose agents are buzzards and crows.

"Immanence" (61) speaks in strikingly similar terms of "Nature's Repackaging System," though this time the poet himself is threatened with such Lucretian recycling. Yet perhaps even that might have been foreshadowed in the two poems just past, for the horse had to be shot because its left foreleg was broken, "shattered below *knee*," while in the last lines of the preceding poem we had awakened to discover that "The pussycat / Crouches at your *knees*, proud, expecting / Praise" and bearing death in its jaws. Precisely, in "Immanence," "something / Plays cat-and-mouse with you . . . though you / Sometimes relax, pretend not to notice, thinking / You'll be the cat, and catch / It unawares."

That game is still going on in "The Corner of the Eye" (63), where "It has stalked you all day, or years, breath rarely heard, fangs dripping. / And now, any moment, great hindquarters may hunch, ready— / Or is it merely a poem, after all?" The vain hope in "Immanence" that the roles of cat and mouse will be reversed is in fact realized in "The Corner of the Eye" except that the reversal is reversed: the thing that haunts the poet—a nameless dread in "Immanence," "The poem . . . just beyond the corner of the eye" in "The Corner of the Eye"—changes from mouse to cat, but the poet undergoes no equivalent transformation. At the end of the poem, in the passage cited at the beginning of this paragraph, the poem may be a great cat ready to pounce, while in the opening lines "It may be like a poor little shivering fieldmouse, / One tiny paw lifted from snow while, far off, the owl / Utters." That that mouse is in danger from a bird and not a cat is not discordant with these (so far) four thematically linked poems, for we have seen how the mouse with the intricate heart in "What Was the Thought?" who was also the poet's thought became the dead horse with the intricate skeleton in "Dead Horse in Field"—whose body was eviscerated by birds, as the mouse in the poem before had been by the cat.

The horse returns, or at least a horse appears, in "The Corner of the Eye" in order to be one of the manifestations, along with the field mouse and the enormous hunched cat, of what is here called "the poem":

The poem is just beyond the corner of the eye.
You cannot see it—not yet—but sense the faint gleam,

Or stir. It may be like a poor little shivering fieldmouse,
....
Or the rhythmic rasp of your father's last breath, harsh

As the grind of a great file the blacksmith sets to hoof.

The father's death has been on our minds in this section, graphically detailed just five poems back, in "Questions You Must Learn to Live Past." Could it be that it, like the dreaded "something" in "Immanence" and the "poem" here, has been haunting this section of the sequence all along? And could it also be that there is, as these lines suggest, some connection between the horse and that death? A comparison of what Warren says about the horse and what he says about the father makes this possibility all the more likely. In "Dead Horse in Field"

> The day
> After death I had gone for farewell, and the eyes
> Were already gone—that
> The beneficent work of crows. Eyes gone,
> The two-year-old could, of course, more readily see
> Down the track of pure and eternal darkness.

In "I Am Dreaming of a White Christmas: The Natural History of a Vision" (*N&SP*, 180), published seven years earlier in *Or Else*, Warren says precisely the same thing about his father's eyes, as he sees them in a dream of a Christmas homecoming in which only he is alive. His father is there in his customary chair, preserved like some kind of mummy, with his skin "brown / Like old leather lacquered." But the eyes are missing.

> I have not
> Yet looked at the eyes. Not
> Yet.
>
> The eyes
> Are not there. But,

Not there, they stare at what
Is not there.

What is "just beyond the corner of the eye" in "The Corner of
the Eye" is both a corner and an eye, for in the immediately preceding "Immanence" what is immanent (and imminent—death,
in both instances) "may well be // At the *corner*" of a city street,
while we have seen in the poem just before "Immanence" the
hauntingly absent *eyes* of the "Dead Horse in Field." Given those
two immediate anticipations (not to mention all the others to be
found in Warren's late sequences), the suggestion in "The Corner of the Eye" that what lies just beyond the corner may in the
end be "merely a poem, after all" may have a self-referential
sense as well. For precisely what lies just beyond the corner of
the eye in one poem is another poem, one that will appropriate
elements of the first poem and find for them uses of its own.
Such recycling eerily resembles what happens when one falls
into what "Immanence" calls "The black conduit of Nature's Repackaging System." Thus the very structure of Warren's poetic
sequences reflects (and reflects upon) the most obsessive themes
of his poems, among which are not only the questionable place
of a sentient, thinking being in a natural world that thrives on
death, but the Oedipal mystery that haunts Warren as the eyes
of the dead father (here glimpsed in those of the horse) haunt
the dreamer of "White Christmas." As we continue to explore
these ironizing, repackaging sequential echoes we will deepen
our appreciation of the degree to which the son in Warren lives
through the father's death and how these succeeding poems
reenact that tragic, but necessary, succession.

One of the forms assumed by the poem beyond the corner of
the eye, together with field mouse, predatory cat, and his father's last breath, is itself a text—to the degree that a discarded
newspaper could be one: "Or the whispering slither the torn
morning newspaper makes, / *Blown* down an empty slum street
in New York, at midnight." The poet listens a bit more closely to
that sound in the next two poems. In "If " (65) it's still a newspaper, though its language has changed: "I shut eyes now, but
still see / The discarded newspaper, across the Piazza, / In a foreign language, *blown* / Over *stones wise* with suffering. . . . I hear /
It scrape the stones." In "What Voice at Moth-Hour" (69) it's the

sound a stream makes as it moves over stone, with a wisdom to which they also contribute: "What voice did I hear as I stood by the stream, / Bemused in the murmurous wisdom there uttered, / While ripples at stone . . . / Caught last light . . . ?"

Seeing, and hearing, that newspaper in the Piazza Navona in "If " "was only a trivial incident of / My middle years. I do / Not even know why I remember it"—the same kind of remark he makes in "Minneapolis Story": "I wonder why / That old white bubble now arises." It's less trivial if he remembers it and doesn't know why; it's even less so for another reason: it's the memory of a memory. "I have stood / Alone . . . in / The dark and unpopulated / Piazza Navona—and I thought: what is the use / Of remembering any dream from childhood? Particularly, / Since any particular moment would be the future all dreams / Had led to. I shut eyes now, but still see / The discarded newspaper." Shutting his eyes now, he can see the newspaper he saw then at the moment when he was remembering a dream from childhood, or trying to, or wondering what was the use of trying to remember one.

Which dream? We don't know, surely—or do we? Warren has in fact spoken elsewhere, in the poem "I Am Dreaming" (in *Or Else*) to which "The Corner of the Eye" and "Dead Horse in Field" have already recently led us, of a particular dream that he had been trying to reconstruct: "the original dream which / I am now trying to discover the logic of." That dream, or part of that dream, is the story of coming home at Christmas to find, among other things, a preserved father with eyes that are not there. "I have not / Yet looked at the eyes. Not / Yet," he tells us, as if he felt he shouldn't look. Just a few lines earlier in "I Am Dreaming" there is something else he is certain he shouldn't see—a newspaper: "the mattress / Bare but for old newspapers spread. / Curled edges. Yellow. On yellow paper dust, / The dust yellow. No! Do not. / Do not lean to / Look at that date." Perhaps the dream he was trying to remember as he stood and watched the newspaper blow by was this dream in which a newspaper, and his father's eyes, were something he knew was there (or wasn't there) but could not, at least at first, bring himself to look at. The newspaper in the Piazza "Carries yesterday with it. . . . It carries yesterday / Into tomorrow." At the conclusion of "I Am Dreaming" we find that to discover the logic of the original dream is to do the same: "This / Is the process whereby pain of the past in its pastness / May be converted into the future tense / Of joy."

The pun in the title of "What Voice at Moth-Hour" suggests an answer to the question it poses—"What voice at moth-hour did I hear calling / As I stood in the orchard . . . ?"—but nothing in the poem confirms it. It may as well have been the father. What the voice actually says gives us no clue: "as I / Once heard, hear the voice: *It's late! Come home*" (Warren's italics). The first stanza resounds, however, with some peculiar echoes:

> What voice at moth-hour did I hear calling
> As I stood in the orchard while the white
> Petals of apple blossoms were falling,
> Whiter than moth-wing in that twilight?

Where have we seen these white petals before? In the "shimmering / White petal . . . at last, in triumph, / Divulged" when the father died, yielding up the "precious secret" of his cancer ("One I Knew"). In "Reading Late at Night, Thermometer Falling" (*N&SP*, 200), in *Or Else*, that precious secret received a different characterization but one whose link to its later incarnation—the century plant's white petal—is forged by the white petals of apple blossoms that fall here as the poet hears the voice: "they discovered your precious secret: / A prostate big as a horse-apple. Cancer, of course."[2] These two versions of what is on both occasions called the father's "precious secret" combine to produce what is falling around the poet in the orchard as he hears the voice: Horse apple plus white petal equals white apple blossom petals plus horse. And the horse is one we have seen before—in the "Dead Horse in Field" whose eyes in their absence were just like the eyes of the dead father in the Christmas dream in theirs.

In "If," the poet can "shut eyes now, but still see / The discarded newspaper." In "What Voice at Moth-Hour," likewise, "If I *close / My eyes*, in that dusk I again know / The feel of damp grass between bare toes," can see the "last zigzag, . . . high, / Of a bullbat" as he once heard and can now "hear the voice: *It's late! Come home*." If "What Voice" seems another version of "If," another attempt to remember something with eyes closed—in

which the discarded newspaper blown over stones wise with suffering, scraping them, making a noise one can hear, is meta-
morphosed into two different phenomena: the falling blossoms,
discarded from the tree (and white, like the paper), and the wise
murmur coming from the water moving over the stones in the
stream—so also does "Another Dimension" (70) seem another
version of "What Voice." For there the white blossoms become
"white / Bloom" powdering long hedges, the poet is lying "on
the grass," and looking upward to see the lark as in "What
Voice," he stands barefoot on the grass and looks up to see the
last zigzag of a bullbat. Once again he has the gift of blind sight:
"I have shut eyes and seen the lark flare upward. / All was as real
as when my eyes were open." Like the dead horse in the field
("Eyes gone, / The two-year-old could, of course, more readily
see / Down the track of pure and eternal darkness"), and like his
father in the dream of Christmas ("Not there, they stare at
what / Is not there"), he too can see certain things better without
his eyes. In "Another Dimension" the sound of the lark the poet
can see with his eyes shut belongs to this category. "Song is lost /
In the blue depth of sky, but / We know it is there at an altitude
where only / God's ear may hear"—only God, or perhaps his
dying father: "I have strained to hear, sun-high, that Platonic
song. / It may be that some men, dying, have heard it."

The first two stanzas of "Another Dimension," like the first
two of "What Voice at Moth-Hour," restate the same thing two
ways and are at the same time a transformation of earlier images. In the first, "the lark / Flames sunward, divulging, in tinseled fragments from / That height, song. Song is lost / In the
blue depth of sky." In the second, "Dividing fields, long hedges,
in white / Bloom powdered, gently slope to the / Blue of sea that
glitters in joy of its being." Clearly the blue of the sky and the
blue of the sea both incarnate Warren's vision of the self-sufficient absolute. The sea revels in the joy of its own being; the sky,
in the third stanza, will be described as "That world which had
no meaning but itself." The tinseled fragments that are divulged
from the lark are its song, though we can't hear it; but if we
could hear it—and the poet almost succeeds in hearing it, later,
when he shuts his eyes—it would come to us from, connect us
to, that blue absolute (which is why he calls it "that Platonic
song"). The equivalent term in the second stanza is the white

bloom powdered on the long hedges that, gently sloping, lead our eyes to the sea. Reading this poem in light of the one that immediately precedes it allows us to see just how closely this white bloom powder is related to those divulged tinseled fragments that fall from the sky. "What Voice at Moth-Hour" in fact makes the connection for us: "the white / Petals of apple blossoms were falling, / Whiter than moth-wing." The petals are like the wings of moths in their whiteness. They are already, that is, emblems of flight. The white blossoms fall like the tinseled fragments that scatter down from the flight of the lark, but as white blossoms they are equally like the white bloom that powders the hedges.

The functional similarity, noted above, of the tinseled fragments and the white bloom on the hedges is thus intimately connected to the echoes linking these two adjacent poems. The tinseled fragments divulged from the lark are the visual representation of something that cannot be heard. "What Voice at Moth-Hour" is likewise a poem about trying to hear something (which can only be heard with eyes closed), and the voice in question is, if not transformed into, at least closely associated with things that are seen and not heard: white blossoms and the moth wing. The voice bears a special relationship to the latter, for it defines the hour that voice may be heard and the homonymity of "moth-hour" with "mother" further suggests that in naming the hour one may also, if unknowingly, be naming the voice ("Code Book Lost," in *Now and Then*, resolves all ambiguity in this regard when it speaks of "the mother's voice calling her boy from the orchard, / In a twilight moth-white with the apple blossom's dispersal").

But there is something else we can hear in the song of the lark that cannot be heard. It's apparent in the "divulging" of those tinseled fragments and in the dusting effect of the white bloom powdering the hedges—the father's precious secret: "The shimmering / White petal . . . Divulged. On the dusty carpet." No wonder that song can only be heard by "some men, dying," for clearly the father's death is present here.

"Glimpses of Seasons" (72) is a poem in four parts, each part numbered and with its own title. As in other such poems—"Mediterranean Basin" and "Paradox of Time"—the allusions to the immediately preceding "Another Dimension" are scattered throughout the poems that compose it or at least throughout the first three of them. While "Another Dimension" had the poet looking "upward / To feel myself redeemed *into* / That world which had *no* meaning but it*self*, / As I, laying there, had only the present, no future or past," in "Gasp-Glory of Gold Light" the poet stares at the gold light of dawn and finds that "Self flows away *into* the unbruised / Guiltlessness of *no-Self*." The sense of being outside the normal process of Time that he felt in "Another Dimension" when he "had only the present, no future or past" returns in "Gasp-Glory" in the form of standing "On the knife-edge of no-Time. / Or is it not no-Time, but Time ful-filled?"

The other dimension in "Another Dimension" was of "That world which had no meaning but itself "—which in the context of that poem seems to be the world the lark inhabits, the blue depth of sky, or sea "that glitters in joy of its being." "Snow Out of Season" (73), the second poem in "Glimpses of Seasons," however, says the same things of the world *we* inhabit: "We / Are old enough to know that the world / Is only the world." In "Redwing Blackbirds" (75) the telling image in "Another Dimension" of the lark so far above that its "Song is lost / In the blue depth of sky" returns in the form of redwing blackbirds whose singing is first perceived by the eye through binoculars: "Throats throb, your field glasses say." And the ability to perceive with eyes closed—familiar from "Another Dimension": "I have shut my eyes and seen the lark flare upward. / All was as real as when my eyes were open" (but also from the two poems before that, "What Voice at Moth-Hour" and "If ")—has not left the poet here: "I again / Awake, not in dream but with eyes shut, believing I hear / That rusty music far off."

The poems within "Glimpses of Seasons" have sequential echoes as well. The "Now forgotten green *bough*-loop" of "Gasp-Glory" returns as "*boughs* hung heavy, white only" with snow in "Snow Out of Season"; "sun stabs the red splash to scarlet on each epaulet" of the redwing blackbirds, echoing the dogwood berries in the preceding "Snow Out of Season" that shock by their sudden redness: "Sudden on white, as on white velvet deployed, / Uncountable jewels flamed to the sun's flame." The redwings return every April, prompting the poet to thoughts of his own mortality: "Next year will redwings see me, or I them, again then?" While in "Crocus Dawn" (77), the last poem in this minisequence (of which all but "Redwing Blackbirds" have taken place at dawn), he worries about "the blank check / Of a heart that flutters vacantly in / The incertitude of the future's breath, / Or blast." As he had wondered if next April would see him still alive, here he asks, "After / Darkness will there come that crocus dawn . . . ?" and prays to see at least one more: "Oh, crocus dawn, / May our eyes gleam once more in your light before / We know again what we must wake to be."

That darkness before the crocus dawn is unrelieved by any dawn in "English Cocker: Old and Blind" (78) for the dog whose name is a near-anagram for the name of the dawn. The cocker is blind, constrained to "whirling dark" and "eternal night." The poet sees him as with "painful deliberation he comes down the stair, / At the edge of each step one paw suspended in air,"[3] enacting a metaphor for the uncertainty of what lies beyond life: "Does he thus stand on a final edge / Of the world?" The poet was similarly uncertain in the darkness before the crocus dawn, anxious about "The incertitude of the future's breath"; here, the dog's only reassurance is the poet himself, sometimes present to him only in the form of something like breath: "Only a frail scent subject to the whim / Of wind."

Both dawn and thoughts of mortality permeate "Dawn" (79), in which the poet imitates the cocker's "own paw suspended in air" in his eternal darkness when in dawn's grayness, wondering if there is enough light to distinguish shadow, "I hold up my hand. I can vaguely see it. The hand." The anagrammatization of "cocker" and "crocus" continues in "Dawn" with the addition of a third term that, like a crocus dawn, signals another day of life, and whose message the poet prays (as he did in "Crocus Dawn" and "Redwing Blackbirds") to receive once more: "Far, far, a *crow calls.* . . . I want to be real. Dear God, / . . . Will I find it worthwhile to pray that You let / The crow, at least once more, call?" Behind this crocus, cocker, and crow call there may be another, unspoken term, one that in Warren's lexicon is a rude word for dying—found, for example, in the very early "Genealogy" (in *Thirty-six Poems*): "For the other young guy who *croaked* too late."

The first light in "Dawn" is watery: it will "seep in as sluggish and gray / As tidewater fingering timbers in a long-abandoned

hulk"—an image transported from salt to fresh water in "Millpond Lost" (81): "the mill, / Now long back, must have rotted
away. One by one, old beams may drop" into the pond. The mill,
having rotted away "*long* back," is, like the boat whose timbers
are fingered by tidewater, "a *long*-abandoned hulk," its beams
the equivalent of those timbers.

"One by one," those "old beams may drop, / Though some,
mossed and leaning, through vine-ruck, may poke still. // They
will drop, one by one, and each individual fact / Will measure
out time." The beams that measure time anticipate a pine tree
that does similar clockwork in "Summer Afternoon and Hypnosis" (83): "the shadow of that tall pine names night, and by //
The moment it touches the mossed stone yonder," he will have
risen from his afternoon drowse to return home (note that the
adjective "mossed" returns as well). While he was there, lulled by
"the afternoon's hypnosis / Of summer," he experienced motionlessness before a mirror—

> . . . lulled thus, your life achieves its honesty,
> . . . And your heart,
> Bemused as though in a mirror's icy duress,
> Seems to suspend its stroke, and your dry lips part
>
> In a whisper of slow appalment to ask: "Was this
> The life that all those years I lived, and did not know?"
> Do you really think now the sun's frozen motionless?
> Do you really think the stream no longer can flow?

—that seems almost a mirror image of the mirrored stasis in
"Millpond Lost": "Lucent, the millpond mirrors September
blue. / . . . motionless air, . . . water motionless too."

"If Ever" (87) tells a quite different story. No longer is a pas-
toral scene the pleasant locus of thoughts about timelessness;
here, the place is one of dread, the one "where once it happened"—"it" representing a distinctly unpleasant event. But
some of the same things happen here that happened in "Summer Afternoon": "If ever you come where once it happened, /
Pause, even briefly, and try to discover / If the heart now stalls,
as once, for a lover, / It did." Or as it did when it seemed "to sus-
pend its stroke," bemused by the mirror's icy duress in the pre-

ceding poem. "What if a mysterious / And throttling fist should now squeeze the heart, / And wrench it, and seem to tear it apart / From your bosom . . . ?"—as in "Summer Afternoon" truth is "torn at last from lies." Here, you may find yourself "frozen in hope—or despair"—as the heart was paralyzed by the mirror's iciness, and the sun "frozen motionless" in the poem before. There, it was precisely the heart's "stroke" that was suspended in the mirror's icy duress, while here strokes are what will bring you back to life: "Seize the nettle of self, plunge then into / Cold shock of experience, like a mountain lake, and let // Stroke, after stroke, sustain you. And all else forget."

The "Scene" in "Have You Ever Eaten Stars? (A Note on Mycology)" (88) (and "Scene" is in fact what it is called here, that marginal indication preceding the first thirty-five lines, while the remaining lie under the rubric "Question") is, like the one in "If Ever," one "briefly" visited. The latter is where you should "Pause, even briefly," if you ever come that way; the former is "that precinct where / The sunray makes only its brief / And perfunctory noontide visitation." It is also the site of the equally "brief" appearance of golden mushrooms:

> Earth, black as a midnight sky,
> Was, like sky-darkness, studded with
> Gold stars, as though
> In emulation, however brief.
> There . . .
> Burst the gleam, rain-summoned,
> Of bright golden chanterelles.
> However briefly. . . .
>
> Later, I gathered stars into a basket.

These poems, particularly these two, leave plenty of clues for us to conclude that, in sequences of twos, they keep returning to the same spot (a spot that, paradoxically, changes into another spot as one moves to another sequence of two—each two poems, for the most part at least, have their *own* spot): "If ever you *come* where *once* it happened" ("If Ever"). "But late, *once* in the season's lateness, I, / . . . *Came*" ("Have You . . . ?"). Here, he gathers stars which are chanterelles into a basket; there, he told us to

gather up another sort of wild flora: "Seize the nettle of self"—
and spoke of, if not a basket, "the grab-bag of pastness." There,
the place "where once it happened" is where one might hear
"contradictory / Voices now at midnight"; here, midnight returns in the sky that is the black earth where these gold stars appear. There, those midnight voices may make "you, nightlong,
in your ignorance, sweat"; here, the site is where "I, sweat-
soaked in summer's savagery, / Might here come."

The chanterelles are "rain-summoned"—brought from the
earth by recent rain. The event "Twice Born" (90) tells is likewise
brought about by rain; in it, a great dead pine is struck by lightning, snatching the poet from sleep. If he was "soaked" by
sweat in the poem before, here, he is, after going out in the
thunderstorm to investigate, also, though not by sweat, "soaked,
and hands / Chilled to the marrow, shoes squishing water." In
the end, "The God-ignited torch, dying, left / Only a faint flicker
on the walls—and the ceiling / That I stared at with a strange
shudder and excitement"—the pine in its fading glow coming to
resemble even more closely the chanterelles with their starlike
"gleam" in the "midnight sky" of black earth.

"Twice Born" cites a portion of a biblical verse (appropriately,
considering its title, from the New Testament) that "The Sea
Hates the Land" (92) begins in its very first words to complete:
"one last and greatest crash, as though / On our roof, as though
God / Was not mocked by any easy assumption" ("Twice Born");
"*Be not deceived* by the slow swell and lull of sea" ("The Sea
Hates"); "Be not deceived; God is not mocked: for whatsoever a
man soweth, that shall he also reap" (Galatians 6:7). The verse
interprets itself, in Warren's handling of it, for he sows part of
it in one poem and reaps that to which it gives rise—part of itself—in the next. That by which one should not be deceived in
"The Sea Hates the Land" is that what the title says is true, despite the "lull of sea lolling / In moonlight," and that "Deeper
process // Proceeds, as blood inwardly flows while you sleep."
But anyone who has passed through the experience of the preceding poem is not likely to be so deceived or likely not already
to know about what can happen while one sleeps.

You cannot blame the sea. For you, as a man,
Know that only in loneliness are you defined.

      . . . even the kiss at midnight,
And the hurly-burly of firmaments and men
Are froth on the surface of deepening need.

That midnight kiss gets fleshed out, a little, in "Afterward" (93),
when the poet discovers the obituary of a woman "Who, *at night,*
used to come to your apartment and do everything but / It."
While the remark about the defining power of loneliness loses
some flesh in its reincarnation here: "Oh, see / How a nameless
skull, by weather uncovered or / The dateless winds, // In the
moonlit desert, smiles, having been / So long alone." It is precisely the skull's having been alone so long that defines its
expression as a smile. Both "The Sea Hates the Land" and "Afterward" end in moonlight, the former issuing the command "so
by moonlight / Swim seaward . . . remembering when // The self
had the joy of selflessness completely / Absorbed in the innocent
solipsism of the sea," the latter issuing the commands "see //
How a nameless skull . . . // In the moonlit desert, smiles" and

      Sit down by a great cactus,
While other cacti, near and as far as distance, lift up
Their arms, thorny and black, in ritual unresting above
Tangles of black shadow on white sand, to that great orb

· Of ever out-brimming, unspooling light and glow, queenly
      for
      good or evil, in
The forever sky.

The cacti's uplifted arms repeat, within this poem, the striking
gesture of

            menhirs, monoliths, and all
Such frozen thrusts of stone, arms in upward anguish of fan-
      tasy,
      images

By creatures, hairy and humped, on heath, on hill, in holt
Raised!

Their upward anguish is shared by the gold leaf in "Fear and Trembling" (97), and the boughs of its tree repeat the skyward gestures of menhir and cactus: "When boughs toss—is it in joy or pain and madness? / The gold leaf—is it whirled in *anguish* or ecstasy *skyward*?"

Thus the sequence ends as it began, with upstretched arms— and as in the last line, in a cave:

> Can the heart's meditation wake us from life's long sleep,
> And instruct us how foolish and fond was our labor spent—
> Us who now know that only at death of ambition does the deep
> Energy crack crust, spurt forth, and leap
>
> From grottoes, dark—and from the caverned enchainment?

For that is where we were in "Chthonian Revelation: A Myth": "there, / In that drizzle of earth's inner darkness, she / Stands, face upward, arms up as in prayer." This linkage gives a new meaning to the last two words of *Rumor Verified*, for what is en-chained is the cave itself: this one to the sea cave in "Chthonian Revelation" as all the poems in the sequence of *Rumor Verified* are, connected like links in a chain, forming an unbroken se-quence in which each poem repeats and transforms elements of the one that precedes it and in which the last links up with the first to complete the enclosed, caverned enchainment.

Interlude: A More Distant Parallel

If Warren's discovery that John Crowe Ransom's poetry exhibits sequential linkage may have had some influence on the devel-opment of sequential echoes in his own work, no such claims of influence may be made for the structurally based echoes I would like to take a moment to discuss here—though they could well have had some influence on my own discovery of the echoing words in Warren. A need to confess lies behind what I am about to say, though of more importance is the fact that it tells us something about the unconscious structure of literary works.[4]

No doubt Warren knows Montaigne as well as anyone, but no one until recently (and therefore not Warren either) has been aware of the extraordinary degree to which words, anecdotes, and arguments in his *Essays* echo in pairs. Though they do so in essays that are symmetrically—rather than sequentially—placed,[5] the ways in which that which is repeated often seems a commentary on the repetition provide an instructive parallel to the manner in which Warren's repeated words seem at times to speak of the very activity in which they too are engaged. Instructive, that is, for someone interested in a general literary phenomenon. What follows is an excursion into comparative literature that will not necessarily add anything to what we know about Robert Penn Warren but may help to place what we are discovering about his poetry in a broader context. The parallel in this instance is due not to historical influence but to what happens when a recurring structure of repetition inhabits a literary text; it is due as well to the propensity of literary texts to tell us in more or less hidden ways what they are secretly doing.

We have seen such self-reference, for example, in the "crackling spread" of "Small Eternity" that spreads to "Basic Syllogism," where it appears as a "crackling rush," as if the crack in the ice were occurring as well in the sequence in which these two poems are contiguously placed. It happens too in "The Corner of the Eye," where the "poem . . . just beyond the corner of the eye" may also be the poem just beyond the corner just passed, the immediately preceding "Immanence" which spoke of what "may well be // At the corner of one of Fifties and Fifth Avenue." As well as in the "Horizon's blue ambiguity" of "Looking Northward" that immediately reappears in "Blessèd Accident" when "The slow bulge of earth purged blue / To join the heavenly blue, no certain // Horizon to be defined"—where the blurring contiguity of blue sea and blue sky is paralleled by the contiguity of these two blurring blue horizons, so similarly phrased as almost to blur into each other.

In Montaigne's *Essays* the verbal echoes apparent in chapters equidistant from the center of the book[6] likewise seem at times to allude to the fact of their repetition. With the difference that these echoes occur over what are sometimes considerable distances (between for instance the first and fifty-seventh chapter or the second and fifty-sixth), so that, while Warren's self-commenting echoes may speak of their contiguity (of a spreading crack, of what is just around the corner, of a contiguity that blurs distinctions), those of Montaigne allude to a mutual communication carried on *despite* long distances. Thus for example in essay 1:23, "Of custom, and not easily changing an accepted law," Montaigne begins by cataloguing all sorts of diverse conditions and customs from around the world in order to demonstrate that "there falls into man's imagination no fantasy so wild that it does not match the example of some public practice" (79);[7] arguing, that is, that for every fantasy we can imagine there is some outlandish custom somewhere in the world that is its real counterpart. And then spends the rest of the essay arguing that it is wrong to change an accepted law because "a government [*une police*] is like a structure of different parts joined together in such a relation that it is impossible to budge one without the whole body feeling it" (86). Now, in the symmetrical counterpart to this essay, essay 1:35 (equidistant from the central chapter 1:29), Montaigne, in typically contradictory fashion, argues that there is a defect in our government that ought to be remedied, as its title suggests: "Of a lack in our administrations" ("D'un défaut de nos *polices*"). Significantly, the word *police*, which means "government" or "administration," figures prominently in the title of this essay and is at the same time the word used in the other essay to name the thing which, despite whatever defects it may have, ought not to be changed.

When Montaigne speaks of "a structure of different parts joined together in such a relation that it is impossible to budge one without the whole body feeling it," he is alluding not only to civil government but also to the complicated structure of the *Essays* themselves, which are much more closely related than they may appear on the surface. And this very issue of changing an established practice or introducing a new one in order to correct a defect in the general *police* is a case in point. For the innovation that Montaigne in 1:35 thinks ought to be introduced—an innovation that necessarily violates the stricture against innovations in our *police* the second half of 1:23 lays down—responds precisely to what the first half of 1:23 says both about (1) diverse customs and conditions from around the world and about (2) matching one's private fantasy with someone else's practice:

> My late father . . . once told me that he had wanted to arrange that towns should have a certain designated place

where those who needed something could go and have their business registered by an officer appointed for that purpose. As, for example: "I want to sell some pearls; I want to buy some pearls. . . . " And it seems that this means of informing one another would be of no slight advantage to public commerce; for all the time there are people with congruous needs [il y a des conditions qui s'entrecher-chent] who are looking for one another, and, for lack of knowing one another, are left in extreme need. [165]

Such an innovation would have had the force of law, as his father was mayor of Bordeaux at the time. To these "conditions qui s'entrecherchent," these conditions that seek each other out, respond the encounters that essay 1:23 predicts between the fantasies of human imagination and "the example of some public practice," some custom in a foreign land that will fulfill the fantasy. Like mathematical fractals that replicate on a microscopic level the same patterns that obtain at larger levels of structure, the encounter of these two essays—an encounter guaranteed by the secret symmetrical structure of the *Essays*—enacts the very encounters of which they both speak. The two essays are themselves "conditions qui s'entrecherchent," conditions that seek each other out over the long distance (the twelve intervening essays) that separates them.

So too are Montaigne's *Essays* and Warren's poetry sequences, distanced by all that separates a sixteenth-century French essayist from a twentieth-century American poet. To list side by side their respective and strangely responding *conditions* may be an innovation in our literary *police*, but it is one of which Montaigne's father at least would have approved.

I'd like to offer one more example, bearing this time on another aspect of the literary self-reference—the tendency of certain texts to call attention to what they are doing by denying its very possibility. We have seen such denial in Warren's "New Dawn," which in the very first line speaks of the removal of "all the 'unauthorized items' " from the bomber, which despite this purgation turns out to be overweight by a factor of ten (of 10 percent: "150,000 pounds, / Overweight 15,000"). Ten is the insistent number in the poem, and in the sequence it forms with

"The Distance Between: Picnic of Old Friends," being both the distance separating the two bombs within in the bomb and the distance separating the two old friends about to come together in adultery. "New Dawn" thus provides an allegory of its own reading, reporting both the attempt to remove all "unauthorized items" unsanctioned by authorial intent and the failure to complete the job—in particular the failure to rid the poem of a certain insistent ten.

Like Warren, Montaigne went through the motions of a such a denial when he said in essay 1:24, "Various outcomes of the same plan," that "sometimes there escape from the painter's hand touches so surpassing his conception and his knowledge [surpassans sa conception et sa science] as to arouse his wonder and astonishment. But Fortune shows still more evidently the part she has in all these works by the graces and beauties that are found in them, not only without the workman's intention, but even without his knowledge. An able reader often discovers in other men's writings perfections beyond those that the author put in or perceived, and lends them richer meanings and aspects" (93). The reader of the *Essays* may therefore find richer meanings than Montaigne intended, and such discoveries, when they occur, can only be attributed to chance. Curiously—and suspiciously—enough, this is just what happens here. For the symmetrically placed counterpart to this essay is 1:34, "Fortune is often met in the path of reason," which as its title indicates is precisely about such fortunate accidents as those accomplished in 1:24 without the painter's intent. In fact it tells the story of a *painter* to whom such a thing happened. And in doing so it repeats the very words *surpassans* and *science* that in 1:24 told of what could happen by chance to a painter's work. "Did [Fortune] not surpass [surpassa] the painter Protogenes in the knowledge [la science] of his art? He had completed the picture of a tired and panting dog to his satisfaction in all parts but one: he was unable to show the foam and slaver to suit himself. Vexed with his work, he took his sponge, which was soaked with various colors, and threw it at the picture to blot it out completely. Fortune guided the throw with perfect aptness right to the dog's mouth, and accomplished what art had been unable to attain" (164). We are therefore to believe that the coincidence between these situational and verbal echoes and the symmetrical placement of the chapters in which they occur is due to the very *fortune* of which they speak, that it is, to adopt Warren's slyly self-referential term, an "unauthorized" phenomenon.

THREE

Being Here

"Life's Long Sorites"

Of *Being Here: Poetry 1977-1980*, Warren has warned us that if we read the poems in this collection without regard for the order in which they appear we will be missing something rather important: "The order of the poems is not the order of composition. . . . The order and selection are determined thematically, but with echoes, repetitions, and variations in feeling and tonality" ("Afterthought," 107). Peter Stitt has made a start toward tracing the sequential movement of the book, arguing that the five divisions of the sequence move from childhood to youth to old age, with the central sections investigating "possibilities within the nature of time" ("Life's Instancy and the Astrolabe of Joy," 725). He argues as well that the overall pattern of the book is circular. But in paying attention to the sequence of divisions rather than to the sequence of the poems themselves, he has not gone as far as he might have done in figuring out what Warren could have meant by stressing the importance of their order nor in justifying his conclusion that *Being Here* is a "brilliant and unified volume—brilliant in conception, brilliant in construction, brilliant in artistry" (731).

If it is a unified volume brilliant in construction, that brilliance will show up in its attention to detail, but to see it we will have to pay similar attention ourselves to some of the more microscopic aspects of its structure. What we have found in *Altitudes and Extensions* and in *Rumor Verified* may lead us to hope that *Being Here* can sustain a reading intensely interested in sequence, and in the metonymic connections to which sequence can seem, almost by chance, to give rise. It is one way, and an intentionally narrow one, of looking at details of poetic construction, but we have seen sufficient evidence by now to warrant the belief that Warren has been exploiting these possibilities for some time; very possibly in our journey backward through his poetry we will come to a time when he did not do so. *Being Here* was not written at such a time.

Part I begins with a gradual venture backward into a cave, the poet a boy who gathers enough new courage each year to penetrate a little deeper. At age twelve in "Speleology" (7) he's able to go all the way—which is to go so far as to allow himself to fall asleep in the depth of the cave, in imitation of death. Perhaps he didn't intend to fall asleep, but the "silken and whispering rustle" of a stream brought him to that state: "the water . . . sang to itself. . . . Light out, unmoving, I lay, // Lulled as by song in a dream" and then, "Heart beating as though to a pulse of darkness and earth," he "thought / How would it be to be here forever."[1] Peter Stitt is right to say that "the feeling of union experienced by the boy in the cave is designed to remind us of the actual and universal experience of union which the baby has while in the mother's womb. The final tip-off may be the insistent nature of the heartbeat" (720). But yet another tip-off is offered by the by now familiar sequential structure of Warren's recent books of poetry. For this is not the first poem in the collection; it is preceded by the liminal "October Picnic Long Ago" (3)—a poem in which the mother sings, as her chthonian and watery incarnation will sing in the cave, while her son is about to fall asleep:

> And a bird-note burst from her throat, and she gaily sang
> As we *clop-clopped* homeward while the shadows, sly,
> Leashed the Future up, like a hound with a slavering fang.
> But sleepy, I didn't know what a Future was, as she sang.
>
> And she sang. [Warren's italics]

The setting here is not a cave but a rented surrey on the way home from a picnic in the woods. Yet such is the transforming power of Warren's poetry and his exploitation of the possibilities of poetic sequence that we can, with the poet, fall asleep in one and wake up in another, hearing the same lulling mother's song throughout.

"When Life Begins" (9) describes his grandfather—his mother's father—as if he were made of stone: "Curl-tangled the beard like skill-carved stone / With chisel-grooved shadow accenting the white." The image here is of a Greek statue—"Erect was the old Hellenistic head"—but could it be that we are once again in the same place, despite the change of scene? Could there be some significance in the fact that the stone, at least, of the scene in the cave is still present here? The grandfather's head, in fact, like the cave, is a place of mystery, a place more real, in some respects, than the bright world outside: "He felt that all reality / Had been cupboarded in that high head," that it was, like the cave, a place of sleeping: "He thought all things that ever lived / Had gone to live behind that brow, / And in their infinite smallness slept." Sitting with his grandfather under the cedar on a summer's afternoon, the boy listens for something like what he had heard in the cave when he "Felt / Heart beating as though to a *pulse* of darkness of earth," when "The silence / There [with his grandfather] seemed to have substantial life / That was the death of the *pulse* of Time."

Years later, he comments at the end of "Speleology," he could still lie in darkness and hear "the depth of that unending song, / And hand laid to heart, have once again thought: *This is me*" (Warren's italics). A similar revelation occurs to the boy when some of those things cupboarded up in his grandfather's head are awakened—memories of the Civil War that the grandfather recounts and the boy experiences as if they had happened to him: the sound of hoofbeats, the boom of the cannon, the smoke, "the gust of grape / Overhead, through oak leaves. Your stallion rears. // Your stallion rears—yes, it is you!" It's not the same thing at all—in one instance the revelation of who one really is, lying in the dark hearing in memory the "silken and whispering rustle" of the water's song that is also the mother's, and in the other the vicarious illusion that one was there when one wasn't. But the expressions—"*This is me*" / "it is you!"—are so alike in their meaning and their italic and exclamatory emphasis that we must wonder what might be behind their juxtaposition (a juxtaposition imposed by the propinquity of the two poems). One could at least say that what comes out of the grandfather's head and what can be found by going into the cave are alike in that they tell the poet who he is. Whether one of them is pure illusion is another matter.

Two more of the things that come out of the grandfather's head had already been encountered in the cave: silk and the fear of death. Back when the poet hadn't been able to make it all the way in, when he was younger than twelve, the age at which he did find that courage, "one summer all I could see was a gray / Blotch of light far behind. Ran back. Didn't want to be dead." The grandfather "once said / How a young boy, dying, broke into tears. / 'Ain't scairt to die. . . . it's jist / I ne'er had no chance to know what tail's like.' " Again, it's not the same thing: the poet was afraid to die; the young soldier wasn't. But it's enough of the same thing for us to suspect that, as will so often be the case when the same sort of echo occurs in Warren's later sequences, there is some meaning to be discovered in the repetition; specifically, that the second tells us something about the first. In this instance, it introduces sexuality into the discussion, and we may well wonder if it hadn't been there already—the expression, if not the substance.

To the degree that the protagonist who is the self of the poet is constant in Warren's poems, that protagonist will again lie down in darkness, though with a woman this time and very possibly as part of a seduction strategy, in "Bearded Oaks" (*N & SP*, 306), a poem Warren regarded highly enough to reprint in each of his *Selected Poems*. The poet and his companion lie not in a cave with an underground stream but under bearded oaks, "subtle and marine," on grass that moves in the breeze like kelp; in this shadow they await "the positive night . . . the graduate dark." Like the boy in the cave, they are trying out death: "we may spare this hour's term / To practice for eternity." As long as the poet is afraid to go all the way into the cave, he will never know what something is like, and that something appears in "Speleology" to be at once death—the kind of practice run for death that one can effect by lying down in darkness in a low-roofed cave and thinking "How would it be to be here forever . . . , part of all"—and the true nature of his mother's voice. Now at this point the boy can't yet know that, not having read the immediately preceding poem nor the others in this section where his mother's voice appears. But the song she sings in the carriage home from the picnic is the one he hears in the cave, the "silken and whispering rustle" that he will hear once more a few poems later in "The Moonlight's Dream" (17), in her sleeping breath: "like *silk* or the *rustle* of lilies that leant / By the garden pool when night breeze was merely a *whisper*." That silk will have already reappeared in the memories stored in the grandfather's stone-carved head, when he speaks of his wife, the poet's mother's mother: "My Mary, her hands were like *silk*."

"Boyhood in Tobacco Country" (11) brings us back into the open again, out from the memories of human events stored up in the grandfather's head with the carved and chiseled beard and into the natural world, where we had been two poems before, in the cave of "Speleology." But in spite of the change of scenery, some things remain the same. In place of a beard shaped by carving and chiseling we see groves of trees "hammered of bronze"; in place of the grandfather's cob pipe's "smoke, more blue than distance" we see "from the curing barns of tobacco, / Blue smoke." That blue smoke "clings / To the world's dim, undefinable bulge," while in the poem before something else blue clings to that same bulge: the grandfather's "blue gaze" was "fixed on a mythic distance. // That distance, a far hill's horizon, bulged."

The culminating event in the grandson's vicarious reconstruction of his grandfather's Civil War memories, in "When Life Begins," after the cannon, the smoke, and the stallion, was the bursting of a shell over the far hill, "Single, annunciatory, like / A day-star over new Bethlehem." So annunciatory is this evocation of the star that announced Christ's birth that it announces its own reappearance in "Boyhood in Tobacco Country," where it is no longer a star that announces a birth but the birth of a star: "a black / Voice . . . utters the namelessness / Of life to the birth of a first star." That birth-announcing day-star is surely central to the argument of "When Life Begins," for what it announces the title announces too. Life will begin for the boy when, or soon after, that shell bursts, for at that moment the Civil War recollection ceases and something else happens: "In the country-quiet, momentarily / After that event renewed, one lone / Quail calls." The correlation between star and birth and the call of a bird is an insistent one, for it returns in the very next poem: when he observes "the birth of a first star," the poet (who is still a boy in this dream of his youth) is walking a dusty lane at dusk, and soon thereafter

> From the deep and premature midnight
> Of woodland, I hear the first whip-o-will's
> Precious grief, and my young heart,
> As darkling I stand, yearns for a grief
> To be worthy of that sound. Ah, fool!

In a gesture that will be repeated just a few poems later in the first section of *Being Here* (in "Platonic Drowse" [20]), the poet will, in the foolishness of youth, find the expression of grief so moving that he desires a grief to express. Such wishes are dangerous, for they are likely to be granted. The correlation of bird note and birth is so striking in these two poems as to suggest that when life begins grief beings too, though it begins as expression only. It's up to the poet, to his ultimate regret, to fill that expression with meaning.

"Filling Night with the Name: Funeral as Local Color" (12) is the first installment of that hard lesson. It's made a little easier by the fact that the grief is not his own. But this poem clearly does provide the grief for which he yearns in "Boyhood in Tobacco Country," for it is precisely the whip-o-will and its self-naming call that here becomes the best and only expression for the deepest grief. Mrs. Clinch had died, and Mr. Clinch must begin to live alone. He refuses the neighbors' offer to cook his supper and spend the night. He doesn't eat. He pulls down the cover of the bed, and "stared at the infinite tundra of / Starched sheets by some kindly anonymous hand pulled tight. / He couldn't crawl in." He decided to write a letter to his son. "But no word would come, and sorrow and joy / All seemed one—just the single, simple word *whip-o-will.* // For the bird was filling the night with the name: *whip-o-will.* // *Whip-o-will.*"

The common element in this poem and the next, "Recollection in Upper Ontario, from Long Before" (13), is those sheets, which in both instances are the sign of, bear the weight of, a dead spouse. The poet is awakened by the nightmare of a brass-bound eight-wheeler locomotive boiling over the hill, a dream of terrifying reality, though there are no tracks there, where he is camped by Hudson Bay, no locomotive within three hundred miles. "The loon / Bursts out laughing again at his worn-out / Joke," as if he had heard it, too, but knew it was a dream. The poet falls back asleep and dreams it again. It's an event recalled from boyhood. Old Zack and his wife Mag were scrounging for coal along the railroad tracks, when Mag got her clubfoot caught in a switch-V—the boy witnessing all this from a ditch where he had been catching butterflies. A train is approaching, whistle and brakes shrieking. Zack finally gets her loose, and she's standing up. But the next second she's down again, over both rails, "Down for good, and the last / Thing I see is his hands out. To grab her, I reckoned." That grab is an ambiguous gesture, doubly so. The boy first reckoned it was his attempt to save her; later he realized it was murder. Later in the recollection the dream prompts, the gesture comes back with a different sense—in which love, of a sort, and aggression are fused, as what the boy presumed was love in the end turns out to be something quite other—when the poet imagines Zack and Mag years earlier, in bed together, Zack trying not to see her deformed foot, Zack lying in darkness looking up at "The shadows dance on the ceiling. And handle himself. / To make himself grab her."

Zack and Mr. Clinch are about as different as can be, but both had wives that died (Stitt notes this as well; both poems, he writes, "are concerned with women, beloved at least by someone, at least at one time, who die" [719]). And for Mr. Clinch what really brought it home for him that his wife was dead was those "Starched sheets by some kindly anonymous hand pulled tight" at which he stared, whose "infinite tundra" bore the weight of her irremediable absence. As he stared at them "It seemed all was happening still." While for Zack—and for the boy watching from the weedy ditch by the tracks—it's bed sheets, too, that convey the reality of death: "The express, I see it back up. The porters, conductors, / With bed sheets, pile out. I see / The first sheet pass. It sags. It drips."

What Mr. Clinch saw in those sheets was an "infinite tundra" of white. In "The Moonlight's Dream" (17) the poet will likewise see snow that isn't there, when he sees "the tracks of my bare / Dark footprints set in the moonlit dew like snow." Like the railroad tracks in which Mag caught her foot and that keep following the poet in his recurring dream, even in the Canadian wilderness, these tracks follow the boy he once was: "I wondered why I had come out and where / I would go, and back-looking, now saw the tracks . . . / And thought: *I go where they go, for they must know where we go.* // It was as though they did know the way in a dream" (Warren's italics). In "Recollection in Upper Ontario" the phantom locomotive came "boiling / Over the hill," about to reduce the poet to nothingness (or at least grind him to bits, as it did Zack's wife). Here, in "The Moonlight's Dream," the same thing has happened for real, except that instead of a railroad track and a brass-bound eight-wheeler it's a modern highway with cars whizzing by at sixty miles per hour: "The highway has slicked the spot the white farmhouse once stood. / At sixty per I am whirled past the spot" where he had left his family behind sleeping and gone out to leave foot tracks in the snowlike dew. The creek has been "bulldozed dry." There is no trace left: "their sorrow and joy, their passion and pain and endeavor, / Have with them gone, with whatever reality / They were."

The two poems begin with almost exactly the same words: "Why do I still wake up and not know?" "Why did I wake that night, all the house at rest?" "The Only Poem" (19) speaks, too, of waking in the night, and once more the sheet returns as the sign of the death of a woman, who this time is clearly identified as the poet's mother: "I've waked in the night. . . . / Till a flash of the dying dream comes back, and I haul / Up a sheet-edge to angrily wipe at an angry tear. // My mother was middle-aged." The dying dream is the memory of a visit he had made in young adulthood with his mother to see the Allen Tates' new daughter, whom they had left with Mrs. Tate's (Caroline Gordon's) mother (RPW to RPR, 9 June 1985). Young Warren was at a loss to know what to do with the baby; he passed it to his mother, who had been waiting for the moment when, "half-laughing, half-crying, arms stretched, she could swing up her prey / That shrieked with joy at the giddy swoop and swirl" (she had done the same with her own daughter in "October Picnic Long Ago" when "she swung the baby against the rose-tinted sky").

The poet's awkwardness with the child, his inability to do much more than "warily [handle] the sweet-smelling squaw-fruit," is one way of expressing his inability to fully express his love for his mother (particularly because in this poem she, though middle-aged, becomes something like that daughter, a child again: "Sitting there on the floor, with her feet drawn up like a girl"); she could express her love, he couldn't. This is especially poignant here, for after he and his mother left the house where the infant was and "wordless . . . wandered the snow-dabbled street" (as the poet, alone, had, "in the moonlit dew like *snow*," followed the path that "*wandered* down to a stream" in the poem before), and arrived home, where she laid out his supper, he left to return to his own world—"My train left at eight [a recollection of the nightmare train in "Recollection" and of the number associated with it: that "brass-bound *eight*-wheeler"] / To go back to the world where all is always the same. / . . . what can alleviate / The pang of unworthiness built into Time's own name?" He didn't know it then, but she was to die not long after; this was nearly his last chance to express the love whose expression came so easily to her. Her words as she fumbled for the key to the door are sadly prophetic: "Shucks! Time gets away."

"Grackles, Goodbye" (21) is a passionately felt meditation on her death, but the intervening "Platonic Drowse" (20) seems at first to separate it unduly from "The Only Poem," from the latter's "dying dream," "angrily" and tearfully remembered, of his mother. "Platonic Drowse" is about lying in the sunlight watching the cat crouching beneath the last rose of the season and the "Sun-glint gold on / The brown of enameled wasps weaving // Around one gold pear, high-hung" that is "far beyond your reach." It is not, at first glance, about his mother.

But in the context of the immediately surrounding poems, it turns out that it is. For we have heard this sentiment, and these words, before: "Fool, don't you remember? / You lay in the browning, tall // Grass, in unaimed pubescent / Grief, but the grief, it / Shriveled to nothing." It was in "Boyhood in Tobacco Country," when he heard "the first whip-o-will's / Precious grief, and my young heart, / . . . yearns for a grief / To be worthy of that sound. Ah, fool!" That whip-o-will grief did take shape in the next poem, as it filled the night with its name and became the only word Mr. Clinch could think of to express his grief at the death of his wife. And the unaimed pubescent grief for which the poet again calls himself "Fool" will find *its* object in the very next poem after this, in "Grackles, Goodbye."

Another year gone. And once my mother's hand
Held mine while I kicked the piled yellow leaves on the lawn
And laughed, not knowing some yellow-leaf season I'd stand
And see the hole filled. How they spread their obscene fake
    lawn.

Who needs the undertaker's sick lie
Flung thus in the teeth of Time, and the earth's spin and tilt.
What kind of fool would promote that kind of lie?

What kind of fool indeed? Perhaps the kind of fool who is guilty
of a symmetrically parallel lie to this grief-concealing one, the
kind of lie that projects grief, yearns for grief, when it isn't, yet,
there. Of the unaimed pubescent variety, the kind that lying on
the lawn can inspire—just as another kind of lying lawn, the obscene fake kind, can hide the other so well (so poorly: "Even
sunrise and sunset convict the half-wit [undertaker] of guilt").
    Other clues in these poems suggest that from angry tears to
unaimed grief to genuine grief, from "The Only Poem" to "Platonic Drowse" to "Grackles, Goodbye," we are in fact in the same
poem. The *"pear*, high-hung . . . beyond your reach" recalls the
strange, but now comprehensible, term applied to the infant:
"the sweet-smelling squaw-*fruit*" that he so unsuccessfully cooed
over and that his mother, "arms stretched . . . could swing up."
There is "Sun-glint gold" on the wasps, but the grackles glint in
sunlight too: "Black of grackles glints purple as, wheeling in
sun-glare." The cat crouches in "Platonic Drowse" "Beneath the
last blowzy red [rose] // Of the season," while in "Grackles,
Goodbye" the poet remembers seeing a first red of the season:
"a first fall leaf, flame-red."

Peter Stitt is absolutely right to characterize part I of *Being Here*
as being concerned with childhood and part II with youth. But
as we have seen, more than childhood links the poems in the
first division of the sequence; if childhood is the setting for
those poems, grief for the mother is what takes place in that setting, projected backward from adulthood (Warren's mother
died when he was twenty-six). And the particular linkages from
poem to poem create a richer field of resonance for that grief
than the poems can singly provide.

Similarly, part II, as the first word of the title of its first poem suggests, is for the most part about youth; yet in a somewhat narrower but surely interesting sense, the first three poems, as their titles reveal, are also about three kinds (at least) of wandering: "Youthful Truth-Seeker, Half-Naked, at Night, Running Down Beach South of San Francisco" (25), "Snowshoeing Back to Camp in Gloaming" (27), and "Why Have I Wandered the Asphalt of Midnight?" (29).

Nevertheless the first of these still looks backward to the poem that had immediately preceded it, despite the fact that this new section will be moving in a different direction from the first—or more exactly, this first poem listens back. For the central image in "Grackles, Goodbye," the "hole filled" and then covered with the "obscene fake lawn" where the mother now rests, reappears in the form of the underground realm on whose surface the poet presses an ear to hear the sound "ma . . . ma" makes:

Below all silken soil-slip, all crinkled earth-crust,
Far deeper than ocean, past rock that against rock grieves,
There at the globe's deepest dark and visceral lust,
Can I hear the *groan-swish* of magma that churns and heaves?

No word? No sign? [Warren's italics]

We have learned to recognize silk as the sign of the mother (Stitt acknowledges this point, too [727]), having heard her breath in sleep rustle "like silk" ("The Moonlight's Dream") and the underground stream's "silken and whispering rustle" lull the poet to sleep in a cave ("Speleology"). So we are not surprised to learn that the soil-slip here is "silken"—nor that rocks here "grieve."

Three other, perhaps less telling, certainly less dramatic, elements are repeated in these poems. (1) In "Grackles, Goodbye" the poet asked of the undertaker's fake lawn "What kind of fool would promote that kind of lie?" He had called himself a fool in the poem just before, under the accusation of unaimed pubescent grief ("Fool, don't you remember?"); here, in "Youthful Truth-Seeker," the word appears for the third consecutive time (the fourth time overall, counting "Boyhood in Tobacco Country," in the passage "Platonic Drowse" so closely echoes). It's what the poet calls himself when he gets up from having fallen asleep with his ear pressed to the sand, trying to hear that underground sound (as in "Speleology," likewise the first poem in its section, where he fell asleep listening to "the depth of that unending song"): "I stand up. Stand thinking, I'm one poor damn fool, all right." (2) In "Grackles, Goodbye" he tells us "once my mother's hand / Held mine" while he kicked a pile of yellow leaves and laughed, "not knowing some yellow-leaf season I'd stand / And see the hole filled"; here, as he lies with one ear pressed to the sand (sand that had been "raw between toes," kicked, perhaps, in his running like those leaves) listening for the sound beneath "the foam-frayed sea / . . . now and then brushes an outflung hand, as though / In tentative comfort." (3) He speaks of the grackles' "rusty *creak* high above"; and here, of how "the ice *creaks* blue in white-night Arctic light."

"Snowshoeing Back to Camp in Gloaming" ends with the slightest of hints looking backward to how "Youthful Truth-Seeker" began. But the precision with which Warren's neighboring poems repeat words is worth watching. In the former, the poet remembers that when he returns from his mountain hike and the door opens and "I, fur-*prickled* with frost, / Against the dark stand" a certain gaze will lift and smile. In the latter, our first glimpse of him running on the beach has "spume yet *prickling* air on // My chest, which naked, splits darkness." It's a word sufficiently unusual, as is *creak*, for its appearance in two sequential poems to be due to something more than chance. And it's accompanied in both instances by darkness against which the poet, prickled by frost or sea air, opposes himself—standing against it in the light that comes from within the door he has just opened, splitting it as he runs down the beach.

If the repetition of that word should at least suggest that within these two poems the same things happen in quite different landscapes—the beach, a snow-covered mountain slope—and suggest, as well (given that one can be found in the first stanza and the other in the closing lines), that what unites the two is something having to do with beginnings and ends, with front and back, then they may have a greater resonance. Consider the following two lines from "Youthful Truth-Seeker":

Far *behind*, the glow of the city of men fades slow.
And *ahead*, white surf and dark dunes in dimness are wed

These lines have a remarkably rich echo in "Snowshoeing":

Ahead was the life I might live
Could I but move
Into the terror of unmarred whiteness under
The be-nimbed and frozen sun.

While *behind*, I knew
        . . . that
The past flowed backward. . . .
Dead leaves lost are only
Old words forgotten in snowdrifts.

(Those last two lines recall this from "Youthful Truth-Seeker": "scraps / Of old wisdom that like broken bottles in darkness gleam at you.") What's behind the poet in one poem is the slow-fading glow of the city of men; what's ahead of him in the other, when he finally returns home (yet behind as well, for it's the place he left), is likewise a glow: "moved on . . . remembering / That somewhere . . . / Beautiful faces above a hearthstone bent / Their inward to an outward glow." What's ahead of him in both instances in white: "white surf" and the "unmarred whiteness" of snow.

In both poems, what ultimately lies ahead is grayness: on the beach, "fog threatens to grow," and the stars will be "swaddled in grayness, though grayness, perhaps, / Is what waits—after history, logic, philosophy." In the mountain landscape, the sun is about to set, and the forces of pink and magenta and those of gray fight a losing battle: "Magenta lapped [like waves on a beach!] suddenly gray at my feet, / With pink, farther up, / Going gray. // Hillward and sky-thrust . . . a huge / Beech clung to its last one twinge / Of pink on the elephant-gray."

"Why Have I Wandered the Asphalt of Midnight?" is concerned with more than asphalt; it asks the same question of the poet's wandering the beach and the snowy slope in the two previous poems. "Why should I wander dark dunes till rollers / Boom in from China, stagger, and break / On the beach . . . ?" it asks, clearly placing the poet back where he was when he ran half-naked down the Pacific beach: "sometimes," the poet tells us, "I have . . . met, / Snowshoed, the trapper"—who could well have been himself in the poem just before: "trap-laid, / Snatching thongs of my snowshoes." "Ahead," we recall, was the life he might live if he could only break out of his motionlessness: "Could I but move / Into the terror of unmarred whiteness." "Why Have I Wandered" directly refers to his standing there, in that particular spot, paralyzed, when it asks, "Why did I stand with no motion under / The spilt-ink darkness of spruces . . . ?" The *spilt*-ink darkness of spruces had been, in "Snowshoeing," "the blackness of spruce forest" and "The shadow of spruces" that "*Bled* at me in motionlessness."

We learn in "Snowshoeing" that at the moment he was standing there, as the spruces' magenta bled at him across the unmarred white, "Time died in my heart." "Why Have I Wandered" retells that scene and, in picking up the thread of the narrative, tells us a little more about what was going on in that heart:

> Why did I stand with no motion . . . and try to hear,
> In the soundlessness of falling snow,
> The heartbeat I know as the only self
> I know that I know . . . ?

The heartbeat he is straining to hear is, surely, his own. But we are reminded, just as surely, of the poet's pressing an ear to the sand in his attempt to hear something else in the poem ("Youthful Truth-Seeker") to which this poem so painstakingly alludes, the sound that "churns and heaves" within the earth, the sound he also heard in the cave in "Speleology" when he "Felt / Heart beating as though to a pulse of darkness and earth, and thought / How would it be to be here forever, my heart // In its beat, part of all" ("Speleology"). That was, among other things, as Peter Stitt has pointed out, the experience of the infant in the womb, its heartbeat in synch with its mother's.

But the synchronization of the poet's heartbeat works in another direction too, as we may also learn from "Why Have I Wandered." Not only might it be in synch with chthonian, and maternal, darkness, but with the stars as well.

Why have I wandered . . . and not known why?
. . . not even to know how the strict
Rearrangement of stars communicated
Their mystic message to
The attent corpuscles hurrying heartward, and from.

Here begins a theme that will develop through three consecutive poems. In "August Moon" (31), the second of these, the
poet is still attuned to the "inner, near-soundless *chug-chug* of
the body's old business" (Warren's italics), and is "dreaming /
There's an inward means of / Communication with / That world
whose darkling susurration / Might—if only we were lucky—
be / Deciphered." He is dreaming this while walking down a
woods lane as "night / Hardens into its infinite being" (and as he
was walking an asphalt road at midnight in the poem before),
wondering "What kind of world is this we walk in?" while
"Slowly stars, in a gradual / Eczema of glory, gain definition." In
the world we walk in, those stars are mysteriously connected to
such internal events as the near-soundless chugging of the bod-
y's old business in much the say way as, earlier in the poem, "the
sky goes deeper blue / By the tick of the watch."

"Dreaming in Daylight" (33) speaks, too, of how "something
mysterious // Is going on inside you, but with no name." "August
Moon" had added a note of dread to that internal activity—"the
body's old business— / Your father's *cancer*, or / Mother's *stroke*"
—that was absent from its appearance in "Why Have I Wandered" but is continued in "Dreaming in Daylight": "like *gastri-
tis* / Or *migraine*, something mysterious // Is going on inside you."
"Dreaming in Daylight" is full of dread. Here, in a kind of nightmare, the poet climbs ever higher to escape the "last flicker of
foam / Just behind" that is the ocean of the past trying to catch
up with him; animal eyes hidden in the brush watch his every
move; when he reaches the highest rock he still expects to see
foam lapping at his feet. "This / Is the end. . . . all you can do is
try to remember, // And name by name, aloud, the people you
have / Truly loved." Those loved ones had been at issue in "August Moon," too, when thoughts of the body's internal chugging, and perhaps as well its analogy to the tick of the watch by
which the sky also conducted its business, had led him to think-

ing about "The counting of years, and who / Wants to live anyway / Except to be of use to / Somebody loved?"

The poet's concern with keeping his feet dry ("You barely escape the last flicker of foam / Just behind, up the beach of // History. . . . Move higher! / For the past creeps behind you, like foam") persists in "Preternaturally Early Snowfall in Mating Season" (35), where he sets his feet toward the coals of the campfire to dry the snow off, like the pioneers who "learned early to beat the chronic curse / Of rheumatism: set wet moccasined feet . . . / Toward fire to sleep." But the tables are turned in another respect: instead of being spied upon by "eyes that from crevice, shade, log, aperture, // Peer," he is the voyeur here, eavesdropping on the mating of deer. He was awakened by the noise—the "blast, wheeze, snort, bleat, / And beat and crash of dead boughs." The next morning he found the spot "where a doe, by a deadfall, had made her huddle. Then / Where the buck had wrestled and struggled to mount / . . . the marks / Of plunge, stamp, trample, heave, and ecstasy of storm."

The story of "Sila" (37) is an astonishing retelling of this one. Again there is a doe, and a "deadfall." And the violence with which the buck in the poem before wrestled and struggled to mount her is present again here, but with the difference that it is only violence. The boy's dog Sila attacks a doe who had leaped "From behind a beech deadfall." Before the boy can stop him he has spilled her viscera on the snow with claws as sharp as a knife. The boy had to finish her off with his knife so that she wouldn't die a slower death, the prey of fox and field mouse. He "cuddles the doe's head, and widening brown eyes / Seem ready, almost, to forgive." There is communication with those eyes: "Twin eyes / Hold his own entrapped in their depth." He painlessly slit her throat, "Aware even yet of the last embracement of gaze." He finds himself "bewitched by the beauty" of her blood petaling on the snow, "curve swelling past curve."

This change in the meaning of the violence the doe suffers is accompanied by a reassignment of roles. The buck's violence becomes the dog's, but his luck comes close to becoming the boy's, who nearly becomes a lover—bewitched by beauty, aware of the embracing power of her eyes. One detail of the husky's attack lends support to this confusion of roles. The poet in the preced-

ing poem wore snowshoes when he ventured out the next morning to investigate the marks left by the mating—"while," in Sila's
attack, "the husky's wide paw-spread / Had opened like snowshoes."

There are two incidents to "Sila," of which this is the second.
The first is the boy's discovery, likewise "past / Deadfall," of a
"ruin of old stonework"—a house where a family once lived, as
much as two centuries before. Snow covers all now, but the boy
thought that in the summer he might come back and look for
gravestones. "Then thought / How letters that crude must be
weathered away—how deeper / A skull must be pulping to
earth." It was the skull of some one *"young as me, maybe"* (Warren's italics). The fact that both the stonework and the doe were
discovered beyond a deadfall suggests two things: that these two
incidents may have more in common than is immediately apparent and that they have some tie to the mating overheard in
the previous poem, for that, too, had taken place "by a deadfall."
Or at least that the two poems read better when read together.

One way to interpret the triple appearance of the word
"deadfall" is to point out that what happens in "Sila" in two incidents had already happened in "Preternaturally Early Snowfall" in one. We have already seen that the two elements of
violence and desire present in the buck's mounting the doe in
one had been separated out and distributed in the other to the
husky (violence) and the boy (desire). Similarly, another aspect
of the mating episode is separated out and distributed to the
first incident in "Sila" (rather than to its second incident, the
death of the doe), for that episode was the story not only of a
mating but of the poet's discovery of it—first at night by eavesdropping, later in the morning by finding "the *marks* / Of
plunge, stamp, trample, heave, and ecstasy of storm." Discovering marks is precisely what the boy does in the first incident in
"Sila": "muscles tighten and clinch / At a sudden impulse of surprise / To find here the old *mark* of life that for life / Once had
sung."

That old mark of life was the "ruin of old stonework, where
man-heart / Long ago" had once labored in joy. Even that old
stone has a prehistory in "Preternaturally Early Snowfall," when
the sky, with no sun, seemed "a dome / Like gray stone crudely
set / In the gray cement of prehistory." That adverb reappears

as the adjective that the boy in "Sila" applies to what's inscribed on the gravestones he imagines must be there somewhere: "How letters that *crude* must be weathered away—how deeper / A skull must be pulping to earth, and now grinless." That's the skull he thinks might have been someone like him: "*Was young*, then he thought, *young as me, maybe*." And that skull, particularly the fact that he identifies himself with the skull, appeared in the poem before, too—when the poet snowshoes out from the wilderness spot where he had witnessed the deer's mating and tells how his head, his skull, began, in the course of that two-day journey, to feel empty (empty as the one the boy in "Sila" imagines grinless in earth): "My skull / Felt scraped inside as though scrubbed with ammonia, / . . . nothing / Inside the skull but the simple awareness of Being."

What analogy we may see between this skull and the one in the next poem, and between the stone crudely set in prehistory and the old stonework and accompanying crudely carved gravestone, receives confirmation from the fact that even within the first poem the stone and the skull were already related: when the poet had observed that the gray, sunless sky resembled a dome of stone and he also found that the inside of his head was like that stony dome of sky: "Your mind hangs gray, like the dome of cloud-stone." So the complaint in the second half of the poem that his skull felt empty should be analyzed, even if one were only reading "Preternaturally Early Snowfall" by itself, without reference to "Sila," as the counterpart to that earlier observation about the stony grayness inside his head. Skull and ancient (if not prehistoric, at least two centuries old) stone come together again on the first page of "Sila." But their conjunction had been prepared by what happened in the poem before.

That first episode of "Sila"—the boy's discovery that someone lived there once, the evidence of the ruin of old stonework, the gravestones he imagined must be there somewhere—is retold in "Empty White Blotch on Map of Universe: A Possible View" (43) in terms of an island on which the poet imagines himself cast, an island with marks of habitation but whose inhabitants he never sees. The boy in "Sila" found a "*ruin* of old stone work"; the poet here finds "a *ruined* cairn [a pile, that is, of *stones*] raised by lost aboriginals / To honor their dead (but who honored the last?)." That concern with honoring the dead whose descendants are all dead, too, and thus unable to honor them recalls the boy's decision to "*come / And hunt for the gravestone*" (Warren's italics) of the lost inhabitants whose trace he found.

The blood of the doe, in the bewitching beauty of "petal by petal, a great rose that bloomed," had a kind of redeeming beauty in "Sila." "Empty White Blotch" speaks, too, of blood that redeems, cleanses evil: "the tide comes in like Christ's blood, to wash all clean." This is precisely the "Function of Blizzard" (45)—snow's ability, like the tide's, to redeem, restore, cover over: "Black ruins of arson in the Bronx are whitely / Re-deemed. . . . Bless coverings-over, forgettings. // Bless snow." This is the third consecutive poem to speak of ruins; those in "Sila" were similarly snow covered: "snow-buried, there— / The ruin of old stonework."

The island in "Empty White Blotch" was the world itself: "The world is that map's white blotch." The world is whitened in "Function of Blizzard," too: "God does the best / He can, and sometimes lets snow whiten the world / As a promise." The world, that island, was "full of faceless voices"; the snow-covered world of the Bronx and its burnt ruins are inhabited by phantom voices, too: "Can't you hear the . . . ghostly echo of childish laughter?" If the snow that covers the ruins of arson constitutes God's promise in "Function of Blizzard," God's promise in "Dream, Dump-heap, and Civilization" (46) is something more like the fire: "Smudge rose by day, or coals winked red by night, / Like a sign to the desert-walkers // Blessed by God's promise."

The poet is speaking of the Norwalk, Connecticut, dump from which this smoke arises because he finds it a perfect metaphor for the fragments, the "residue," of his dream that, like trash, remains and of which he can make no sense: "Like the stench and smudge of the old dump-heap / Of Norwalk, Connecticut, the residue // Of my dream remains, but I make no / Sense of even the fragments." He's still trying to remember what it was he dreamed, and wonders if he has dreamed, again, the memory of how he once "watched a black boy / Take a corn knife and decapitate six kittens." Did he dream, he wonders, of those six kitten-heads staring all night at him and trying to tell him something, and "still now trying / By daylight" as he remembers the residue of the dream? The poems we have just read, like his dream, leave a residue that persists, from poem to poem, and one incarnation of it is precisely that knife in that black hand. In the poem just before, located in the Bronx and Harlem, one of the things the snow can bless is "Needle plunging into pinched vein." And in the poem before, one of the things the poet enacts on the island that is the white blotch on the map of the world as he sees the whole of human history pass as delusion before his sight is the Crucifixion, but because he was alone, there was "no Roman ready with nails for the feet / Or to pierce my side with a spear—as God intended." Though in "Sila," the poem before that, the coup de grâce that the spear stroke would have achieved was in fact performed, and well, by the boy with his knife on the doe. The dream's residue persists at least into "Vision" (47), where the blade is in black hands again, as it was in "Dream, Dump-heap": "A black orderly, white-coated, on rubber soles, enters at 5 A.M. / The hospital room, suds and razor in hand, to shave, // . . . the area the surgeon / Will penetrate."

The great "Globe of Gneiss" (49) which is seemingly precariously poised high on a granite ledge in Vermont in the poem of that title, but which the poet found impossible to budge, was, punningly, preceded by the two "highballs" the poet ordered in a dingy cafe in the opening scene of an adulterous liaison in "Vision."

"Part of What Might Have Been a Short Story, Almost Forgotten" (51) finds the poet again in a high place, though in Idaho this time; still, what remains poised at that altitude, ready to descend, appears equally threatening. He couldn't make the gneiss globe budge an inch but found himself a fool for trying ("Don't, / For God's sake, be the fool I once was, who / Went up and pushed"), for if he had succeeded, the result would have been disastrous. Thinking of how it could, perhaps, at any moment fall all the same from the effects of erosion—"the infinitesimal / Decay of ledge-edge"—*Suddenly,* / I leaped back in terror. / Suppose!" In the next poem, as he stared down at Shoshone Falls and up at the sunset, "*sudden- / ly,* glare of the car's headlights bursts," warning him of a mountain lion (I assume—the species of cat is not named) crouched nearby, fangs exposed and eyes glaring, directing their gaze directly at him.

"The tail, in shadow, slow swung / From side to side. My blood was ice. // But no reason. With insolent, / Contemptuous dignity," it turned away and leaped "Like flight into blank darkness past / Lip of the chasm. That was all." It's worth remarking that, like the globe of gneiss, the cat posed a threat that existed only in the mind of the poet. Or at least that's the way the story is told. Just in case we missed the analogy between cat and globe, the poet generalizes the menace the crouching beast exemplifies and wonders "What beast with fang more white . . . patient / As stone in geological / Darkness, waits, waiting, will wait / Where and how long?"—attributing to that beast the quality of stone, and of patient waiting measurable only in geological time, qualities the globe of gneiss exemplified. It has waited a very long time to assume its perch on the ledge, ever since it was formed "in a mountain's womb." That uterine imagery returns at the conclusion of "Part of What Might Have Been," when the poet sees the ultimate menace as a "foetal, fatal truth" toward which we move.

We are told of the crouching menace at Shoshone Falls that "The tail, in shadow," slowly moved. In the following "Cocktail Party" (54) we likewise "sense a faint / Stir, as of a beast *in shadow*." To adopt the lingo of the Confederate boy soldier whose death the grandfather recounted in "When Life Begins," the beast itself *is* tail. In fact, "Cock*tail* Party," by casting woman as the beast in shadow, builds upon the hidden connection in that earlier poem between its two uses of that word: the first was what the dying soldier said—"it's jist / I ne'er had no chance to know what tail's like"—while the second comes in the last line, when the boy who became the poet sat and waited for life to begin, not knowing that just beyond the horizon "Time crouched, like a great cat, motionless / But for tail's twitch. Night comes. Eyes glare." At the Falls, "The *eyes, catch-* / *ing* headlight glare, glared" back; at the party, "You *catch* some *eye*-gleam . . . as of a beast in shadow. . . . / And you see, of a sudden, a woman's unheard laugh *exposing* // *Glitter* of gold in the mouth's dark ghetto like unspeakable / Obscenity, but not sound." That glitter in the mouth was exposed as well in the cat at Shoshone: "upper / Lip drawn slightly back to *expose* / White *glitter* of fangs." If it all seems like a bad dream, that's because it may be one—the nightmare in "Dream, Dump-heap, and Civilization" about felines that, like the laughing woman, seemed to be silently saying something unspeakable: "six kitten-heads staring all night at me [that] try to say something—still now trying / By daylight." Later, in "Vision," the poet would find that "lynx-scream . . . / Freezes the blood."

"Deep—Deeper Down" (55) is, like the two poems before it, a confrontation with the beast, this time in the form of poisonous snakes. The poet, with his friend Jim, would spend after-hours hunting them down in the bayou with a pistol. He also took his dog, whose powers of scent are described in terms that suggest that the beast hunted here is ultimately the same beast that lurked in shadow at the cocktail party: the dog "could smell / A cotton-mouth on a bridal wreath as well as on cypress roots."

Poison—already evoked in "Deep—Deeper Down" by the menacing cottonmouths—returns in "Sky" (56) as arsenic. Thanks to a change in the weather, trees and grass are "arsenical now in [the sky's] / Acid and arsenical light." And the cotton-mouth that had been a *"dark* arabesque wavering down, *belly white* as it died" reappears in the sky as "a *blackness* . . . towering / Toward you—sow-*bellied*, brute-nosed, coiling, / *Twisting itself in pain*, in rage, / And self-rage not yet discharged"—as if it were the unidentified form the poet at the conclusion of "Deep—Deeper Down" brushed past in a dream that was "yet *twisted in pain*, / Its belly paling in darkness" or as if that dream persisted into "Sky." The "self-rage" that needs to be "discharged" here had already appeared in the preceding poem as the rage that belonged to the poet's shooting companion—"Jim, who'd cursed all day at a desk in town," and who felt the need "To purge earth of evil, and feel thereby justified" by slaying snakes whose bodies displayed a "cleansing beauty" ("the cleansing beauty / Of the dark arabesque wavering down, belly white") as they died.

These two poems are cloaked in mystery—the twisting form in the dream is never identified: a vision of the snake? a woman? The last lines of "Sky" insist that whatever it is we fear, we do not know its name: "What most we fear advances on / Tiptoe, breath aromatic. It smiles. // Its true name is what we never know."

"Better Than Counting Sheep" (58) breaks this mood completely. Yet something of that last vision still persists. No longer is one menaced by snake, woman, or any other beast in shadow—something nevertheless does advance upon us gently, timidly. And we don't know its name, either. Better than counting sheep when you can't sleep is to try to recall all the dead you've ever known. They will stand around you, filling all available space, "and some, // Those near, touch your sleeve, so sadly and slow, and all / Want something of you, too timid to ask." Only gradually do you realize what they want: "Each wants to know if you remember a name"—their own. But you can't remember, not even your mother's name, not even your own, and then you fall asleep.

"The Cross" (59) is likewise a confrontation, and communication, with the dead. The poet has found a drowned monkey "hunched by volcanic stone / As though trying to cling in some final hope," on the beach (in Italy, one might presume, considering the language the monkey speaks) after a night of storm. He stares into his eyes, "With a glaucous glint in deep sightlessness, / Yet still seeming human with all they had seen." The dead in the poem before wanted the poet to tell them something, their name; the monkey, it seemed, desired the poet to say something particular to him, too: He needed a "friend to come and just say *ciao*." The poet couldn't oblige the dead's request in "Better Than Counting Sheep," but this time it's easier: "So, like a fool, I said *ciao* to him."

And then sat with him there, watching the afternoon fade. When evening came he dug a little grave, put a "little cairn on top. / And I enough fool to improvise / A cross— // Two sticks ties together to prop in the sand." The cross and the cairn bring this poem, which ends part III, into an intriguing relation with "Empty White Blotch," which began it. There the poet raised a cross, too, though not in commemoration of the dead: "I have even erected a cross, looped my wrists, hung suspended," and later, came down from that cross, bathed his wrists, and "crept to lie / In my cave, with no prayer, and no hope of change of condition." The cairn, however, which he placed on the monkey's tomb had a similarly commemorative predecessor in that other poem: the "ruined cairn raised by lost aboriginals / To honor their dead (but who honored the last?)." What he does for the monkey may be his answer to that parenthetical question. The storm-tossed and -beached monkey in "The Cross" bears an interesting resemblance to the poet himself in "Truth" (63), the first poem in part III, who exclaims, "What a landfall the world!—on which to be naked cast / By the infinite wind-heave, and wind-shoveled sea."

Peter Stitt says of the poems in section IV that they "are all concerned with varieties of sound" and serve the poet's quest for meaning "by focusing on the potential of sound." It is true that all the poems in this section *are* about sound, or more precisely, about listening—to the dead and to the voice that speaks in the natural world—but as Stitt himself observes, other poems in *Being Here* are just as much about sounds (he cites the silken whispers of "Speleology" and "The Moonlight's Dream," and the *groan-swish* of "Youthful Truth-Seeker" [727]) as any here. It is not entirely right to assume that the structure of the book is visible only in the structure of its division into five parts, as Stitt appears to do when he writes that "The structure of the volume loosely parallels the structure of life" and then goes on to link each of the five sections with one of the ages of a man's life (715)—for although his linking of section to time of life is in each case accurate, it is nevertheless not the case that *that* is, by itself, "the structure of the book."

The consistent manner in which each poem takes and re-works something from the preceding poem must be counted too as part of that structure. It is an aspect of the sequence's structure that does not respect the separation between divisions and might even be considered to be at odds with those structural divisions. That tension is especially evident in passing from the last poem of part III to the first in part IV, which concludes with these lines:

> Truth is the long soliloquy
> Of the dead all their long night.
> Truth is what would be told by the dead
> If they could hold conversation
> With the living and thus fulfill obligation to us.
>
> Their accumulated wisdom must be immense.

What more fitting conclusion could there be to a sequence of three poems of which the first ("Better Than Counting Sheep") depicts the poet trying to sense what the departed souls who approach him, in their "grieving susurrus, all wordless," want; the second ("The Cross") shows him figuring out that the wide-eyed corpse of a drowned monkey wants him to pronounce a particular word of greeting, an unspoken wish he grants, after which he holds silent colloquy for the rest of the afternoon with that shipwrecked simian; and the third, this poem ("Truth"), maintains that truth could be had by holding conversation with the dead? If we thought that because "Truth" began a new section it also began a new train of thought, we would have missed out on a significant aspect of the sequence; it would be just as erroneous, however, to conclude that the section divisions have no purpose. Clearly Stitt's characterizations of them are broadly true. But here, it seems, they have yet another role to play, that of being at odds with the sequential structure of the larger poem: the meaning of "Truth" would be different if we read the poem in isolation—as we would be encouraged to do by a reading that considered the sections to be independent units. For then we could take the sentiments it expresses in its final lines with a sense of finality. But having just read the account of the poet's one-sided conversation with a dead monkey, we must wonder what is really meant, in a way we might not otherwise, because of the line "Their accumulated wisdom must be immense." Does "Their" include the dead of which the poet had just been speaking?

Yes, certainly. But not just because the monkey is a creature who has seen death and not because Warren believes that all God's creatures are endowed with wisdom. This monkey, "most desperately hunched . . . in some final hope," is more than a monkey; it is representative of the mysterious fetal figures that haunt many of Warren's texts—the fetus that appeared to Perse Munn in a dream in *Night Rider*, for example, the fictive one Isaac Sumpter invents in *The Cave*, or the one in a glass jar that Miss Pettifew buries and later digs up in *Flood*.

The monkey in "The Cross" to whom the poet says *ciao* in fact recalls what should have been an aborted fetus in "To a Little Girl, One Year Old, in a Ruined Fortress," from *Promises: Poems 1954-1956*. It is the "child next door" that the mother tried to abort because she had seven already: "Took a pill, or did something to herself she thought would not hurt." But the botched abortion turned into a monstrous, defective child. Its sister "Has taught it a trick, to make *ciao*, Italian-wise. / It crooks hand in that greeting." The poet, in response, makes the same gesture he will make a quarter century later to a dead monkey in "The Cross": "I smile stiff, saying *ciao*, saying *ciao*, and think: *This is the world.*" The association of fetus with monkey that these two *ciao*-saying poems suggest was already apparent in Warren's second novel, *At Heaven's Gate* (1943). For the fetus in that instance was at once monkeylike, hunched and wise: Jason Sweetwater there imagines what the fetus—"the little *hunched*-up creature"—in the womb of the woman he is about to murder (and thereby kill the fetus too) must look like. And he "remembered fetuses in jars, the wizened, little, *simian-wise* faces, intent and, for all their *wisdom*, contorted in profound puzzlement." He thought, too, of American Indian mummies, likewise "hunched," because they were buried in a fetal position, whose faces were like the faces of the fetuses, whose eyelids were "squinting because there was nothing under them any more" (317).[2]

Through this meditation Sweetwater is granted an insight into how meaning can arise from nothing, as the closed eyelids' expressiveness comes from the very fact that there are no eyes for them to cover—as Jack Burden will discover, in *All the King's Men*, that "reality is not a function of the event as event, but of the relationship of that event to past, and future, events." It is a paradox, he says, "that the reality of an event, which is not real in itself, arises from other events which, likewise, in themselves are not real" (384). Likewise I am arguing here that each of Warren's recent poetic sequences is the site of just such a creation of meaning out of what seems to be nothing more than mere juxtaposition. Indeed, both this way of reading Warren's sequences and the paradox Jack Burden expressed find significant justification in a pronouncement Warren once made as a literary critic, in his essay "Pure and Impure Poetry": "Does this not, then, lead us to the conclusion that poetry does not inhere in any particular element but depends upon the set of relationships, the structure, which we call the poem?" (24) Because the poems appear in sequence, they partake, as do Burden's events, of time: the poem just before is past, the poem beneath our gaze is present, and the poem ahead is future. Combining Burden's paradox about events immersed in time with Warren's critical pronouncement about how poetry inheres in the relationship and not the elements could indeed give us the analytical method I have been employing here to account for how a certain new reality seems to emerge from the *now* and *then* of Warren's interwoven sequences. Thus out of the relationship between "The Cross" and "Truth" we may see a certain wisdom emerge. Though simian, in the cumulative effect of so many other such sequential relationships, it can be immense.

Cumulus clouds adorn the afternoon sky of "On into the Night" (64) ("how soundless crunch / Cloud cobbles of bright *cumuli*"), providing their own echo to that resounding last line ("Their *accumulated* wisdom must be immense"). In "Truth" the "long *soliloquy* / Of the dead all their long *night*" becomes in "On into the Night" the "night's voices" to which the poet gives his attention: the bear's sexual hoot from the ruined orchard, the thrush's "last music," the owl's "mystic question." That afternoon in "On into the Night," the owl had been doing what God was doing in "Truth" "when He drowses": "taciturn, / The owl's adrowse in the depth of a cedar / To pre-enjoy the midnight's revel."

But when "the last of night's voices is heard," even that silence is not complete. There's still one sound left, "one sound / Defined now by silence. The pump in your breast . . . declares // Its task in undecipherable metaphor." The heart sound was always there; earlier in the poem, lying beside a stream as silent as the windless trees, where even "No insect hums," and looking up at the trees, the poet is made aware of his dark-flowing blood by the darkness of shade: "Shadow and shade of cliff sift down / To darken the dimmest under-leaf, / And in the secret conduits / Of flesh I feel blood darker flow." In "No Bird Does Call" (66), as the poet lies in similar shade, it is not shadow but light that makes him aware of his blood, and it's not the darkness of its flow that he thinks of but its (bright) redness: "one noon-ray strayed through labyrinths of leaves, / Revealing to me the redness of blood in eyelids, / And in that stillness my heart beat."

In "On into the Night" "No insect hums" (and "The thrush-throat only in silence throbs now"); in "No Bird Does Call" "no bird ever calls"; and in "Weather Report" (67) the single warbler left motionless in the rain, his beak "unmoving as death," gives the poet "No note of ignorant joy."

"Weather Report" and "Tires on Wet Asphalt at Night" (68)
are both rain poems, and both reproduce their rain texts in italics, sounds the poet hears the rain make and tries to interpret.
In the first it's the drops hitting the roof: "This the code now
tapped: *Today is today*" (Warren's italics); in the second, the hiss
of tires passing outside his bedroom window: "That sound like
the *swish-hiss* of faint but continual / Wavelets far down on the
handkerchief beach-patch" (Warren's italics). While the rain on
the roof declares "*Today*," the swish in the street declares *yesterday*, making him remember when once he had climbed down a
crag to a Pacific beach to watch the sun set over the ocean and
then climbed back up.

> Once up, exhausted, face-down, arms outflung,
> I lay clutching old clumps of summer-burned grass.
> ....
> That was long ago. Till the hiss of the tires,
> Like last wavelets, I had forgotten it.
>
> I wish I could think what makes them come together now.

Warren has posed us a puzzle that I think we can solve: what
makes lying prone on a Pacific beach, outflung arms, summer-
burned grass, and the sound of tires in the rain come together?
The answer is the juxtaposition of the last poem in part I and
the first in part II, "Grackles, Goodbye" and "Youthful Truth-
Seeker," a juxtaposition justified by the way in which Warren exploits the possibilities of sequential structure. On that Pacific
beach the poet lay prone, the wavelets now and then brushing
his "outflung hand" as he pressed his ear to the sand to hear a
sound that the *swish-hiss* of the tires in the rain could well have
reminded him of: the *groan-swish* of the magma beneath the
earth's silken surface. And the summer-burned grass? We have
already seen, in realizing the parallel between his yearning to
hear, "past rock that against rock grieves," that subterranean
sound and his grieving for his mother in the ground, the significance of grass. It was the "obscene fake lawn" that the undertaker placed over "the hole filled" that most affected him in
"Grackles, Goodbye." Because it was October, "yellow-leaf season," this "sick lie" fooled no one, for the too-green fake lawn

would not have matched the surrounding summer-burned brown grass in the cemetery; no one looking at it would not have known there was a freshly dug grave beneath.

The summer-burned grass persists in "Timeless, Twinned" (70), where the poet feels "to my back, thin-shirted, brown grasses yet bring / The heat of summer." Even this supineness has its antecedent in "Tires on Wet Asphalt," for it was when he was lying on his back in bed, "eyes ceilingward, / Open to darkness," that the poet was reminded, by the swish-hiss of the tires outside, of the time he once lay face down and arms outflung on the grass.

In "Timeless, Twinned" he lies staring up at a single white cloud in the azure sky of autumn, in a silence in which "No voice / Speaks." The next poem, in both its title and its first line, reverses the situation and turns it into a question: "What Is the Voice That Speaks?" (71). One incarnation of that voice is heard long distance, over the telephone:

"I thought that you loved me—" And I:

"I do. But tomorrow's a snowflake in Hell."
And the phone went dead, and I thought of snow falling

All night, in white darkness.

Love is never certain, just like the weather, though the poet in the poem just before had been able, in the timeless state staring at the cloud induced, not to care that snow would, inevitably, come:

As though I've now forgotten all other nights and days,
Anxiety born of the future's snare. . . .

What if, . . .
                    . . . beyond the perimeter northward, wind,
Snow-bellied, lurks?

In "Language Barrier" (72), where his telephoned eloquence (from "What Is the Voice That Speaks?") about a snowflake in Hell still resounds, we see the inverse of that answer to love: "Hell frozen, where snow / Lingers only in shadow." And the poet is still listening and asking about what he hears: "What grandeur here speaks?" Thinking back to when he saw "Hell frozen" in the tangle of stone falling down from one edge of a great *cirque* among snow peaks, he tells us that "at *night* you may dream-*wake* / To that old altitude" and ask, "What / Long ago, did the world try to say?" What is the voice that we hear in the poems trying to say, the one that keeps repeating both the question and the words? In "Lesson in History" (73), "you, *night-waking*," see a meadow in moonlight, trees and a stream. Do you "know what, in whisper, the water was trying to say?"

The poet asks some questions history doesn't answer in "Lesson in History." Some of their elements reappear in "Prairie Harvest" (74), which is not at all about history. "Did the lips of Judas go dry and cold on our Lord's cheek?" The prairie takes on some of the aspects of such a cheek: "miles of wheat *stubble* . . . , the *shaven* earth's rondure." "What thought had Anne Boleyn as the blade, at last, rose? / Did her parts go moist before it fell?" Sexual arousal reappears in "Prairie Harvest" when "the star the Kiowa once stared at will requite // Man's effort by *lust*, and lust by the lead-weighted eyes"—it appears that that star is the sun, at which the poet had, likewise, been staring. "And what did Hendrik Hudson see / That last night, *alone*, as he *stared* at the Arctic sky?" The poet, similarly, is "standing *alone* in starlight" after having stared at the star "the Kiowa once *stared* at."

In "Eagle Descending" (77) the eagle, too, "Stares at the sun" as it sets. Both this poem and "Prairie Harvest" concentrate on the moment of the sun's disappearance—the latter by the poet's realization that, though he thought the sun was hanging "Apparently motionless" above the horizon for the longest time, he actually missed seeing it disappear: "The sun, / It is gone. Can it be that you, for an instant, forget / And blink your eyes as it goes?" Just before he realized it had already set he had been gazing at some high-flying birds: "in last high light the bullbats gyre and twist, / Though in the world's emptiness the sound of their cries is // Nothing." That moment between the sun's motionless hanging and its disappearance is expressed differently in "Eagle Descending": here, the eagle, riding "air currents, switch and swell," is so high that he can still see the sun as if it hadn't set, though that sun is "invisible to us, / Who downward sink."

The eagle becomes a parody of itself at the same time that it becomes the poet in "Ballad of Your Puzzlement" (78). Reviewing his life before death comes, he envisions the lives he has led projected onto a silent movie screen, of which the first is a man on a tightrope, so high that the spectators, far below, look like ants—as the eagle was so high it could see the sun, "invisible to us." As the eagle "rides airs currents," the acrobat, "clutching his balance-pole, / . . . sways, high." "Why doesn't he skyward gaze, / Then plunge . . . ?" the crowd asks—as the eagle, who "westward gazes," would also, finally, return to earth. "How soon?" the poet had, likewise, asked then. Perhaps, the poet concludes in "Ballad of Your Puzzlement," "you are only // A wind-dangled mirror's moment / That flickers in light-streaked darkness." Perhaps only a heliograph—like the eagle, though less glorious: something suspended in the wind that by reason of its position in the scheme of things and not for any personal virtue happens to catch the light of the sun. Or like the crow that concludes "Antinomy: Time and Identity" (81), that, "caw lost in the sky-peak's lucent trance, / Will gleam, sun-purpled, in its magnificence."

That film unspooled in silence, returning to blackness in the end, "but blackness / Slashed by stab-jabs of white / That remind you of lightning bolts" but are only scratches on the emulsion. "Antinomy" begins in blackness, too, and silence: "Alone, alone, I lie. The canoe / On blackness floats . . . ghost-white on blackness. / . . . Silent, / As entering air, the paddle, slow, dips. Silent, / I slide forth. . . . Slow / As a dream . . . I move."

It's slow going as well in the dust bowl on the way west in "Trips to California" (83): "Dust on the highway piles so deep / Mules had to drag the car." The association of ghost-whiteness with boat returns here in the form of "Faces stunned *white*. Eyes blank like those // Of people picked up in a *lifeboat*." In the canoe in "Antinomy" the poet, floating in that canoe in the darkness, is moving "Forth into, / What new dimension?" One in which Timelessness spreads like oil on black water to make past and future the same, to "spread / On the time that seems past and the time that may come, / And both the same under / The present's darkening dome." It may be that the dust covering everything in Kansas is the equivalent of that oil; in any case past and future are in "Trips to California" reduced to the same thing too, to the status of a dream: "California"—the goal of the trip, the future—"Waits like the dream it is, and mother / Of dreams. Reality past may be only // A dream, too." If, as both poems suggest, the past and the future are the same, perhaps this explains why birth and death, which may also be the same, appear at the same time, at dawn: "Dawn burst like the birth pangs of your, and the world's, existence" ("Antinomy"). "Dawn / Then showed the hundred new naked corpses" ("Trips to California").

The corpses were of the buffalo the poet knows were slaughtered in these parts in the last century, not only for their skins and their meat but also because killing would help kill off the Indians who depended on them for food: "General Sheridan was a realist: // The only good one, he said, is a dead / One—not buffalo, but redskin." Sharps rifles blazed all day in an immense and merciless shooting gallery.

Gunpowder served a more merciful impulse in "Auto-da-Fé" (85), when executioners charged with burning martyrs at the stake would sometimes affix a packet of gunpowder to the belly to bring on a quicker and less excruciating death: "This, perhaps, / From some fumbling thought of the holiness or // Beauty of body." The poet is in awe of that beauty: "Beautiful the intricacy of body! / Even when defective." Yet beautiful as it may be, he knows as well that the body is but flesh, "a bag of stercory, a bag / Of excrement, the worm's surfeit"—a truth that the dead mule by the roadside in "Trips to California" graphically incarnates: "bloated like an / Enormous winter squash, green-blue." "Auto-da-Fé" is about the scream that comes from the body itself, and not the "I," at the moment of painful death. "All history resounds with such / Utterance—and stench of meat burned: / Dresden and Tokyo," he cites; but if our memories are not too short, and since meat is what these bodies become, we might think as well of the stench of buffalo meat in the poem before, their "naked corpses." In what may or may not be an autonomous (that is, unmotivated) pun on the title of the poem, one of the victims whose death-scream he calls to our attention is the half-drunk "soft-bellied citizen, / With swollen ego" who, testing out his new Cadillac, "*piles* on- / to the goddam overpass buttress." But this is a joke, too—a pun on how dust put a stop to the poet's auto in "Trips to California": "once / Dust on the highway *piled* so deep / Mules had to drag the car."

In "Aspen Leaf in Windless World" (87) he wonders what will be the last thing he will see before death: "What image . . . / Will loom at the end of your own life's long sorites?" A sorites is a pile, "a heap," literally, in Greek, and is defined by the *Oxford English Dictionary* as "1. *Logic.* 'A series of propositions, in which the predicate of each is the subject of the next, the conclusion being formed of the first subject and the last predicate' (Mansel) . . . 2. *transf.* A series, chain, or accumulation of some thing or things . . . 3. A sophistical argument turning on the definition of a 'heap' . . . 4. A heap, pile." The last of the last images the poet here proposes for the one that will appear at the end of life's sorites, after a rising sun, a face, and a "great, sky-thrusting gray menhir," is "the last elephant turd on the lot where the circus had been"—clearly another kind of pile, but one that "Auto-da-Fé," with its insistence on the at once stercoraceous and intricate nature of the body, has prepared us for. But the way each poem in *Being Here* takes something from the poem before and reworks it into an image of its own, the process that it has been the principal object of this reading to reveal, has prepared us for sorites in another sense, sorites as "series, chain" (as in the "caverned enchainment" that will in fact be the image at the end of the sorites that is *Rumor Verified,* as we saw in the last chapter)— "sorites" as the term that describes extraordinarily well both life as he sees it and poetry as he writes it.

Perhaps puzzled all this time about *why* Warren was doing this, now we may realize the reason: *Being Here* is, in fact, as Warren says in his "Afterthought" to the sequence, "a shadowy narrative, a shadowy autobiography." And this statement is not to be interpreted only in the sense in which the five divisions pass from childhood to age and incorporate from time to time elements transposed from his own life experience but also in the sense in which it is, like life, a sorites in which each moment is metonymically connected with, is contiguous with, is for a brief instant copresent with, the moment just before. It is a poetic sequence with narrative qualities, not just because it in some general way tells the story of a life but, more significantly, because it works like a narrative, each poem as tightly connected to the one before as are the sequence of events in a well-told story.

The "intricacy" whose beauty the poet extols in "Auto-da-Fé" when he sees it in the body is a case in point, for it immediately reappears in "Aspen Leaf," in the form of a text that may or may not be a text:

> Look how sea-foam, thin and white, makes its Arabic scrawl
> On the unruffled sand of the beach's faint-tilted plane.
> Is there a message there for you to decipher?
> Or only the joy of its sunlit, *intricate* rhythm?

Is this repetition in two consecutive poems of intricacy itself a text, a message for us to decipher? That, too, is surely a function of the soritic structure of such a sequence as *Being Here*—to make us ask of it what Warren asks of the world: Does the rain indeed tap out a code on the roof? Do bat and bullbat indeed "scribble" on the sky? Is there a sound to be heard beneath all silken soil-slip?

And we should ask it as well of the tilt on the plane of the beach that, precisely, caused the foam to linger long enough in its return to the sea to trace out what looks like writing. For earth's tilt appears in the next poem, "Acquaintance with Time in Early Autumn" (89), as the tilt of the terrestial globe on its axis that caused seasons—and makes the poet acquainted with time. It's that tilt that makes the leaf the poet stares at fall, though he prays it won't: "Oh, leaf, // Cling on! For I have felt knee creak on stair," for I have felt the onset of age and your falling will make me know all too well that I, too, will die. He sees, to his chagrin, "in / The golden paradox of air unmoving / Each tendon of that stem, by its own will, / Release / Its tiny claw-hooks, and trust / A shining destiny." It lets go, does not fall as much as slide, sustained by air, in total calm, and, "While ages pass, I watch the red-gold leaf, / Sunlit, descent to water I know is black"—black as death. "It touches. Breath / Comes back, and I hate God / As much as gravity or the great globe's tilt." For the poet's thoughts are still, as they were in "Aspen Leaf in Windless World," on death, and these thoughts are expressed again here in very much the same way they were when he said in the immediately preceding poem that one's span of days is a sorites in which the last term, simply because it is last, is the final predicate, the one that will link up with the first even though one would have thought it didn't deserve to, even though it is as unseemly as the memory of the last elephant turd on the lot where the circus had been. Who would have thought that *that* would be life's last image? Who would have thought today would be the last? "Who once would have thought that the heart, / . . . might . . . / Have picked today as payday, the payment // In life's dime-thin, thumb-worn, two-sided, two-faced coin?"

Something like the two-faced quality of that coin may be glimpsed in the contrary ways these two poems treat the sight of a single leaf moving of its own accord with no help from the wind. In "Acquaintance with Time" when the poet sees "in / The golden paradox of *air unmoving* / Each tendon of that stem, by its own will / Release" it makes him hate God, gravity, and the tilt of the globe. But in "Aspen Leaf in Windless World" that sight had done just the opposite, had given him joy: "Watch how the aspen leaf, pale and *windless*, waggles, / . . . And think how delicate the heart may flutter / In the windless *joy* of unworded revelation."

He calls that windless movement of leaf a "golden paradox" in "Acquaintance with Time," and it is. In "Safe in Shade" (91) we are posed another one, as his grandfather tells how he lived as a man must, performing "Acts evil or good, or even / Both in the same gesture, in / That *paradox* the world exemplifies." And the following "Synonyms" (93) will pose yet a third, that of the white noise of silence in the "sempiternal roar" of a waterfall: "Chaos of white in dark *paradox*. What is the roar // But a paradox in that / Tumultuous silence— // Which *paradox* must be a voice of ultimate utterance?" "Synonyms," divided into seven numbered sections, is in large measure about the paradox of opposites that are in the fact the same—synonyms, in the paradox the title expresses: The roar that is silence; or, in section 2, the writing "bats scribble" on the sallow western sky at twilight: "minuscule murder, which, / From one perspective, is beauty, too," or, in section 3, the "something / Funny and disastrous" that the magpie with shoe-button eyes has been waiting to happen.

These paradoxical synonyms ultimately lead to two kinds of insights—themselves at odds with each other, since one is less an insight than clouded sight, since to suffer from one is worthy of condemnation, while to realize the other is wisdom. Yet they are essentially the same: the first, in section 6, is what a drunk who has been witness to cruelty shouts, accusingly, at God: "can't You see the hour to smite!— / Or lost Your nerve, huh? Can't longer tell wrong from right?" The other is what the poet, in section 7, concludes after bearing witness to all that has gone before in this poem—including the waterfall's white noise, the bats' scribble, the cruelty, the drunk, and the drunk's prophetic exclamation:

> Some things in the world are beautiful, and I
> Have seen some. But more things are to come,
> And in the world's tangled variety,
> It is hard sometimes to remember that beauty is one word for
>   reality.

These lines make two statements, of which the second contradicts, supersedes, the first. The first points out the obvious, that some things in the world are beautiful—with the implied corollary that some things are not. But the second states that reality itself is beautiful, and reality would have to include a great many things, not all of which fell into the first statement's category of beautiful ones. The resolution of this apparent contradiction can be derived from what a few pages earlier I called Burden's paradox, after the Warren hero who enunciated it in *All the King's Men*: "the reality of an event, which is not real in itself, arises from other events which, likewise, in themselves are not real." The things, in other words, in the world of which some are beautiful and some are not are not real. Reality comes at the same time as beauty, only when those things, and those events, are combined, and a certain perspective arises—the kind of perspective that allows bats' insectivorous murder to become "beauty, too."

The kind of reading practiced here of Warren's poetry offers a similar perspective. Given enough distance, the bats' movements, though motivated in each instance by other, more immediate reasons, will look like "scribble"; given enough distance—which in this instance is just far enough back from the page to see two poems where we had seen one—words, images, turns of phrase that had in any single poem their own more immediate reasons for being will now look like they form part of a larger script.

One example is the recurring image of hands that in part 3

enable one to "Lean back, one hand on saddle-horn, if you must" on a mountain trail, that in part 4 "still ache from the pitchfork heft," in part 5 are locked in a "desperate handgrip" on the cap shroud of a yawl in a Mediterranean storm, and in part 6 belong to "a grubby old dame [with] one hand on a cane [while] / The other . . . / Clutches the iron rail" of a stone staircase. Another example is the eyes that in part 5 have tears in them and suffer in part 6 when "spume / Burns eyeballs" and in part 7 when "fumes burn the eyes." Still another example, more like the high-flying bats, is the gull in part 5 that "on a pivot of wing-tip, Nijinski-like, *swings* / To a motionless, lateral joy" that is parodied in part 6 by the poor injured cat that a garbage man "*swings* . . . high, choking with laughter to think / How she tries to climb air."

Then, too, there is "Time" that "will *slip* in silence past" in part 2 of "Synonyms" as, "eons back, earth *slipped* and cracked" in part 1 and "stones and gravel *slip* and cascade / Down each side of the knife-edge trail" in part 3. What slips in parts 1 and 3 is earth, dirt and stone, while the subject of that verb in part 2 is Time. "Swimming in the Pacific" (101), however, the poem immediately after the seven-part "Synonyms" brings those all together in "Time, / That trickles like sand through fingers"— thereby commenting, through its own repetition, on a repetition within a poem ("Synonyms") that is made up of poems (seven of them) as sequentially related as the larger sequence of which it is a part.

"Swimming in the Pacific" takes as well part 5's image of a foot in the sea—"the big yawl, hard-driven, / Thrusts merciless forefoot / Through tasseled silk-swell"—inverting its connotation from aggressivity to fearful avoidance: "At sunset my foot outreached the mounting Pacific's / Last swirl as tide climbed." And the "westward height" where bats wrote their murderous script in part 2 returns in "Eyes *westward*, sea graying, one gull at / Great *height*."

It returns once more in "Night Walking" (103), the account of how the poet spied on his son wandering alone in the moonlight, ultimately to lift his arms to its whiteness: "His gaze / Turns slow . . . over / The light-laved land, over all / Thence visible. . . . // Last, the next range to *westward*. // High, calm, there the moon rides." The boy's night walking resembles in more ways than one his father's beach wandering in "Swimming in the Pacific." When the poet came out of the ocean, made his way to his "land-mark— / Gray cairn to guard duck pants" and the rest of his clothes, and dressed, he "wandered the sand." This was long ago, in his youth, at the time of "Youthful Truth-Seeker, Half-Naked, at Night, Running Down Beach South of San Francisco." Thinking back on it in old age, he sees himself emerging from the sea again, finding his cairn and his clothes and again pondering the nature of Time.

> What answer, at last,
> Could I give my old question? Unless,
> When the fog closed in,
> I simply lay down, and on the sand supine, and up
> Into grayness stared and, staring,
>
> Could see your face, slow, take shape.
>
> Like a dream all years had moved to.

Whose face? He doesn't say, but the proximity of "Night Walking" suggests it may be his son's, who likewise can be seen looking up at the sky: "Moving upward, and on, face upward as though / By stars in an old sea he steered" (that it may be the same sea as the one from which the father emerged is hinted at by the return of that adjective: the poet saw himself rising "from the *sea* as of *old*"). The son steers by the stars; the father sees the future in the sky—the future that is, I think, the star-guided son.

The son becomes his father as the father becomes his (the father's) grandfather—for the grandfather of "When Life Begins" and "Safe in Shade," and not the father of the poet, is the figure for the past in these poems. This takes place as the poet does the same thing in "Night Walking" that he does in "Swimming in the Pacific," but with a significant difference. And by now we have learned to read Warren's sequences with precisely an eye for what, within sameness, is not the same. In "Swimming" he made his way to his cairn of stones to find his "duck pants" (and his T-shirt, shoes, and wallet); in "Night Walking," as he quickly gets up from bed when he hears his son go outside, what he puts on are a different kind of breeches: "My Levis."

But are they really his? Or do they belong to his grandfather, who is pictured wearing them on both of the occasions we see him here: "blue-jeaned" in "When Life Begins," clad in "washed blue-jeans" in "Safe in Shade." The poet is more like his grandfather now, in "Night Walking," than he was in his youth, when he wore a different kind of pants on the beach. For now, he has a son, a future that is not his:

> I do not guess
> How far he will go, but in my
> Mixture of shame, guilt, and joy do know
> All else is his—and alone.

Costume detail is significant here for another reason: within "Night Walking" the father and the son, who are about to change places in the larger scheme of things, are similarly clothed. The son is "booted and breeched but bare / From waist," and the father too is shirtless, breeched, and booted: "My Levis now on, and boots, I wait."

The transmission of paternity from grandfather to poet had already been the substance of an allusion in "Safe in Shade" to the poem immediately preceding it, "Acquaintance with Time in Early Autumn." In the latter, the poet had "plunge[d], / With delicious muscular flexion and heart's hilarity, / White to the black" water of the mountain pool into which he would later watch, to his regret, the first dying leaf fall. "Voices of joy how distant seem! / I float," he writes, "pubic hair awash" in that black pool of death, the future oblivion that awaits that leaf. This hilarity, this joy of muscular exertion, as well as this dark hereafter and this allusion to that part of the poet's body that will connect him to that future all reappear in the next poem ("Safe in Shade") when he speaks of his grandfather as

> one who, like all men, had flung,
> In joy and man's maniacal
> Rage, his blood
> And the blind, egotistical, self-defining
> Sperm into
> That all-devouring, funnel-shaped, mad and high-spiraling,

Dark suction that
We have, as the Future, named.

("Swimming in the Pacific" will call the future by the same name:
"the suction of years yet to come.")

"Night Walking" is the last poem in *Being Here* save for the en-
voi, "Passers-by on Snowy Night" (105), a farewell to the reader
which is also a poem about walking at night. Like "To a Face in
a Crowd," the poem that closes each of Warren's near-decennial
anthologies (the *Selected Poems* of 1943, 1966, 1975, and 1985), it
is a poem in which the poet crosses paths with the "you" he is
addressing—and who, it seems, is the reader. In the context
Being Here's sequence provides—that of the intersection of these
two poems and the way the second obliges us to reread the
first—that reader is, implicitly, compared to the poet's son. The
continuity linking these poems, already apparent in the repeated "Night" of their titles and in the walking that transpires
in both, is particularly evident as well in the third and fourth
lines of "Passers-by"—"And the moon, skull-white in its stark-
ness, / Watches upper ledges lean. . . . " These lines echo both
the "*ledges* and rock-slides" past which "the *moon* rides" when the
father tracks his son in the poem before and the osseous pale-
ness of the latter's "crags bone-white" that is reassembled in the
moon's skull-whiteness here.

In "Night Walking," moreover, the poet could not guess
"How far *he* [his son] *will go*"; here, in the last line, in the same
words, "each [the poet and the passer-by] goes the way *he will
go*." The intersection of these two poems in the larger poem's
soritic structure (an intersection echoed by the apparently
chance encounter the second of these poems recounts), and the
echoes between them that put into question the notion that their
encounter is a chance one, compel us to ask how we might compare the passing stranger—who is us, the reader—with the
poet's son. Already in "Night Walking" the poet must relinquish
his parental espionage and allow the son, like the passer-by in
the poem that follows, to continue his way on his own:

I do not guess
How far he will go, but in my

Mixture of shame, guilt, and joy do know
All else is his—and alone.

That "alone" will soon return in his address to the stranger:

> . . . Alone,
> I wish you well in your night
> As I pass you in my own.
> . . . each goes the way he will go.

May the reader of Warren, the passing stranger who, like his
son, must in the end go his own way, beyond the poet's ken, in-
herit something of a filial nature? The novels do in fact teach,
as I elsewhere show,[3] that the intersection of sonship and read-
ership in Warren is very real. It is there, in the novels, that Warren's predilection for making his protagonists, and his readers,
into sons who must find their own path with a father's taciturn
text for a guide is most evident. Yet even here, in the poems, it
can surface, as the intersection of the last two poems of *Being
Here* reveals.

Interlude: The Father's Mark

It is no wonder that Harold Bloom is very high on Warren,
whom he has consistently named this country's "most eminent
man of letters" (review of *New and Selected Poems*). For Warren
extraordinarily exemplifies Bloom's theory of the *agon* of the
poet who must struggle with his literary father to affirm his own
identity. According to Bloom in "Sunset Hawk: Warren's Poetry
and Tradition," this father is T.S. Eliot. Though we have reason
to believe that another one is John Crowe Ransom (and another,
in a different way, Robert Franklin Warren, who also wrote
poems, the discovery of which was for his son "a profound and
complex surprise" [*Portrait of a Father*, 41]). As far as Eliot is concerned, Bloom would appear to be right to argue that Warren
struggled against his influence, and eventually succeeded, even
if that "prime precursor" is still present, though "repressed"
(76), in as late a poem as "Heart of Autumn" from *Now and Then*.
Warren's poetry of fifty years ago, as Bloom illustrates by quot-

ing "pretty much at random from Warren's earliest verse, . . . is the purest Eliot" (77).

The case of Ransom is in a way the inverse, for Warren says in "Notes on the Poetry of John Crowe Ransom" that he had early on rebelled against his influence (as he did not, at least from the evidence of his early poetry, appear to rebel against Eliot), but from the uncanny coincidence between what he then in that essay goes on to find in Ransom's poetry and his own recent poetic practice it would appear that *that* literary precursor has come to assert a new claim of influence. For to the degree to which Warren's poetic sequences have become increasingly interwoven, their structure has come increasingly to resemble the one Warren found in Ransom's *Two Gentlemen in Bonds*.

One story Warren has been telling all his life is that of the son who must struggle to make sense of a text his father wrote while simultaneously acknowledging the power it will always hold over him. Warren would appear to have been living out this struggle throughout his poetic career, fighting to break free of Eliot, returning in the end to something like Ransom—as if, perhaps, one father could protect him from the other. I would like here to sketch briefly how this story is told in two texts other than the four poetic sequences considered elsewhere in these pages—one a representative novel, the other a long narrative poem that Warren has quite recently published (and was thus writing as he was writing these strongly sequential poems).

In the novel *Wilderness: A Tale of the Civil War*, which appeared in 1961, Warren's protagonist, Adam Rosenzweig, in at least one respect resembles Warren the poet. For he too is struggling against a literary father. Leopold Rosenzweig was, among other things, a poet, and after his death his son carries engraved on his memory the opening lines of one of his poems: "If I could only be worthy of that mountain I love, / If I could only be worthy of sun-glitter on snow, / If man could only be worthy of what he loves" (5). Adam's journey to America and his attempt to join in the war against slavery is clearly a search for worth, in particular a search for a definition of the worth that is the subject of his father's poem.

He finds it in the end, in the curious inscription of the letter W on the skin of the man who has become his closest friend, a former slave named Mose. What's curious about it is its interpretation: "W—W for worthless! That's what the Yankees put on 'em. Put on a soldier that ain't worth a damn," Jed Hawksworth tells Adam Rosenzweig (217). Mose, that is, was a deserter from the Union army, and had managed to keep the W on his thigh covered up from sight until this moment of revelation. The interpretation remains unquestioned, which on the level of the plot poses no problem, given its doubtless historical accuracy. But on the deeper level that concerns Adam's search for an adequate definition of the worth inscribed on his father's text one might well wonder why a W couldn't just as easily stand for worth itself instead of its absence.

An essential part of the plot—of the subplot in which Adam tries to make sense of what his father wrote—that comes into play here is the fact that this son was very disappointed in his father's inability to live up to the promise of his poem. Six months before he died, Leopold Rosenzweig had yielded to his brother's insistence that he give up his hope in secular humanistic ideals (he had taken part in the Revolution of 1848) to return to the faith of his fathers, to a Jewish faith in the promise of the Torah. To trust, as his brother put it, in God rather than in man. Adam's decision to go to America is his attempt to live up to the ideal his father had abandoned, to find the worth his father had given up seeking. The denouement of this subplot is his discovery of the W on Mose's thigh. For it is surely not by chance that the former slave bears the name of the presumed author of the text to which his father had switched his allegiance. What the son succeeds in doing is to read worthlessness onto the surface of the Mosaic text and thus teach his father a lesson in reading, namely that he should have been true to his own text, and not to *his* fathers'.

Some twenty years later in Warren's career, another son feels betrayed by his father's decision to abandon his personal ideals and switch allegiance to a worthless text. That is the essential subplot of *Chief Joseph of the Nez Perce*, which appeared in 1983, between *Rumor Verified* and the *Altitudes and Extensions* of *New and Selected Poems*. The poem celebrates the heroic exploits of Chief Joseph's struggle against the U.S. Army's effort to make his people abandon their ancestral lands and fathers' graves for the reservation at Lapwai. But part of the reason the Nez Perce find themselves in these desperate straits is the fact that Joseph's father had been guilty, twice, of what we could well term a textual betrayal. For he had twice been corrupted by a white man's text, at the expense of his devotion to the tribe. The first was his un-Indian interest in the Bible:

> My father—Old Joseph, whites called him—had heard
> Of the "New Book of Heaven" the whites had brought
> To Lapwai. . . .
> . . . So went there.
> Lapwai was then not named reservation
> As later it was for those who sold
> Their land to the white man. [6]

Once in Lapwai, Old Joseph longed to return to the land of his people, and did so—but took the Bible with him:

> And came there, yet carried the "New Book of Heaven,"
> New in our tongue now. But could he forget
> The bones of his fathers, and the Old Wisdom?
> Nor eyes of the fathers that watch from darkness? [6]

Indeed he could, it seems. And be corrupted thereby. For in 1855 Old Joseph signed a treaty with the white man which promised him possession of the tribal lands; in retrospect his son realizes that it was a mistake.

> I, a boy, stood and watched my father.
> His hand reached out. It made the name-mark.
> ....
> A promise, how pretty!—but our sacred land
> They trod. They spat on our earth. It was like
> A man's spit on your face. I, then, a boy,
> I felt the spit on my face. [7]

The son now knows better: "For now you know what a treaty is— / Black marks on white paper, black smoke in the air" (13). The essence of the ancestral text the father had abandoned, the "Old Wisdom," could be described as antitextuality: a wisdom that knew how little "Black marks on white paper" meant, that knew "how the Great Spirit / Had made the earth but had drawn no lines / Of separation upon it" (14).

Like Adam Rosenzweig, the protagonist of *Chief Joseph of the Nez Perce* proves to be a better reader than his father of the father's text—the text that in *Wilderness* the father wrote and that in the poem he inherited. The profound ambivalence Warren bears toward the father's fathers' text is evident here, for in the novel the son calls it worthless, but in the poem it's the only thing worthy of allegiance.

The poem that Bloom calls "the essential Warren, as much his own invention as 'The Course of a Particular' is Stevens' or 'Repose of Rivers' is Hart Crane's" (76) is "Heart of Autumn," with which this reading of Warren will conclude in the next chapter (and in this poem, despite its being Warren's own invention, "Eliot, prime precursor, is so repressed" that one would hardly think of him, although he remains in Bloom's opinion somehow there). At the risk of anticipating myself, I would like to point out one special way in which this poem is indeed "the essential Warren." The wild geese are heading south: "watching / How tireless V upon V arrows the season's logic, // Do I know my own story? . . . they know. . . . / The path of pathlessness, with all the joy / Of destiny fulfilling its own name."

The season's logic, as *Being Here* tells us, is a soritic one, and so is the logic of Warren's own life—the logic of "life's long sorites," as we read in "Aspen Leaf in Windless World." The enchained logic where each predicate is the subject of a predicate yet to come, the logic of a life in which closure and therefore ultimate meaning is continually deferred until we see the last image we'll ever see. Then perhaps we'll know what in *Audubon* "Is the dream he had in childhood but never / Knew the end of," (*N&SP*, 218) as perhaps we may by now have discovered the logic for which Warren is looking in "I Am Dreaming of a White Christmas" when he seeks to know what is in the present under the tree he doesn't get to open in "the original dream which / I am now trying to discover the logic of." For the logic of dream, the logic of dreamwork recycling the residue of the preceding day, is likewise the logic of these soritically sequential poems.

The V upon V that "arrows the season's logic" is something the geese know—it is "destiny fulfilling its own name." It is perhaps indeed the inscription of a name, the poet's own, for V superimposed upon V becomes W, the initial of Warren's and Warren's father's name (and the initial his protagonist read in the Civil War novel whose initial it also is). Warren's patronymic destiny thus becomes in this concluding poem "destiny fulfilling its own name." And the name of the father writ large becomes the structure of his text. A text that replicates the textual struggle itself between father and son, as each moment, each poem, rereads (and thereby ironizes—that is, neutralizes) its predecessor. For as Warren makes abundantly clear in "The Use of the Past" (in the recent *New and Selected Essays*), he sees successive literary generations as sons struggling with their fathers:

> Petrarch, speaking of the proper relation of the new Italian literature to the old Latin literature, said that the resemblance of the new and the old should not be that of a portrait and the sitter, but of a son and the father. But Petrarch's description, though it tells a truth, is incomplete— incomplete because static. It omits one aspect of the relation of the writer to the past. The more he knows about the past, and the more he reveres the great creators of the past, the more he must struggle against them. . . . The self . . . can be discovered only in the attempt to assert it against a powerful opponent from the past. [47]

In this same passage Warren gives his wholehearted endorsement to Harold Bloom's version of this agon in *The Anxiety of Influence* ("a . . . fascinating book"). And he offers one more analogy: the struggle is not only one of a son with a father, it is also that of "Jacob, who wrestled with the angel all night . . . and, though at the break of day he received the mystic wound in the thigh,[4] would not let go of the mysterious stranger until he had extracted the blessing he craved and could say that he had 'seen God face to face' " (47). In *Now and Then* we will see how Warren situates Jacob's struggle with his "necessary angel" (48) in two dreams (in two sequential dream poems: "Dream" and "Dream of a Dream") of which the second works the first "Into the braiding texture of dream" into which Warren tells us "my name . . . is gone." It is another way of inscribing that name into the very fabric of his text.

FOUR

Now and Then
"In Its New Ectoplasmic Context"

Now and Then: Poems 1976-1978 begins with a biblical epigraph—
"Let the inhabitants of the rock sing" (Isaiah 42:11)—that, like
the quotation from Dante inscribed at the beginning of *Rumor
Verified*, finds its way into the first poem of the collection. It's not
the inhabitants that survive but the rock—in the form of the one
that someone had thrown at a skull the poet and his boyhood
friend K find in a marsh. The rock is "cracked in star-shape
from a stone-smack." Near the end of this poem ("American
Portrait: Old Style" (3) another stone is thrown, the one K, now
sixty years older, "Like young David at brookside . . . swooped
down, / Snatched . . . wound up, and let fly" to illustrate that,
big league baseball pitcher that he once had been, he still had
control. He hit his target with precision, "And high on a pole
over yonder the big brown insulator / Simply exploded."

Within the context of this poem alone, one stone answers the
other; within the larger context that includes this poem as well
as the epigraph that precedes and, as we are about to see, the
poem that follows it, those stones are answered, or anticipated,
by others. In the face of the echoes, repetitions, and variations
that abound in such sequences as the ones we have been reading, the notion that any single poem can be insulated from the
effects of, and from communication with, the other poems in
the sequence (or in the rest of the Warren corpus) is one that
Warren's poetic practice, like K's pitching arm, explodes.

Peter Stitt has nevertheless argued that *Now and Then* "is even
less sequential" in structure than *Incarnations: Poems 1966-1968*
and *Or Else—Poem/Poems 1968-1974* ("The Grandeur of Certain
Utterances," 57). While it may indeed be the case that those two

earlier collections are not sequentially structured to the extent that we have found *Being Here, Rumor Verified* and *Altitudes and Extensions* (the last two had not appeared when Stitt wrote those words) to be, *Now and Then* is. Part of the proof lies in those stones.

Within the first line of the second poem, "Amazing Grace in the Back Country" (8), the combination of star and stone that had first appeared in the "star-shape" crack that a "stone-smack" had caused reappears, rearranged: "In the season of late August star-fall." "Star-Fall," likewise set in August, and the penultimate poem in "Nostalgic," the first of *Now and Then*'s two sections (with ten poems; the second, with twenty-seven, is entitled "Speculative"), will speak in greater detail of the same annual meteor shower, the Perseids: "They fell / Like sparks in a shadowy, huge smithy, with / The clang of the hammer unheard." What is important to note here is that falling stars are not in fact stars, but stones—meteors. And that the stone that left the imprint of a star on the skull in the first poem reappears in the next in the form of celestial stones that, as they fall through the atmosphere, leave starlike traces too.

The poet becomes stony himself when, menaced in "Amazing Grace" by "some old-fool dame" crouching in black silk by his knees at a tent revival and tugging him down to pray for his unsaved soul, "he hardened his heart, / Like a flint nigger-head rounded slick in a creek-bed," stood up, and ran away. While the other, stellar, connotation of the first line's "late August star-fall" returns at the end of the poem when, having safely escaped the revival enthusiasm but not so safely escaped the worry about dying that was the basis for the enthusiasm, the poet as a boy "lay / By the spring with one hand in the cold black water / That showed one star in reflection, alone" and wondered how many mornings he had left to live. "Wondering and wondering how many / A morning would I rise up to greet, / And what grace find." And well he should worry, if he knew what could await a young man who catches a glimpse of a reflected star in a cold black spring. In "The Ballad of Billie Potts," Billie, whose parents didn't recognize him when he returned home, went down to the spring with his father and saw

> the spring as black as ink,
> And one star in it caught through a chink

Of the leaves that hang down in the dark of the trees.
The star is there but it does not wink. [*N & SP*, 296]

As he knelt for a drink, and the reflection of his face obscured
the star, his father set a hatchet in his skull. The Pottses' profes-
sion was robbery, accompanied by murder, and their returning
son was, to them in their ignorance, just another customer.

"American Portrait: Old Style" also ends with thoughts of
death. The poet, having returned to the scene of his childhood
haunts six decades later, lies down in the six-foot long trench
that was a sunken grave for one they named "Pap" ("Pap must
have died of camp fever, / And the others pushed on") and that
had served him and K for war games and wonders "What it
would be like to die, / Like the nameless old skull in the swamp."
K and the poet, then, were playing pioneers and Indians and
Yankees and Rebels on what was, or what they took to be, a father's grave. It served a dual purpose, sinking in time, as the
body within turned to dust, to a trench with military application
("Bluebellies / . . . came charging our trench. . . . But we held").
Similarly, "Amazing Grace" is about a tent that could have
served, and maybe did, two discordant purposes:

> the tent
> Had been pitched, no bigger than one of
> Some half-bankrupt carnival come
> To town with fat lady, human skeleton, geek,
> . . . plus a brace of whores. . . .
>
> The tent old and yellowed and patched,
> Lit inside by three wire-hung gasoline lamps
> That outside, through threadbare canvas, were muted to
> gold.
> Here no carnival now—the tabernacle
> To the glory of God the Most High.

Warren's sequential poems are like that tent and that trench:
polyvalent and multipurpose, open to more than one use, inhabitant or enthusiasm, depending on what shifts in context
their sequence reveals.

"Boy Wandering in Simms' Valley" (11), for example, the

third poem in *Now and Then*, recasts the scene in which the revived issued from their tent at the end of "Amazing Grace" and
went back to their ordinary lives: "Found bed *and lay down*, /
And tomorrow would rise and do all the old things to do, / Until
that morning they would not rise, not ever." "Boy Wandering"
recasts the scene, that is, in terms of a farmer whose wife has
died of a long illness and who "turned out his spindly stock to
forage at will, / And took down his twelve-gauge, *and* simply *lay
down* by her side." The words these poems repeat encourage us
to wonder how alike these actions are. For those who did lie
down in their beds, both for the farmer and for the saved who
sang their way home to dark houses, death is clearly the next
event in their lives of any significance. For in "Amazing Grace"
the narrator is struck by the fact that the grace the tent meeting
affords did not really enliven the revived. Their existence would
still be just a meaningless wait for death; they would continue to
lie down and rise "Until that morning they would not rise, not
ever."

"Boy Wandering in Simms' Valley" is about a religious experience, too, but the only way to realize this is through reading its
reference to another poem in *Now and Then*. When the poet
came to wander in Simms' Valley and the house in which Simms
had lain down by his wife to die, he found that "old furrows
were dim" (as in "American Portrait" he had found that "the
trench of our valor," the one he and K used to play in, was "now
nothing / But a ditch full of late-season weed-growth"), that the
"farm had contracted," gone back to wilderness, leaving only the
house standing. He stood in the bedroom upstairs, thinking
about what had happened there, saw the sun sinking, took one
last look around,

                then suddenly
Saw the old enameled bedpan, high on a shelf.
I stood still again, as the last sun fell on me,

And stood *wondering* what life is, and love, and what they may
    be.

This last line recalls the conclusion of the poem before, where
he "lay / *Wondering and wondering*" how many mornings he

would still wake up. The bedpan reminds him, as Watkins points out (116), of the dedicated care with which Simms must have watched over his wife's last days, of that life and that love. This is clearly what the bedpan *obviously* means, but it is not all that it could mean. Later in the collection, in "When the Tooth Cracks—Zing!" (45), something like what happens here to the poet is said to have happened to a sixteenth-century religious mystic:

> Do you
> Remember that Jacob Boehme saw
> Sunlight flash on a pewter platter on
> The table, and his life was totally changed?
>
> Is the name of God nothing more than
> The accidental flash on a platter? But what is accident?

Is it just accidental that this sudden view of sunlight striking a place should occur in the same sequence in which the poet himself suddenly saw, with sunlight falling on him, a shiny piece of dishware, and that both would have had a significance beyond their homely appearance? And is it just an accident that the only other time Warren speaks of Jacob Boehme in his poetry it was in connection—as it ultimately is here, in the connection between these two poems in *Now and Then*—with a certain Simms? "Dragon Country: To Jacob Boehme" (from *Promises: Poems 1954-1956*, and consistently reprinted in the *Selected Poems*) claims that a dragon once haunted the poet's native terrain: "I was only a boy when Jack *Simms* reported the first depredation." (*N & SP*, 275)

Floyd Watkins, whose study *Then and Now: The Personal Past in the Poetry of Robert Penn Warren* is devoted to showing the extent to which Warren's poetry is based on personal experience, particularly his childhood in Guthrie, Kentucky, expected that the Simmses of Simms' Valley would have been "old citizens of Todd County," Kentucky (116), and was therefore surprised to hear from Warren himself that the deserted farmhouse was really in Vermont. Watkins's feeling that there is some personal and private landscape behind the poems is surely accurate, but it is not

necessarily one that ever existed on any map. In that interior
landscape the mystic Boehme, who discovered God in the hum-
blest things, lies not far distant from the Simms who left the
enameled bedpan so that the poet might make the same discovery, who may have been the same Simms who first discovered
the trace of the dragon (whose spoor is sometimes stool, to
which the particular use to which the enameled bedpan is devoted responds: "The slime on the railroad rails is where he had
crossed the track. / On a frosty morning, that field mist is where
his great turd steams") whose existence caused the "Baptists [to]
report new attendance" (as well as, one may presume, the tent
revivalists) and justified Jacob Boehme, who, Watkins reports,
"saw the divine and demonic in the daily reality" of his world
(83).

"Old Flame" (13) provides another sunlit revelation. The poet
recalls having been awed by the glory of a certain girl's twin
braids when he was a boy. He would dog her tracks to school,
watching the braids twitch over each shoulder as she walked, his
"Gaze fixed on the sun's stunning paradox which / Gave to
blackness a secret flaming that blackness denied." Here what
fixed his gaze was something akin to Jacob Boehme's experience: not just the braids, but what happened when the sunlight
and those braids came together, as for Boehme it had been the
accidental flash of sunlight on pewter. The "secret flaming that
blackness denied" was the sexuality that the burning blackness
suggested was hidden inside, in the dark—the flame of the "Old
Flame." As he had when he stood in the light of the setting sun
and suddenly saw the enameled bedpan at the end of the preceding poem, he would surely have found himself wondering
"what life is, and love, and what they may be" as he gazed at the
sun's paradox enacted on those bouncing braids and fantasized
about the girl who wore them.

In "Boy Wandering in Simms' Valley," the poet came, "years
later," to the place where it all had happened and found the
ghostly detritus of the life, and the love, that had once been
lived in that house: "saw sheets hang spiderweb-rotten, and
blankets a mass / Of what weather and leaves . . . had done, /
Not to mention the rats." In "Old Flame" he had found what he
calls there a "pile of age-litter," too: the "grisly old dame" with

gray hair and false teeth who a half-century later stops him in the street of his old hometown to say, " 'Why, it's you! . . . Don't you know me?' it wailed. *Then suddenly*, by Christ, I did." This sudden recognition, whatever it may have been for the poet, is a case of déjà vu for the reader, for Warren has told the story in such a way—with such words—that it is in fact a retelling of the incident at the end of the preceding poem. For there, too, he had been standing in the presence of the detritus of time and "*then suddenly* / Saw the old enameled bedpan."

"Old Flame," "Amazing Grace," and even "Boy Wandering" are haunted by images of women intimately associated with death. The "grisly *old dame*" that the old flame had become echoes the "*old*-fool *dame*" clothed in funereal black who tried to drag the boy down to his knees to confess his sins in the tent and come face to face with death (in the latter she succeeded, as we see at the end of the poem). "Amazing Grace" featured other menacing women as well, the carnival whores ready to dispense fatal diseases: "ready to serve / Any late-lingerers, and leave / A new and guaranteed brand of syphilis." In the middle of all this, Mr. Simms's wife, despite the apparent sentimentality the poem conveys of a husband too lonely to carry on by himself, could, and perhaps should, be seen for what she was: a woman who led a man to his death.

In the interval between the time he saw the girl with the braids and the time he saw her again fifty years later, the poet had already nearly wished her into the grave: "Then I was gone, and as far as I cared, she could moulder, / Braids and all, in the grave, life carved in compressed notation." Even after the recognition scene, he still can't retain her name in his memory, or even her face; the most he can conjure up is a pair of legs and that pair of braids: "When her name escapes, I can usually call to mind / Sausage-legs, maybe some kind of braids. Never, never, a face." In the following "Evening Hour" (14) he's still unable, as he puts it, to add two and two and come up with anything more than two twos: hanging about the graveyard looking for arrowheads, he doesn't really think too much about the dead.

Not thinking of flesh and its nature, but suddenly still
For maybe two minutes. . . .

Not morbid, not putting two and two together
To make any mystic, or fumblingly philosophical,
Four. . . .

Putting two, if not two and two, together is what the sequential
structure of Warren's late poetry encourages us to do; in this instance, what we might put together is the way "Evening Hour"
returns to the fascination of "Old Flame" with twos: with the
twin braids in which all the erotic attraction of the girl who wore
them was concentrated (as well as another set of two, "the rather
sausage-like trotters" that he mentions even before the braids—
only to say that at first he had *not* noticed them), in a kind of
"compressed notation" like that into which the grave would
transform her entirely. "Evening Hour" makes explicit that im-
plicit analogy between one kind of compressed notation and another by expressing the boy's obliviousness to the death that
surrounded him in the terrain where he searched for arrowheads in terms of adding two and two together (an arithmetici-
zation that is itself an instance of compressed notation) and not
getting the four that was there but that he did not recognize.

What else might be there in that graveyard that we, like the
boy, don't see? Something about it should remind us of "American Portrait: Old Style": the way the boy used the graveyard for
another, more playful purpose than the one for which it was intended—"Here the Indian crouched to perfect his arrowhead. /
And there was a boy, long after, who gathered such things /
Among shiny new tombstones recording the first-planted dead."
In the same way he had used the sunken grave of old "Pap" as
a trench for a last Confederate stand. And something about the
Indian might remind us, too, of someone in "Amazing Grace,"
the old lady in black who tried to save the poet's soul. Like the
Indian, she appeared in a crouching position: "And now by my
knees crouched some old-fool dame / In worn-out black silk,
there crouching with tears / In her eyes as she tugged me to
kneel." What connection there might be between the two is suggested by the poet's reaction to her appeal—he became like the
material with which the Indian was working and which he would
later come looking for in the graveyard, flint: "But the Pore Little Lamb, he hardened his heart, / Like a flint nigger-head
rounded slick in a creek-bed." Here flint was the alternative the

poet chose when confronted with the kind of question the woman meant to ask, namely "Where will you spend eternity?" The same opposition lies at the base of "Evening Hour," where the poet could ignore the death all around him in his search for flint, for the arrowheads which were as plentiful there as graves, as those who dug them knew: "and the spade at the grievous chasm / Would go *chink* on chipped flint in the dirt, for in times forgot // Here the Indian crouched" (Warren's italics).

The echo of that chipping and *chink* resounds in "Orphanage Boy" (15) in what Al was doing as he taught the boy who was to become the poet all the dirty words he had never heard before: "*chop- / ping* stove-lengths" at the woodpile. The orphanage boy Al worked as a hired hand on the poet's uncle's farm, and his best friend was (not, perhaps, the poet but) Bob, the white bull-dog with whom he sat and watched the sun go down or the moon rise every evening after supper. But a copperhead bit Bob, and the poet's uncle told Al he had to put him out of his misery. He

> handed a
> Twelve-gauge to Al, and said, "Be sure
> You do it right back of the head."
> He never named Bob's name.

Al took Bob into the woods, the boy following, and did the deed. He gave the still smoking gun to the poet and told him to go away. "And I got away and he lay / On the dead leaves crying even / Before I was gone." Al never came back. Six months later, the poet went back to the spot and found that Al had dug a grave ("There was a real grave / There," he tells us, echoing the first words of the poem before: "There was a graveyard once") and erected a wooden cross, and that Al must have taken the trouble to come back to the barn for the shovel and hammer and back again to return them. "It must have taken nigh moonset."

The poem is so simple and direct that it is difficult to say much about it. Floyd Watkins finds it to be "an account of tend-erness in a boy who superficially appears to be a hoodlum and a master of obscenities" (117) and believes that "It is a poem of nu-merous afterthoughts, many of them possible, none of them provable beyond dispute from the text itself. The conditions it reflects may be attributable to a Southern or rural way of life, man's theological condition, the haphazard luck of the world, or the status of man—or dog" (112-13). But when we read it in the context, indeed in the larger poem, in which Warren has placed it, something more emerges. It comes directly before the deservedly famous "Red-Tail Hawk and Pyre of Youth" (17)—the poem about the pride and sorrow that comes from shooting a great hawk and memorializing it by taxidermy. Warren's decision to place these poems side by side impels us to consider how one might help us read the other. The tears Al shed ("he lay / On the dead leaves crying") the poet shed too when the great bird fell: "in / Eyes tears past definition . . . the bloody / Body already to my bare flesh embraced, cuddled / Like babe to heart, and my heart beating like love." What he felt was both grief and joy ("Heart leaping in joy past definition"), but it was also something like love, which was the emotion Al had felt for Bob.

The poet's uncle "never named Bob's name" when he told Al what he had to do; when the poet in "Red-Tail Hawk" looked down at the rifle in his hand "It was as though / I did not know its name," and when the hawk first appeared it, too, was "nameless," though as it got close enough to shoot, "suddenly I knew the name." Al's industrious and memorializing use of "shovel and hammer" is answered by the poet's skillful manipulation of razor, "scissors, / Pliers and needles, waxed thread, / The burlap and salt, the arsenic and clay, / Steel rods" and the rest of his taxidermic apparatus, all for the sake, too, of a certain funereal transformation, the hawk becoming a memorial to itself—its own tombstone and grave. The *dog* had to die because he would never recover from the effect of a snake's *teeth* ("It was a copperhead / Bit Bob"); the hawk had to die to become what the poet would make of his body, and though after it was all over he would look as if he were ready "to take to the air," he was in reality "now / Forever earthbound, fit only / For *dog tooth*, not sky." Reading the two poems side by side would almost allow something like that to happen, would permit the dog to sink its teeth into the hawk, would let one poem consume, or at least work its will upon, the other.

We destroy what we love, or at least we have to sometimes. Al had to learn this lesson, but surely in his case it was not a truth of universal application, since had it not been for the snake matters would never have turned out as they did. But in "Red-Tail Hawk" this truth is genuinely at issue, for the thing the poet both loved and killed was something that if he hadn't killed he wouldn't have loved (and vice versa). "Red-Tail Hawk" is the real thing for which "Orphanage Boy" is the practice run, telling a paradoxical and essential truth for which the poem that precedes it, in giving an accidental, contingent version, provides the prelude.

Poems, as I said, can eat other poems. Take, for example, the detail of the advice the poet's uncle gave to Al: "Be sure / You do it right back of the head." And think, two poems back, of the insistence with which the boy stared at the back of the head of the girl whose name he didn't name either (and couldn't) and whom he as good as wished to an early grave: "as far as I cared, she could moulder, / Braids and all, in the grave." In retrospect, if we allow "Orphanage Boy" to influence our reading of "Old Flame," might not the paradox of love and murder be as much present in one as in the other—and in "Red-Tail Hawk and Pyre of Youth"?

In "Mountain Plateau" (22), as in "Red-Tail Hawk," the poet confronts a bird, a crow perched on the highest branch of an oak "At *the center of* acres of snow-whiteness"—as the hawk had first appeared at "*the center of* / That convex perfection." The crow "Uttered // Its cry to the immense distance," and the poet wants to respond but can't. Like the encounter with the hawk (and Al's with the necessity of killing Bob), this one with the crow leads the poet to tears.

> I can make no answer
> To the cry from the immense distance,
>
> My eyes fill with tears. I have lived
> Long without being able
> To make adequate communication.

The hawk had uttered no cry, but the poet, shooting it, had done so: "I screamed, not knowing / From what emotion, as at that insane range / I pressed the cool, snubbed / Trigger." There was, if not communication, a common bond between the hawk and the boy, even in that pull of the trigger that bound them together: "The old .30-30 . . . knows / How to bind us in air-blood and earth-blood together / In our commensurate fate." Yet there was communication too, at least in one direction, for even with his eyes closed the boy "knew / That yellow eyes somewhere, unblinking, in vengeance stared. // Or *was* it vengeance? What could I know?" (Warren's italics).

No bird and no gun appear in "Star-Fall" (23), but making communication, or rather not making it, is the subject of this poem as it was of "Mountain Plateau." The poet and someone else—his wife, given the context the next poem will provide—are lying on a cliff in August watching the Perseid meteor shower. While the poet complained in "Mountain Plateau" of not being able to "make adequate communication" with the crow, here he is content not to make communication with the person lying next to him. Their fingers are touching but immobile, sending no messages.

> for hours
> The only contact was fingers, and motionless they.
> For what communication
> Is needed if each alone
> Is sunk and absorbed into
> The mass and matrix of Being that defines
> Identity of all?

While he was saddened to the point of tears because he could make no answer to the cry of the crow, here he is again silent but with no need to speak: "We found nothing to say, for what can a voice say when / The world is a voice, no ear needing?"

"Youth Stares at Minoan Sunset" (25) finds the poet again with his wife, once again by the sea and near a cliff, and once again in a situation where communication does not take place. In "Mountain Plateau" it did not take place between him and the crow even though the poet wished it could; in "Star-Fall" it doesn't transpire between him and his wife because it doesn't need to; while here in "Youth Stares" it does not, at least not at first, take place between the poet and his wife, on the one hand, and their son, on the other. That son is some distance away, a "frail human figure . . . minted black" on the "great coin" of the setting sun. "The black / Silhouette, yet small, stares seaward. To

our cry / It does not turn. Later, / It will." These three poems
form a continuous series of gradually transforming situations,
with the last term echoing the first, the "frail" and "black" silhouetted son recalling the black bird on the "black, frail" top-
most twig of the tree in "Mountain Plateau." By a symmetric
reversal, the "cry" the crow uttered that the poet could not answer is answered by the "cry" to which the silhouetted black figure does not turn ("Youth Stares" even appears to allude to the
mountain and bird of "Mountain Plateau" when in another passage it speaks as well of the parents' fruitless attempt to call to
the son: "Mountainward, / No bird cries. We had called once, /
But we were too far, too far").

   If in this poetic sequence the crow becomes the son, it should
also be noted that the crow had been the hawk, and that the red-
tail hawk is at once his father (the father he killed, whose venge-
ful eyes are always on the son, expressive—as are the eyes of so
many fathers in the novels—of something they cannot, by
rights, express, since they are fake, are glass eyes the poet in-
serted himself), his child ("cuddled / Like babe to heart"), and
the poet himself ("one eye long gone—and I reckoned / I knew
how it felt with one gone"). Warren's fondest dream, expressed
in such poems as "The Leaf " (in *Incarnations*) and "Sunset Walk
in Thaw-Time in Vermont" (in *Or Else*), is that the roles of father and son become exchanged, inverted, interchangeable.
And the name of the dog whose death prefigures the hawk's is,
as it happens, a familiar form of the Robert the son and father,
in this instance, share.

   Familiar, in particular, to his own experience. In the quite recent autobiographical essay *Portrait of a Father*, Warren informs
us that "Bob" is in fact what his mother called his father: "Once
or twice, as a child, I overheard my mother say to some friend,
or to a sister, something like this: 'Oh, yes, a happy marriage is
simple. Everything outside the front gate is Bob's concern and
everything inside is mine' " (55).[1] A few pages later, he recounts
a remarkable incident in which his father sadly reproaches him
for suppressing the name that son and father share: his father
had once tried to be a poet and had had something printed in a
vanity publication that he had kept hidden from his son. "My father had known what it was to sweat over poems. I had long
since seen the hidden book. . . . I had begun to publish what I

hoped were poems. . . . one of them, in some sort of reflex against the triple names of many nineteenth-century authors, was signed 'Penn Warren.' My father had read the poem and made a friendly but critical remark. Then, still holding the little magazine (what, I forget), he asked me whether I did not like the name 'Robert.' With an instant of shame—it must have been shame—I remembered that he had once signed his full name" (62-63). (I have already quoted this passage once in a slightly different light.) The father's name, and the son's name that is inescapably the father's, is what, in practically his first act as a writer, Warren refuses to name. This refusal gives peculiar resonance to the refusal in "Orphanage Boy" to name the victim that bears so strong a similarity to what this son will murder in "Red-Tail Hawk": "He never named Bob's name."

The second of *Now and Then*'s two sections—"Speculative"—begins with "Dream" (29), which transforms the striking image of the poet's son's frail human figure "minted" in black on the "great coin, flame-massy," of the setting sun into a version of the poet's self seen also in the west (as "the Morning Star / Westward will pale") and likewise overwhelmed by the sun, a "ghost without history" wandering "A desert trackless in sun-glare." The son is, as such poems as "The Leaf " and "Sunset Walk in Thaw-Time in Vermont" show in detail, in some sense another self of the poet's self, and so also is this ghost in sun-glare the dream self that, according to the argument of this poem, would become that ghost bereft of history if the dreamer did not grapple his dream, did not wrestle it for a blessing as did Jacob the Angel—"For the dream is only a self of yourself."

The title of the following poem—"Dream of a Dream" (30)— makes its continuity with "Dream" abundantly clear. In the first of these two poems, *"Heels slashed* at soft knee-backs" as Odysseus fought with Ajax in a struggle the poet encourages dreamers to imitate ("So grapple your dream! Like Odysseus the Cunning, who leaped / On the mountainous Ajax"); the second begins and concludes with echos of that dreamlike struggle:

Moonlight stumbles with bright *heel*
In the stream. . . .
. . . .

By this time the moonlight's bright *heel* has *splashed* the
   stream;
But this, of course, belongs to the dream of another dream.

It does belong to another dream: to the "Dream" in which
"Heels slashed"—to the poem immediately before this one.
"Dream of a Dream" speaks of the structure of dream, of "the
braiding texture of dream," and such texture seems to be what
these poems, in their intertwining sequence, are made of too.
For in the same way that "In my dream Time and water interflow, / And bubbles of consciousness glimmer ghostly as they
go" these poems interflow, and braid their texture, as the slash-
ing and splashing heels do here—of which another instance is
the manner in which the "ghost without history" in one reappears in the other as the "ghostly" glimmer of consciousness.

In the second half of "Dream of a Dream," the poet wonders
"From what dream to what dream do we / Awake when the *first
bird stirs* . . . ?" "First Dawn Light" (32) poses a similar question:
"not yet *first bird-stir*, first bird-note, only / Your breath as you
wonder what daylight will bring." "Dream of a Dream" in asking
that question presupposes that waking reality is a dream too;
"First Dawn Light" goes even farther in that direction when it
suggests, in its concluding line, that only dreams, and not what
we perceive when awake, are real: "You must wait to resume, in
night's black hood, the reality of dream."

The light in "First Dawn Light" is gray: "By lines fainter gray
than the faintest geometry / Of chalk . . . day's first light / Defines the window edges." "Ah, Anima!" (33) speaks of a different
kind of gray light, the "gray and splintered light" of a storm that
exposes "the gray underside of leaf." "First Dawn Light" spoke
of "the true emptiness of night" for which daylight is not
necessarily a respite, "For day has its loneliness too." Similarly,
in "Ah, Anima!" sleep, for reasons of its own, is not necessarily
a respite from the troubling storm: "But, meanwhile, sleep / Is a
disaster area, too." As it was in "First Dawn Light," sleep is succeeded here too by gray light: "And when, in the dark, you
wake . . . / You may wish that you, even in the wrack and pelt of
gray light, // Had run forth, screaming as wind snatched your
breath away / Until you were nameless."

To run out into the storm like that, this poem concludes,
would be "to leave // The husk behind." "Unless" (35) begins

with that husk, with the realization "that what you think is Truth
is only // A husk for something else" and the example of the rattlesnake who scrapes off his old skin "and flows away . . . // Unhusked for its mission." The setting for "Unless" could hardly be
more different than it is from that of "Ah, Anima!"—the latter
a forest close enough to the ocean to be buffeted by a hurricane
(and therefore, quite possibly, near one of Warren's homes in
New England—in Connecticut most likely, or Vermont), the former a desert with cactus and no storm, no rain. Yet there is a
storm in "Unless":

> At night I have stood there, and the wide world
> Was flat and circular under *the storm of the*
>
> *Geometry of stars.* The mountains, in starlight, were black
> And black-toothed to define the enormous circle
>
> Of desert of which I was the center.

And that storm of stars recalls not only the storm in the poem
before ("Ah, Anima!") but by its geometry the one before that
("First Dawn Light"): "By lines fainter gray than the faintest *geometry* / Of chalk, on a wall like a blackboard, day's first light."
The light here compared to geometry and the light of the storm
in "Ah, Anima!" were already intertwined, braided together in
the way these poems imitate "the braiding texture of dream,"
because they were both gray and both the alternative to sleep
and dream. The "storm of the // Geometry of stars" thus alludes
not only to the two preceding poems but precisely to the manner
in which those poems alluded to each other.

And this passage from "Unless" alludes as well to the poem to
follow, "Not Quite Like a Top" (37), where the sensation of
being the center of an enormous circle is transformed, by ine-
briation, into that of feeling decidedly off center:

> Did you know that the earth, not like a top on its point,
> Spins on an axis that sways, and swings, from its middle?
>
> Well, I didn't know, but do now, and often at night,
> After maybe three highballs, I lie in my bed,
>
> In the dark, and try to feel the off-center sensation.

Later in the poem, in bed on a Pullman sleeping car (where
he could not have been able, as he had been in his bed at home,
to maintain "head north"), "I desperately prayed // To God to
exist so that I / Might have the exalted horror of denying //
Him." "Waiting" (39) continues this theological discourse with
talk of a decision "to take Catholic / Instruction." In "Not Quite
Like a Top" the poet "Wept because / I couldn't be sure something precious was true"; he is still weeping in "Waiting," though
with apparently mixed emotions, at a certain divine comedy:

> You realize, to your surprise, that our Savior died for us all,
> And as tears gather in your eyes, you burst out laughing,
>
> For the joke is certainly on Him, considering
> What we are.

But the most interesting allusion from one poem to another is
the way the prayer he makes to God in "Not Quite" to exist so
that he might have the exalted horror of denying Him is answered in the conclusion of "Waiting" by the realization that
"God / Has allowed man the grandeur of certain utterances. //
True or not. But sometimes true." In "Not Quite" he had wept
because he couldn't be sure something precious was true; what's
true is still at issue here and not resolved, either ("True or not").
But God has allowed man, and the poet, the grandeur of certain
utterances, among them the denial that He exists. He would
have to exist before He could make such an allowance; but then
He would also have to exist before the poet could have the ex-
altation, and the grandeur, that comes from denying Him. The
two poems, then, are really talking about the same thing, a kind
of divine Epimenidean paradox about truth and falsity, their
undecidability, and the impossibility of proving the existence of
God.

"The Mission" (41) opens with a similar paradox about the
possibility of making statements predicated on the existence of
knowing beings that don't exist: "I wake from a dream of horses.
They do not know / I am dreaming of them. By this time they
must be long dead." God doesn't know, either—if He doesn't exist—that He is being asked to exist so that the poet might have
the exalted horror of denying His existence. The horses in the

dream are in France: the dreamer knows that—and he also knows "They are dead"—because he saw the gold horse head above the door of the village's "*boucherie chevaline*" (Warren's italics). All this is made plain in the dream, which thus provides clues to its own interpretation. The analogy "Dream" and "Dream of a Dream" provided between "the braiding texture of dream" and their own interweaving texture, a braiding structure *Now and Then* and all Warren's subsequent sequences share, reminds us that dream clues may also be poetic ones. And precisely here the "*boucherie chevaline*" is not only part of the dream but part of the braiding texture of the sequence, for "Waiting" spoke, as if it were as much a thing to worry about as the other instances it gives of dread (getting bad news in the hospital, hearing one's wife say she never loved you, seeing floodwaters rise when there is no escape) of becoming "uncertain of French // Irregular verbs."

Mention of French, in other words, an apparently minor detail of the poem before, comes back here to play a part in the dream of the horses. And in that chevaline dream it plays precisely the role of something remembered, as if it were partly in the dream and partly outside it. ("Later, the manes will rustle," the poet says, narrating the dream, "But ever so little, in wind lifting off the Bay of Biscay. But no— / They are dead. *La boucherie chevaline*, in the village, / Has a gold horse-head above the door"—their manes can't be rustling, in other words, because they must be dead, and they must be dead because I saw the sign of the horse butcher. There is logic here, and causality, though it is the kind of logic that seems plausible only while it is being dreamed.) If the sequence in which these poems appear is respected, then that earlier mention of French will play the same role in the poem that follows that fragments of the day's events play in the formation of the dream that that second poem is and tells. Within the kind of Warrenian sequence in which each poem picks up elements from the one before, it will be very much, as Freud puts it, like the "recent and indifferent material" from the waking events that immediately precede a dream and are transformed that night into dream material ("in every dream it is possible to find a point of contact with the experiences of the previous day" [*The Interpretation of Dreams*, 197]).

It will also be very much like what Warren himself, in the very early poem I cited in the first chapter ("Images on the Tomb"), calls "Poor fragments of the day" that remain piled in the dark "until there come / Dreams to release from the troubled heart and deep / The pageantry of thoughts unreconciled." The forgetting of French irregular verbs is here just such a poor fragment of the day, piled up in the dark of sleep and then released into the pageantry of warring thoughts that is the fabric of dream. What is remembered, in this instance, is the act of not being able to remember ("Until you become *uncertain*").

But there is something else nagging to memory. It is not in the dream, but it *is* in the poem (it is in the dream that the poem is, which is not the same as the dream the poet recounts). "In the dark kitchen the electric icebox rustles. / It whispers like the interior monologue of guilt and extenuation, / And I wake from a dream of horses." That rustling is clearly the exterior stimulus for the sounds the manes make in the dream, though whether that sound is really heard in the dream is something of which the dreamer is, curiously, not entirely sure. At first they don't rustle, then they do, and then, again, they don't: "horses . . . like gray stone, stand, / Heavy manes unrustling in the gray sea wind. / . . . Later, the manes will rustle, // But ever so little. . . . But no— / They are dead." The reason that, in the end, they don't rustle is because they are dead, and I (the dreamer) know they are dead because I saw the sign of the *boucherie chevaline*. But we (the readers) know what the dreamer does not know (though the poet may know): that there is a reason behind the *boucherie chevaline*, namely the French forgotten in the poem before.

But the rustling of the icebox, as an outside stimulus to the dream, is something very much like that forgotten French, analogous to some poor fragment of the day piled in the dark of the unconscious. Given how closely Warren's description of the dreamwork in "Images on the Tomb" parallels Freud's in *The Interpretation of Dreams*, it is not unreasonable to suppose, certainly by the much later date at which he wrote "The Mission," his familiarity with that text. Freud there declares that such sensations received during sleep as the rustle of the icebox serve the same purpose as the fragments of the day that reappear, transmuted, in dreams. He writes: "In my opinion, somatic sources of stimulation during sleep . . . play a similar part in the formation of dreams to that played by recent but indifferent impressions left over from the previous day. I believe, that is, that they are brought in to help in the formation of a dream if they fit in appropriately with the ideational content derived from the dream's psychical sources, but otherwise not. They are treated like some cheap material always ready to hand" (271).

"The Mission" is practically a case study, conducted by the poet, of how a dream is made. This point becomes especially evident when one realizes how the rustle of the icebox becomes the rustle of the horses' manes. But we have been given yet another clue: the revelation that the sound of the icebox itself carries an emotional charge. "It whispers like the interior monologue of guilt and extenuation" (a guilt that very possibly carries over into the dream, for it is a dream the poet does not want to have to dream again: "if I stare at the dark ceiling / And try to remember [not the dream but "the nature of my own mission"], I do not have to go back to sleep, / And not sleeping, will not again dream // Of clumps of horses"). Freud held that somatic stimuli during sleep could be used as raw material for the dream "if they fit inappropriately with the ideational content derived from the dream's psychical sources"—how then might this whisper of guilt fit with the dream of horses that transforms it into the rustle of their manes? And what are the psychical sources of that dream?

Now and Then holds at least one key to the interpretation of the dream and with it an answer to the riddle of the guilt the icebox speaks. For "Red-Tail Hawk" had already told us what guilt that icebox holds:

> So at last
> I dared stare in the face—the lower beak drooping,
> As though from thirst, eyes filmed.
> Like a secret, I wrapped it in newspaper quickly
> And hid it deep
> In the ice chest.

Calvin Bedient has forcefully argued that the guilt the poet felt for shooting the hawk is not, as Dave Smith would have it, the

guilt the Ancient Mariner felt for killing the albatross but an
Oedipal guilt. Reminding us that the hawk was Godlike, having
"Gold eyes, unforgiving, for they, like God, see all," Bedient asserts: "There is a real father in the fictitious God, the fiction of
God in every father. Hate alone would not have shrieked in
transgressive joy to bring this hot-blooded father down; terribly,
love wanted the transgression just as much, and love weeps in
the tears past definition. As the unforgiving father-god falls, as
the winged phallus plummets, the boy's heart leaps in joy" (190).
If the hawk is the father, hidden like a crime, like a dirty secret,
in the ice chest, then what are the horses whose manes the rustle
of the—now electrified, updated—icebox makes him dream of?
Standing by the sea "like stone primitively hewn," the horses
bear a significant resemblance to the ancient (the mark of "an
ancient band") "taciturn tall stone, / Which is your fathers'
monument and mark" that stands by the sea in "To a Face in a
Crowd" and looms at the end of each of Warren's *Selected Poems*.
But it is not only in their stoniness that they recall the taciturn
father, for the father in Warren's poetry has been shown, particularly in death, to have equine qualities—consider what he
left his son, that "precious secret," in his dying as "Reading Late
at Night, Thermometer Falling" in *Or Else* recounts it: "A prostate big as a *horse*-apple."[2]

A close reading of certain poems in *Rumor Verified*, as we have
already seen, provides even more evidence of the connection between father and horse: (1) In "Dead Horse in Field" the horse,
its eyes gone, could "more readily see / Down the track of pure
and eternal darkness" just as the father's own eyes in "I Am
Dreaming of a White Christmas" in *Or Else*, "Not there, . . . stare
at what / Is not there." (2) In "The Corner of the Eye" the sound
of the father's dying breath resembles a sound that comes from
a horse (as well as the whisper a newspaper makes—and we recall that the icebox "whispers" its rustle of guilt and extenuation,
as well as the fact that what the hawk- and father-slayer put in
the ice chest was wrapped in newspaper): "the rhythmic rasp of
your father's last breath, harsh // As the grind of a great file the
blacksmith sets to hoof. / Or the whispering slither the torn
morning newspaper makes." (3) In "What Voice at Moth-Hour"
the white petals that fall around the poet as he stands in the orchard recall the white petal of the century plant that takes the

place of the horse-apple in the scene of the father's death as it is recounted in "One I Knew"—yet these white petals at the same time allude to the earlier version of that death scene told in "Reading Late at Night" (where the father's "precious secret"—a phrase present in both accounts—that in "One I Knew" will have become a century plant had been a horse-apple), for they are, precisely, "the white / Petals of *apple* blossoms."

"Code Book Lost" (43), the poem immediately after "The Mission," supplies a rather startling confirmation of this interpretation—specifically of the contention that the horses in the dream suggest the father, in particular the death of the father and the horse-apple that was the precious secret of that death. For it tells precisely what "What Voice at Moth-Hour" will tell when it will speak in a book not yet written (*Rumor Verified*) of "the white / Petals of apple blossoms . . . falling, / Whiter than moth-wing in that twilight" and suggests—in the context of the sequence *Now and Then* provides in which it comes immediately after the dream of the horses—the same hidden pun on horse-apple and apple blossom:

> Or what in the mother's voice calling her boy from the orchard,
> In a twilight moth-white with the apple blossom's dispersal?

"The Mission" is a poem about trying to remember something: "the nature of my own mission." If I stare at the ceiling and try to remember what that mission was, the poet writes, I will not have to go back to sleep and dream that dream of the horses. At the end of the poem he suggests what that mission might be: "Perhaps that lost mission is to try to understand // The possibility of joy in the world's tangled and hieroglyphic beauty." That "*lost* mission" is pursued in the following "Code Book *Lost*," wherein the missing key is precisely what would have made it possible to decipher the world's hieroglyphic beauty that "The Mission" speaks of in its final line. The world is full of undeciphered messages. Some are birdsong: "What does the veery say, at dusk in shad-thicket? / There must be some meaning . . . // . . . the message spins on like a spool of silk thread fallen" (a spool that, fallen, will likely become "tangled," like the "world's . . . hieroglyphic beauty"). Some of them are dreams, like the one dreamed in "The Mission," and like "all dreams being dreamed in dark houses. . . . What do they signify? // Yes, message on message, like wind or water, in light or in dark, / The whole world pours at us. But the code book, somehow, is lost."

"When the Tooth Cracks—Zing!" (45) accepts the loss of the code book and even accepts the memory loss that made it impossible to recall in "The Mission" what the mission was by suggesting that forgetting is an essential part of knowledge:

> Must we totally forget a thing to know it?
> Perhaps redemption is nothing more than the way
> We learn to live with memories that are no longer remembered.
>
> But it is hard to know the end of a story.

"Sister Water" (47) answers that last line by beginning with a story whose *beginning* is hard to know (and the ellipsis with which the first line begins is the poem's, not mine): " . . . and to begin again, the night was dark and dreary, and / The Captain said to his trusty Lieutenant, 'Lieutenant, // Tell us a story.' And the Lieutenant: 'The night was dark and—.' "

The first line of "Memory Forgotten" (49), as well as its title, reminds us that the question "When the Tooth" asked about the necessity of forgetting a thing to know it is still echoing in our ears:

> Forget! Forget it to know it. It sings!
> But it is too true to sing its name. Afar,
>
> In a thicket, it sings like
> Some unidentified warbler. . . .
>
> . . . more liquid than thrush,
>
> It sings. How beautiful it is!—
> Now that it is only a memory
>
> Without a name.

As a memory without a name, the song of the thrush is what "When the Tooth" was talking about when it spoke of having to "learn to live with memories that are no longer remembered." Those memories—not remembered yet lived with, and therefore present, like empty ghosts—are clearly paradoxical and in that way resemble the "concept bleached of all content" (a way of talking about Time) of which Warren will speak in "Heat Wave Breaks" (73) later in *Now and Then* and the "metaphor / For which I could find no referent" (the blank, glittering snow) of "Time as Hypnosis" (in *Or Else*). As a thrush (which I think it is said to be, even though it sings like an "unidentified warbler"), it may be what "Code Book Lost" proposed as its first example of the world's undecipherable messages, the veery ("a brown and cream-colored thrush [*Hylocichla fuscescens*] of the E U.S.") that, like this bird, sang in a thicket ("What does the veery say, at dusk in shad-thicket?").

Despite the fact that the bird in the thicket "sings like / Some *unidentified* warbler" in "Memory Forgotten," to the very extent that it is unidentifiable it is *identifiable,* for in the immediately preceding poem the poet had recalled a time when "a finger, // Soft as down and with a scent / *Unidentifiable* but stirring your heart to tears, // Like memory, was laid to your lips." The warbler was "only a memory // Without a name"; similarly, the scent in "Sister Water," as unidentifiable as the warbler's song, has acted upon the poet "Like memory." The unidentifiable scent, like a dream within a dream, is memory within memory— memory itself, the essence of memory, devoid of content, like the concept bleached of all content that is Time and the metaphor without a referent that was the snow.

Unidentifiable/unidentified not only connotes by its very meaning the absence of content, but, appearing in two sequential poems like so many other instances of echoing words and images in these sequences, it is itself something very much like a concept without content, a referentless metaphor, and a memory without a name that must be forgotten—must be emptied of content—before it can be known. For by its repetition it loses what content it had in its first appearance, and by being repeated so soon after its first appearance it exposes its inherent instability, loosening its connection to whatever meaning it is supposed to have in its second appearance—with the result that what remains constant, what appears to mean anything at all in the end, is only what is repeated and not what meaning it may temporarily have in any given instance. But this statement does not mean that nothing remains in the end or that such repetition leads away from the truth. Rather, it leads into the truth, for what happens here is what Warren finds happens in the realm of memory (yet in talking about what happens in the poems we *are* speaking of memory, for we are speaking of remembered words), and in that realm a greater truth arises by the emptying of content that comes from forgetting: "How much do we forget that is ourselves— // . . . And in the forgetting to make it all more true?"

Consider the different connotations waking up at dawn can acquire. In "Sister Water," "dawn light defines the bars of your window [itself a recollection of "First Dawn Light," where "day's first *light* / *Defines* the *window* edges"] / And you hear the cough and mastication of // The garbage truck in the next block." That cough recalls what the poet heard outside his room at the beginning of the poem, the "chain-rattle of phlegm" in the painful respiration of an old man climbing the stairs outside his door. "I never know whose father it is, or son, / Or what mission leads to my locked door." In "Memory Forgotten" he asks "Did you ever / Wake up at dawn, heart singing, and run out // Barefoot in the dew, and dew blazed like diamonds of light?" "Waking to Tap of Hammer" (51) is about waking up to see the effect of the light on the dew, too, but recalls as well that moment in "Sister Water" when the poet heard a noise made by someone's son:

> Waking up in my curtain-dark bedroom, I hear,
> Cottoned in distance, the tap of a hammer:
>   . . . Yes,
> I know what it is. My boy, this early
> At his five-tonner at work, the schooner.
>   . . . Dew-gleaming,
> It swims in the first light.

This father once awoke from a dream in which he, "like a spirit, hung in the squall-heart— / There saw" his son sailing his boat in the storm, his face staring at his unseen father, that ghost suspended in the rain, through the plexiglass dome. "Slowly, it smiled. // I dreamed it was smiling at me."

If the poet is in the rain in that poem because of paternal love, a spirit hanging suspended in the heart of the squall, "you" are the snow, and love, in "Love Recognized" (52): "the happening that / Is you keeps falling like snow . . . you, like snow, like love, keep falling."

That snow covers everything in the landscape, "hiding hideousness, until / The streets and the world of wrath are choked with snow" In "The Smile" (53) the note (again) of the thrush fulfills the same function, calming wrath and rancor, swelling "to redeem all— / Sweat and swink and daytime's rancor, / And the thought that all's not worth all."

The smile in "The Smile"—

Your hand-back, task-tired, pushes up
Damp hair to show the flickering smile.

—(along with "you" and "-back") returns in "How to Tell a Love Story" (54): "You running ahead and a smile / Back-flung."

The telephone in "Little Black Heart of the Telephone" (55) is "screaming its little black heart out" because no one will answer. It cannot tell its story, as the poet could not in "How to Tell a Love Story": "There is a story that I must tell, but / The feeling in my chest is too tight. . . . // If only the first word would come and untwist my tongue! / Then the story might grow like Truth." In "How to Tell" the poet wants to speak of love but can't find the first word; in "Little Black Heart" he empathizes with the telephone's wordlessness: "My heart would bleed too, for I know how pain can't find words."

The scene of the telephone and its "little black bleeding heart" is full of blood. The room itself where the telephone screams, alone and unanswered, *"Bleeds* for the little *bleeding* black heart / Of the telephone. If, in fact, it should scream, / My heart would *bleed* too." For the poet knows what it is like to scream like that, having "looked up at stars lost in blankness that *bleeds* / Its metaphysical *blood*." All that blood returns in a wholly other context in "Last Laugh" (57), where the young Sam Clemens sees, peeping through the keyhole, his father, naked, spread on the family's dining room table for the autopsy:

> split open, lights, liver, and all
> Spilling out from that sack of mysterious pain, and the head
>
> Sawed through, where his Word, like God's, held its deepest den,
> And candlelight glimmered on blood-slick, post-mortem steel.

Could this be the story the bloody heart of the telephone was screaming to tell? A story the poet did not want to hear? "Have you ever . . . at night waked up with a telephone screaming, / And covered your head, afraid to answer?" he had asked in "Little Black Heart."

What's most remarkable about "Last Laugh" (beyond its title) is little Sam Clemens's ultimate response (which is the same thing) to this scene of the death and deconstruction ("It's not every night / You can see God butchered in such learned dismemberments") of the father. After the shock he went upstairs to bed, "wept on the pillow, surprised at what he thought grief, / Then fixed eyes at darkness while, slow, on his face grew a grin." The grin was for the joke that God was dead, and it turns into a laugh, the last one—"So took then to laughing and could not / Stop. . . . // And was left alone with his joke, God dead, till he died."

But does that grin not witness the deconstruction of more than the father in these poems? Does not this filial grin seem a horribly negating parody of the smile the poet, as a father, longed to see in his son—that he dreamed of in "Waking to Tap of Hammer," when he had left his bodily form to become a ghost, "a spirit, hung in the squall-heart?" "Behind plexiglass dome, hands on wheel, the face, / Carven, stared forth: gannet-gaze, osprey-eye. Slowly, it smiled. // I dreamed it was smiling at me." And how could the warmth of that boyish smile be restored after the intervening "Last Laugh," even by the "boyish grin" that will appear a few poems later in "Diver" (69)—especially in light of the fact that it will then be not a smile but a grin, like

young Clemens's? And even though the grin in "Diver" is so joyful a one that, in response, "we smile, too?"

In retrospect, at least one other aspect of "Waking to Tap of
Hammer" now reads differently, in light of what happened to
the father in "Last Laugh," whose head was "*Sawed* through,
where his Word, like God's, held its deepest den." After the silence following the tap of his son's boat-building hammer:
"Then anguish / Of band*saw* on white oak." This son wields
these instruments as skillfully as the dismembering physician
did on the senior Clemens. We have twice elsewhere encountered a hammer in these poems. One is "the hammer unheard"
in "Star-Fall" that makes stars fall like sparks, and which, too, is
connected to the son, through the connection we saw with the
following poem, "Youth Stares at Minoan Sunset." The other
hammer is the one Al used to nail the cross on Bob's grave, and
we have seen the degree to which that Bob may be a substitute
for another, more paternal figure. And it is perhaps not by accident that the other poem in this sequence in which the poet's
son is glorified ("Youth Stares") places that son "At the break of
the cliff-quarry where / Venetians had once *sawed* their stone." A
poem in *Or Else*, "Chain Saw at Dawn in Vermont in Time of
Drouth," makes some startling statements about such a tool: listening to the song of the saw, the poet can hear the "Lash and
blood-lust of an eternal present" that "Murders the past" (30).
In the second half of that poem, a man lies dying; he "Wakes /
In dawn to the saw's song"—as the poet will wake to the tap of
a hammer and then hear the anguish a saw can cause—and
"wonders / Why his boy turned out bad." The song of the saw,
we are told, is "the scream of castration" (32).

Sam Clemens's father's death undergoes a remarkable transformation in "Heat Lightning" (59). Blood, which in "Last
Laugh" glimmered in candlelight on the post mortem steel (and
which figured so prominently in the telephone's suffering in the
poem before that), is let here too, visible in "the faintest blood-
smear at the mouth's left corner." Eyes are the visible symbol of
death in both poems, "two dead fish-eyes" that "stared steadily
ceilingward" becoming, "In shudder and sprawl, only white //
Of eyes showing, like death." The shudder and sprawl are those
of a woman to whom the poet is making love with such passion

and violence that all this "exploitation of orifices and bruised flesh" seems "but / The striving for one death in two." "Last Laugh" and "Heat Lightning" together seem themselves to be striving for one death in two as well, seeking to discover what hidden similarities underlie sexual passion and death, the death of the father and the triumph of the will in sex.

Yet "Last Laugh" was already, without the help of the poem that follows it, a meditation on that subject, for though it starts with the death of the father, it ends with that of the bride. It was "quite a tussle" to convince Livy of the joke that God was dead but in the end "at her bedside / He watched dying eyes stare up at a comfortless sky"—as he once peeped through the keyhole at "two dead fish-eyes [that] stared steadily ceilingward"—"And was left alone with his joke, God dead, till he died." Through this internal echo "Last Laugh" was already itself, perhaps, "striving for one death in two." In any event, the death of this woman is followed, in "Heat Lightning," by the actual death of the woman who imitated death in the tussle of love. The poet stumbled across "The newspaper obit, years later."

The "blood-slick" aspect of "Last Laugh" returns, in "Inevitable Frontier" (61), in the surreal vision of a land where one must be "mindful how / Slick the blood of shadow can be." It is a place with an *heure sexuelle*, devoted to the pleasures of the flesh to which the poet in "Heat Lightning" showed more than passing interest. To understand it fully, one might have to go back to the moment in "Little Black Heart of the Telephone" when the poet asks, "Have you ever stopped by the roadside at night, and couldn't / Remember your name?" as if it had happened to him, for here those convicted of criminality are "Mystically deprived of the memory of their names."

The name of Pascal (along with those of Plato, St. Paul, Spinoza, and Freud) must not be spoken, though in the immediately following "Heart of the Backlog" (63) it is essential to the description of what is experienced "When you go to the door, snatch it open, and, cold, / The air strikes like steel down your lungs, and you feel / The *Pascalian* nausea make dizzy the last stars."

Sitting cozily by the fire, the poet imagines what the track of the vole must look like on the new snow. "How fleeting and thin / Its mark of identity . . . !" "Identity and Argument for

Prayer" (66), too, will be concerned with the relation between foot-tracks and identity. Returning to a place he had once left years before and to which he had thought he would never return, the poet finds it "odd that my feet fit old foot-tracks. . . . I'm *there*, now again!" But is it really the same place it was, or could it be "that / *There* is not there any more, / Having dropped through Time into otherness?" (Warren's italics). It is a question of identity: "For that old *I* is not I any more" but a "ghost," though "the *I* here now / Is not dead, only what / I have turned into" (Warren's italics). Sam Clemens had his joke—"And was left alone with his joke, God dead, till he died"; the poet has his, Time's undermining of his identity: "This / Is the joke you must live with."

The vole's "mark of identity," his track in the snow, was "How fleeting and thin . . . !" The fleeting nature of the poet's identity is revealed to him when he thinks of his own foot-tracks. In the end, he comes even closer to seeing himself in terms of that field mouse, when he recalls "the shadowy thought that / Man's mind, his heart, live only by piecemeal, like mice / On cheese crumbs."

"Diver" (69) too is about the trace feet leave and about identity, expressed here in terms of a diver whose "heels flash as water closes" and after whose dive the "board yet quivers where feet struck" (that "struck" recalling how the poet's own feet had been "*crushing*, / Freshly again, the fresh sea-rose" in the preceding poem). He leaves a wake of "mathematic accuracy," the concentric circles that "widen targetwise" from his point of entry. Watching him, "we"—and in every other instance ("Star-Fall," "Youth Stares at Minoan Sunset," and "The Smile") this first-person plural has meant the poet and his spouse, and the "he" who is the object of their regard has been their son— "know / An unsuspected depth and calm / Of *identity* we had never dreamed."

The poem ends with the "boyish grin" on the face of the diver when he emerges from the water, a smile reflected in those who have observed his performance: "And we smile, too, in welcome back / To all the joy and anguish of / The earth." "Rather Like a Dream" (70) begins with a boy, too, and the boy's wish to resolve a question about identity: Wordsworth, who, "a boy, reached out / To touch stone or tree to confirm / His own reality."

These three poems, then, present three ways of exploring the concept of a personal identity. In "Identity and Argument for Prayer" that identity is brought into question by the poet's realization that he is no longer entirely the person he once was. This truth is brought home to him when he steps in his old footsteps and, though he feels a kind of déjà vu—"How is it that I am *there* again? / Space and Time are our arbitrary illusions: even so, / How odd that my feet fit old foot-tracks"—knows he is no longer the same and that *there* cannot be *here*. *There* doesn't even exist any more,

> Having dropped through Time into otherness.
> But what did happen *there* is—just now
> In its new ectoplasmic context—
> Happening again, even if
> The companion who smiled in that dusk long ago, and
> Smiles now again . . .
> Is long dead. . . .

Warren's sequences have a remarkable way of appearing to speak about themselves, and in particular of their sequential structure while really talking about something else. "Dream of a Dream," with its talk of "the braiding texture of dream" and with the way it intertwined with the preceding "Dream," permitted us to speak of the analogy between the way each poem uses elements from the poem before as raw material for its own construction and the way the unconscious uses elements from the experience of the day before to construct its dream; "Sister Water" and "Memory Forgotten," by speaking of the necessity of forgetting in order to remember and to know and by making unidentifiability into an example of such forgetting, provided yet another instance. And here it's happening again, for in speaking of what happened once happening again in a new context, "Identity and Argument for Prayer" is not only speaking of the poet's own apparent experience in confronting his past but is at the same time addressing the phenomenon of sequential repetition that is so extraordinarily pervasive in Warren's late poetry. For that is exactly what keeps happening: some event in the past—in the preceding poem—happens again in the present, in the present poem, but with a new context, thereby raising the very question that the poet is asking here with regard to his own experience: Is it the same or not? Is it here or is it there?

And in an even more remarkable instance of self-reference, the example the poet cites with regard to his own experience, the smile of a companion who smiles again now, even though he cannot really do that because he is dead, serves in its own new context the very same purpose. That new context is the one formed by the sequential structure that leads us to read "Diver" just after "Identity and Argument for Prayer." In that new context we discover that, just as the smile returns in the poet's own experience to tease him into thinking that *then* is somehow *now*, and *there* somehow *here*, that returning smile itself returns in the very next poem—"Diver"—on the face of the boy whose plunge into another, underwater, world makes "our watching hearts . . . know / An unsuspected depth and calm / Of identity." It takes the form of the "boyish grin" on his face as he emerged from the water. "And we smile, too, in welcome." Yet that boyish grin, as we have seen, is not so innocent. For it is already the haunting return of another—the one on Sam Clemens's face the night he saw the death of God.

Warren focuses our attention on the hands of the boy whose progress through the water revealed that unsuspected depth and calm of identity: "In timeless peace / The mover that shows no movement moves / Behind the prow of a diver's hands." It is by outstretched hands too that the boy's revelation came in "Rather Like a Dream": "Wordsworth, a boy, reached out / To touch." Yet the identity exhibited in "Diver" is different from the reality revealed here. There it wasn't the diver who was uncertain of his identity but the poet watching him who was reassured by what he saw. Yet that moment returns here, at the end of the poem, when the poet will "stand, hands at sides, and wonder, / Wonder if I should put out a hand to touch // Tree or stone— just to know."

The haunting smile so closely associated with death in "Last Laugh," where it signaled young Clemens's awareness of all that could die, and that in "Identity and Argument for Prayer" belonged to the companion who, though dead, smiles again, appears once more, with the finality of death, in the seaside resort in "Departure" (72): "Smiles / Are frozen with a mortuary precision to seal friendships. Time is up." It's the end of the sum-

mer tourist season—"The sun goes earlier low"—and the guests
have packed to depart. It was the end of summer in "Rather
Like a Dream," too, being the "season / When the first maple
leaf falls red . . . and the promise // Of another summer is already a dream."

The end of the day too—in both poems. In "Rather Like a
Dream" "I *walk* in the mountain woods, / Alone, hour *sunset*"
while in "Departure"

> . . . if, toward *sunset*, at low tide, you *walk*
> Near the shoals, you will find the sea-grass
>
> Combed scrupulously in one direction only
> As if some fundamental decision,
> Involving us all, had at last been reached, but
>
> Not yet released for announcement.

In fact each of the last four poems in *Now and Then*—these two,
followed by "Heat Wave Breaks" and "Heart of Autumn"—are
about sunset, the change of seasons from summer to fall, and
the inevitable march of time, embodied in the lines just cited in
the "one direction only" that points to an ominous future that is
ultimately death. The "Heat Wave Breaks" (73) at the moment
summer's heat is about to yield to the chill of fall, as the immediately preceding "Departure" marks the moment "the mistral
levels in." The "hour sunset" of "Rather Like a Dream" was followed, as we have just seen, by the "toward sunset" of "Departure," to be succeeded by the moment hoped for in "Heat Wave
Breaks" "when . . . / The day will redden to flame, like the phoenix, to die." While the last line of "Heart of Autumn" (74)
echoes with some precision the manner in which "Departure"
spoke of the end of day: "*Toward sunset*, at a great height."

In "Heat Wave Breaks" the heat is so intense that "The warbler sits ruffled, beak open but music-less." And the poet wonders "does Time itself, in that timeless and crystalline heat, /
Hang transparent, a concept bleached of all content?" This con-
tentless concept, together with the songless warbler and the
phoenix about to die, are all reincarnated in "Heat of Autumn"
as high-flying geese that are about to perish from the hunter's
gun—

> . . . wild geese
> Head for a land of warm water, the *boom*, the lead pellet.

> Some crumple in air, fall. Some stagger, recover control,
> Then take the last glide for a far glint of water.

These birds, like the warbler and transparent Time, enact a paradox of emptiness, sound, and silence:

> . . . I stand, my face lifted now skyward,
> Hearing the high beat, my arms outstretched in the tingling
> Process of transformation, and soon tough legs,

> With folded feet, trail in the sounding vacuum of passage,
> And my heart is impacted with a fierce impulse
> To unwordable utterance—
> Toward sunset, at a great height.

The "sounding vacuum" the poet wishes to emulate here is not only another way of expressing the "concept bleached of all content" but at the same time a very literal embodiment of what, in an earlier discussion of this poem (in the preceding "Interlude"), we had found this poem to name when it spoke, alluding to the geese's pattern of flight, of "How tirelessly V upon V arrows the season's logic." The W, that is, of the poet's own name that superimposed V's can form. The geese, we recall, have "the joy / Of destiny fulfilling its own name," and the poet would like to know what they know, would like to know *his* own name. And indeed seems to hint that he does know it by superimposing his successive poems—or sequencing their echoes so that the reader will do the work for him—in a way that "arrows the season's logic." Arrows that consistently point ahead, like V's, to an uncertain future that he would like to meet with some degree of assurance—the one "at the end of . . . life's long sorites." A sequential structure, these last poems of *Now and Then* appear to tell us, informed by the fear of death.

For this *vacuum* that sounds may be the only word any of us could immediately call to mind in which the letter the superimposed V's form is actually names—as a double *u*—in something like "*u*nwordable *u*tterance": letters, not words; writing, not speech. Similarly, the poems in their repetitive sequence utter much of what they have to say in patterns dispersed (and thereby not immediately perceptible) in what is written in the text of the sequence itself, not just in the words of the poems.

Phoenixwise, moments of these poems perpetually disappear yet return, like the phoenix itself that returns as the geese about to die. Like the sea-grass in "Departure" that was combed "in one direction only" these sequences point inexorably toward a future—and at the same time direct us to read them with a taste for the ever-renewable paradox, announced by the title of the sequence, of *now* and *then*.[3]

Afterword

Could this way of reading Warren continue indefinitely backward into his poetic oeuvre? Are all his collections sequences in the sense in which the four considered here are? It would be difficult to prove that they are not, and I have no interest in doing so, but it would be useful to point out that the earlier collections are generally organized along different lines, in ways that seem to preclude the discoveries the last four sequences make possible. For in the latter the poems are on a roughly equal footing, each—at first glance—an independent entity in an apparently discontinuous (though ultimately quite closely linked) sequence. The apparent discontinuity forces the continuity that is in fact there to work its way through to the surface. And this tension contributes to their aesthetic power.

A glance at the table of contents of *Promises: Poems, 1954-1956*, the first collection to appear in more than a decade of poetic silence (except for the long narrative poem *Brother to Dragons*) and the first in the recognizably new style that has much more in common with the way Warren wrote in the 1980's than with the poems he wrote before 1943, would show that the equality and surface discontinuity to be found in the later sequences had yet to make its appearance. For almost half the poems in *Promises* are part of sequences already united in a fairly obvious way by subject or story; poems in such a sequence, for example, as "Ballad of a Sweet Dream of Peace" would naturally repeat the same elements, since they are sequential moments in the same unfolding narrative—or "Dark Woods," where the "*All right*" (Warren's italics) that concludes "1. Tonight the Woods Are Darkened" immediately returns, again italicized, as the first two words of "2. The Dogwood" (the boy narrator is talking to himself, gathering the courage to venture forth alone into the dark woods to revisit the spooky cow's skull and the dogwood ("White-floating in dark-ness"). Likewise the poems in the "Mortmain" sequence in *You, Emperors, and Others: Poems 1957-1960* are clearly already about his father, while those in "Penological Study: Southern Exposure" and "Internal Injuries" in *Incarnations: Poems 1966-1968* are, respectively, parts of the story of a convict dying of cancer and a black woman struck down by a car in New York City. It is thus not surprising that words from "Keep That Morphine Moving, Cap" in "Penological Study"—"Each drop upon that gray cement / Exploded like a star"—should reappear two poems later in the same sequence in "Wet Hair: If Now His Mother Should Come"—"sweat drips, and each drop, / On that gray cement, explodes like / A star." For the second passage is quite intentionally quoting the first. It is, however, more surprising (and interesting) that a passage from "Internal Injuries"—"meaning / In my guts blooms like / A begonia"—should echo one from "Penological Study"—"Inside his gut, inside his gut, / The pumpkin grows and grows." For it forces us to wonder what other parallels there may be between the injured black woman and the dying convict.[1] It is just the kind of verbal repetition his later sequences would exploit.

Tale of Time: New Poems 1960-1966, which appeared at the beginning of *Selected Poems: New and Old, 1923-1966*, is like *Promises* and *You, Emperors, and Others* less a sequence than a collection of sequences, some of which ("Tale of Time" and "The Day Dr. Knox Did It") are narratives (like "Ballad of a Sweet Dream of Peace") and therefore made up poems that are already continuous. *Or Else—Poem/Poems 1968-1971*, on the other hand, has a structure that differs radically from that of the collections that precede it: twenty-four numbered poems interrupted at irregular intervals by eight (also numbered) *Interjections*. As its subtitle claims, it is a poem as well as a collection of poems. That unity, though, as far as I can tell, is not one of sequential repetition; many echoes are there, but they are not particularly contiguous echoes. The same is true of the ten-poem sequence (whose brevity does distinguish it from the four that would follow) *Can I See Arcturus from Where I Stand?—Poems 1975* (the first section of *Selected Poems: 1923-1975*).

Yet it is clear that the unity of a poetic collection has been a long-standing concern of Warren's, at least since the revealingly

titled *Eleven Poems on the Same Theme* (1942). I personally am in-
clined, however, to believe that Warren's desire for his poetic
collections to be both poem and poems has found various forms
of expression over the years, as there is more than one way to
construct unity out of diversity: variations on a theme in *Eleven
Poems*, unity of subject and a multitude of (not necessarily sequential) echoes in *Or Else* and elsewhere. And that his collections have come to exploit the possibilities of sequence only
recently.

If his poems began to exploit sequence, as it now appears, in
1978 with the publication of *Now and Then*, and if they have continued to do so through *Altitudes and Extensions 1980-1984*, then
is that principle still at work in 1985 when Warren made the selection from all the collections preceding *Altitudes* that went into
New and Selected Poems: 1923-1985? The "1985" in the subtitle is
otherwise puzzling, for no single poem in that book dates from
that year; perhaps the selection itself, if made in 1985, is what
justifies it, Warren having made a new poem from some of his
old ones. Since I can find no evidence of sequential echoing pri-
or to 1978 in the separately published collections, it does not
seem worthwhile to search for evidence of it in the three previous *Selected Poems* published before that date (in 1976, 1966,
and 1944). But if it is present in the four sequences published
since then, could it not also have guided, perhaps unconsciously,
the selections that Warren made in 1985?

Of the 130 poems in *Rumor Verified, Being Here,* and *Now and
Then*, only thirty-six reappear in the 1985 *New and Selected Poems*.
Their overall order remains unchanged, but the new combina-
tions that result from the omission of so many intervening poems give rise to some interesting confrontations. I would like to
give some account of them briefly here; fortunately, we will be
going over familiar ground.

In the selections made from *Rumor Verified*, the first two poems, "Chthonian Revelation: A Myth" and "Looking Northward, Aegeanward: Nestlings on Seacliff," again appear side by
side, but the next poem is now "Going West" (seven poems including the moving account of his father's death, "One I Knew,"
thus sacrificed). The gulls exploding into flame from volcanic
eruption in "Looking Northward" ("feathers of gull-*wing* / From
white flash to flame *burst*") now find reincarnation in the "wing-

burst" and "bloody explosion" of the pheasant that crashes into the poet's windshield in "Going West." The darkness of noon experienced on the road in the Great Plains—"I have seen blood explode, blotting out sun, blotting / Out land"—now, in this new arrangement, answers the sudden daytime darkness the poet imagined in "Looking Northward": "sky / At noon darkened, and darkness . . . fell, / And in that black fog gulls screamed as the feathers . . . to flame burst." The difference is that then the darkness preceded the birds' bursting, while now the avian explosion precedes, in fact causes, the blotting out of the sun. These newly contiguous poems, at least through these images, now complement each other.

The father's "x-ray glance" in "Rumor Verified" and the eyes of the dying man into which "you" there imagine staring ("You yearn to look deep into his eyes and learn wisdom") recall the sun and its powerful eye in "Going West": "The sun, / Man to man, stares you straight in the eye" (before, that is, the bird hit the windshield). The wine ("discussing wine with the sommelier") "you" will no longer be discussing in "Rumor Verified" reappears in the wine for which "you" in "Mountain Mystery" have an immense desire ("You open your lips in infinite thirst for // The altitude's wine"); it may be remembered that that high-altitude wine originally echoed the "high-proof " of the then-preceding "Minneapolis Story."

In "Mountain Mystery" "you" (a "you" more clearly the poet himself than the "you" in "Rumor Verified") look down from the mountain track to tangled water below: "Far down distance, a stream uncoils, / Like nothing more than a glittering wire / Tangled in stone-slots." In "Vermont Ballad: Change of Season" the poet likewise gazes at tangled, knotted water: "All day the fitful rain / Had wrought new traceries, / New quirks, new love-knots, down the pane." And through it, "I . . . stare up the mountain track / Till I see . . . // A man with no name" up where (mutatis mutandis, for the mountain in "Mountain Mystery" was evidently not in Vermont), in the previous poem, he had been ("On the mountain trail . . . track"). These two poems now stare at each other too, from the new vantage point afforded by the deletion of four intervening poems.

The "tracery" of "love-knots" the rain made on the window

returns in the threading of the love vine that grows through the eyes of the skull in "Dead Horse in Field": "Then, / . . . I'll see / The green twine of vine, each leaf / Heart-shaped." It is called love-vine because of that heart shape. Though not here named as love vine, it was so named in what is essentially an earlier version of this poem, "The Dogwood," from *Promises* (named too in the more recent "Boy Wandering in Simms' Valley," in *Now and Then*: "Through brush and love-vine"). For what is now a horse's skull was once a cow's. Buzzards clean the carcass in both instances, transforming it into an "intricate piece of / Modern sculpture, white now" in "Dead Horse," into "A cathedral for ants" with a "white dome" in "The Dogwood." In the latter, "All taint of mortality's long since wiped clean as a whistle. / Now love vine threads eyehole. . . . / . . . leaf of the love vine shuts eyehole, as though the eye slept." The horse, its "left foreleg shattered," had been put out of its misery by "A .30-30 in heart"; the poet in "Vermont Ballad" had thought of turning a gun on myself: "If I set muzzle to forehead / And pull the trigger, I'll see / The world in a last flood of vital red— // Not gray—that cataracts down"—comparing the red liquid that would be the last thing he would see to the gray rain tracing its "love-knots" down the pane. The last view of life, or the first (and only) glimpse of death. What fascinated the boy about the dead horse (as I have earlier remarked) was *its* privileged view of the nothingness of death: "Eyes gone / The two-year-old could, of course, more readily see / Down the track of pure and eternal darkness."

What the eye cannot quite see is the subject of "The Corner of the Eye," which begins "The poem is just beyond the corner of the eye. / You cannot see it—not yet—but sense the faint gleam." The identification of horse with father (especially visible, as we have seen, in the eyes, for the father's in "I Am Dreaming of a White Christmas" "Are not there. But, / Not there, they stare at what / Is not there") is reiterated in "The Corner of the Eye": "the rhythmic rasp of your father's last breath, harsh // As the grind of a great file the blacksmith sets to hoof." The "gleam" that is here, that which cannot yet be glimpsed, and which recalls the finality that only absent eyes can see in "Dead Horse in Field," is itself recalled in "What Voice at Moth-Hour" by a gleam that, like the "last flood" before the poet's dying eyes in "Vermont Ballad," is a kind of last light: "While ripples at stone, in the steely gleam, / Caught last light before it was shuttered." In another parallel, the field mouse's "One tiny paw lifted from snow while, far off, the owl // Utters" in "The Corner of the Eye" anticipates the poet's own foot in "What Voice at Moth-Hour" that likewise waits (though not, as did the field mouse, in terror) for the owl to speak: "Each foot set soft, then still as stone / Standing to wait while the first owl spoke."

"What Voice" is followed by "Another Dimension," as it was in the original sequence. There the lark sings at so high an altitude that the poet cannot hear it ("Song is lost / In the blue depth of sky . . . at an altitude where only / God's ear may hear"), but he knows the song is there, that the lark as it rises is "divulging, in tinseled fragments from / That height, song." Now the poet's dog in "English Cocker: Old and Blind" finds himself in an extremely, indeed terrifyingly, high place, frozen in fear at the top of the stair as if he stood "on a final edge / Of the world . . . one paw // Suspended above the abyss." But if his owner's hand should lightly touch his head, "old faith comes flooding back—and // The paw descends." Though he cannot see the stair, he knows it's there—as the poet knows the lark is singing even though he cannot hear it or as, a little later in "Another Dimension," he knows what is real even though, like the dog, he cannot *see* it: "I have shut my eyes and seen the lark flare upward. / All was as real as when my eyes were open."

The dog gave out a "musical whimper" "at the edge of the stair" (and *musical* and *stair* are in fact quite close here: "at the edge of the stair, / And remember that musical whimper"), while in "Have You Ever Eaten Stars?" we may "hear, somewhere, a summer-thinned brook descending, / Past stone, and stone, its *musical stair*." The dog, in his blindness, dwelled "*in his eternal night*" while we are told in "Have You Ever" to "Let brain glow / *In its* own *midnight* of darkness." The poem concludes with several commands: "Eat. Swallow. Absorb. Let bone / Be sustained." "Afterward" ends by giving orders too: "Try," we are told, to return the smile of a "nameless skull" in a moonlit desert. While the brain that glows in the preceding poem does so "Under its own inverted, bowl-shaped / Sky, *skull*-sky." Having eaten, that is, the "stars" of bright golden mushrooms on a forest floor "black as a midnight sky," we may see the parallel between the sky in our skull and the skull of the sky. As the "you" addressed in "Afterward" is asked to see what he may have in common with the skull in the desert: "Perhaps you can start a conversation of mutual comfort. // There must be so much to exchange." "Fear and Trembling" follows "Afterward" as it did before.

About a third of the poems of both *Rumor Verified* (fourteen of forty-three) and *Now and Then* (twelve of thirty-seven) reappear in *New and Selected Poems*, but only a fifth (ten of fifty) of those in *Being Here* survive. And while the first and last poems of the other two are also the first and last here, Warren begins his selection from *Being Here* with "When Life Begins" and ends it with "Safe in Shade"—poems that are practically mirror images of each other, each recalling the time he sat at his grandfather's knee under the cedar and listened to his stories of the past. "When Life Begins" is now followed by "Grackles, Goodbye," where the grackles "pepper the blueness of distance" as Civil War rifle fire "Prickles the distance" in his grandfather's recollection. "Youthful Truth-Seeker, Half-Naked, at Night, Running Down Beach South of San Francisco" follows "Grackles" as it did in the original sequence, followed by "Why Have I Wandered the Asphalt of Midnight?" where the poet wanders not only asphalt but, as in the immediately preceding poem, the Pacific beach and its "dark dunes" (in "Youthful Truth-Seeker": "ahead, white surf and *dark dunes* in dimness are wed"; in "Why Have I Wandered": "Why should I wander *dark dunes*, till rollers / Boom in from China").

Crust appears at strategic moments in these two poems as well as in "Sila." In the first, the poet wonders whether he can hear the sound of the heaving magma beneath "earth-crust"; in the second he wonders whether he clambered the cliff "Just to feel blood dry like a crust on hands"; in the third the deer's glittering hooves knifed "the ice-crust as deep / As a trap" just before the husky's attack, and when the boy bent his knees to cradle the doe's head they broke "the snow-crust like prayer."

The boy in "Sila" administers the doe's coup de grâce with surgical skill: "set / The knife's needle point where acuteness / Would enter without prick of pain"; in "Vision" the poet himself must undergo surgery: "A black orderly . . . enters . . . razor in hand, to shave, // . . . the area the surgeon / Will penetrate."

"Cocktail Party" likewise invokes the surgeon's knife: "a tumor grows / Somewhere inside your brain. Oh, doctor, please, oh, / Remove it!"

Alcohol and erotic eye contact inhabit both "Vision" ("you order two highballs, // . . . Drinks come, but / There is nothing to say. . . . Each stares / Into the other's eyes, desire like despair") and "Cocktail Party" ("Beyond the haze of alcohol and syntax and / Flung gage of the girl's glance"). At the cocktail party there is a problem in communication, for the poet can see "a woman's unheard laugh exposing // Glitter of gold in the mouth's dark ghetto like unspeakable / Obscenity, but not sound." And he tries to speak, "but no sound comes." Communication is just as problematic in "The Cross," for the poet does manage to say *ciao*, but he says it to a "wide-eyed, bewildered" drowned monkey—who, like the wide-mouthed woman, seemed to be saying something one could not hear. In "Antinomy: Time and What Happened" (subtitled "Time and Identity" in *Being Here*), the poet wonders, "Do I hear stars speak . . . ?" while in "Safe in Shade" he sat by his grandfather and "waited for him to speak. / . . . I waited for him to speak. . . . / I waited for him to speak. He spoke."

The first three poems of *Now and Then* are also the first three poems of the selection made from that sequence in *New and Selected Poems*. The fourth is "Red-Tail Hawk and Pyre of Youth," whose first words—"Breath clamber-short"—are a rearrangement of the "clambered, breath short" of the third poem, "Boy Wandering in Simms' Valley." In the original sequence, the .30-30 that slew the "Red-Tail Hawk" echoed the shot of the "twelve-gauge" that the "Orphanage Boy" used to put Bob out of his misery. In the new sequence, it echoes the report of another "twelve-gauge," the one Simms used upon himself.

In "Star-Fall" the stars are like sparks falling to earth, descending "Like sparks in a shadowy, huge smithy, with / The clang of the hammer unheard," answering the ascending sparks of the bonfire of the red-tail hawk. While the smith's work of forging answers, too, the work the poet performed on the hawk, in which he must have used a hammer too: "steel / Driven through to sustain wing and bone."

"Star-Fall" is followed, as it was in the original, by "Youth Stares at Minoan Sunset," where the poet saw his son's "form

. . . black . . . minted black" against the backdrop of the setting sun. In "Ah, Anima!" "The tall / Pines *blackly* stagger. Beyond, / / The bulk and backdrop of mountain is / Obscured." His son stood in black silhouette against the sun in a purity of communication with nature, spreading "his arms to the sky as though he loves it"; while in "Ah, Anima!" in the wake of a hurricane "You may wish that you . . . / Had run forth" into the storm "to leave // The husk behind, and leap / Into the blind and antiseptic anger of air."

"Unless" is, as before, the next poem, repeating (as we have seen) the notion of leaving one's husk behind in the image of the skin-shedding snake "Unhusked for its *mission*." But in this new sequence the next poem is, precisely, "The *Mission*": "the brook, / Black, crawls under ice. It has a mission, but . . . has forgotten what. I, too, // Have forgotten the nature of my own mission." "Perhaps," the poem concludes, "that lost mission is to try to understand // The possibility of joy in the world's tangled and hieroglyphic beauty." "How to Tell a Love Story" begins with a tangle (and a crawling, recalling the brook): "There is a story that I must tell, but / The feeling in my chest is too tight, and innocence / Crawls through the tangles of fear."

"Little Black Heart of the Telephone" is, once more, the next poem. The telephone's inarticulate desire, which the poet feels in his heart too—"If, in fact, it should scream, / *My heart* would bleed too, for I know how pain can't find words"—anticipates the last stanza of the next, and last, poem, "Heart of Autumn": "*my heart* is impacted with a fierce impulse / To unwordable utterance." Some of that unwordable utterance comes through, it seems, in what remains unspoken, or almost, in the silence between contiguous poems—even among these same poems given new contiguities.[2]

There are implications here for the study of other poets, for as Fraistat argues, there are probably more poetic collections in which the place of the poem has itself a significance than we at present realize. J. Hillis Miller's recent discussion of the poems of Thomas Hardy, for example, turns upon this very issue. Hardy is, as it happens, a poet of supreme importance for Warren. Like Hardy, Warren abandoned, in his old age, novels for the poetry that was, perhaps, his first love. His interest in Hardy goes back to the very beginning of his poetic career—Warren has spoken in interviews of how he was "struck very early with an affinity . . . of some kind there which I sensed right away" (*RPW Talking*, 13), of how he, like Ransom, was "mad for Hardy . . . as a boy, and still am" (177). In "Red-Tail Hawk and Pyre of Youth" Hardy is there on his boyhood's bookshelf, guarded by the stuffed hawk: "Blake and *Lycidas*, Augustine, Hardy and *Hamlet*, / Baudelaire and Rimbaud." Now Hardy, in his "Apology" to *Late Lyrics and Earlier* (1922), wrote: "There is a contingency liable to miscellanies of verse that I have never seen mentioned. . . . I mean the chance little shocks that may be caused over a book of various character like the present and its predecessors by the juxtaposition of unrelated, even discordant effusions; poems perhaps years apart in the making, yet facing each other. . . . I admit that I did not foresee such contingencies as I ought to have done. . . . But the difficulties of arranging the themes in a graduated kinship of moods would have been so great that irrelation was almost unavoidable with efforts so diverse" (quoted in Miller, 271-72). Taking Hardy at his word, Miller argues that, because the poet's own philosophy denied the possibility of "speaking of 'Hardy' or of 'the mind of Hardy' as a single entity" (273), given that Hardy is "the inheritor of that native British tradition of skepticism about the unity of the self which is most notoriously present in David Hume" (275), it is wrong of the critic to try to see connections between his juxtaposed poems: such a critic "tries to make them related in meaning as well as in physical location. It cannot be done" (274).

But if Miller believes that such a unity of mind does not exist in Hardy, why does he depend for his argument upon a unity in Hardy's mind between what he says in the "Apology" and his poetic practice? It is as if in his eagerness to deny the possibility of meaningful order in Hardy's poems he had abandoned his own unity of mind. Even if Hardy had not claimed that he (or anyone else) was bereft of such a unity, we would not necessarily be obliged to take his word for it, for all he could really be in a position to inform us about is his conscious intent; what the rest of his mind has to say is really quite another matter. With regard to the meaning that can emerge when poetic collections are read for more than what the poems taken singly can provide, Neil Fraistat argues that "having recognized in principle the right of poets to determine the shape of their books, we ought not allow them further to dictate the *meaning* of this shape. That is, interpretations of a book should not be limited to the author's conscious intentions (though these surely must be taken into account)—since there are a wealth of unconscious connections and fortuitous circumstances that contribute to the meaning of a contexture, just as they do to an individual text" (9). As a character in a novel of Warren's once said, speaking precisely of how something can come into existence that was not there before (was not there, as far as a reading of these four poetic sequences is concerned, in the author's conscious intent) when things get combined: "Reality is not a function of the event as event, but of the relationship of that event to past, and future, events. We seem here to have a paradox: that the reality of an event, which is not real in itself, arises from other events which, likewise, in themselves are not real" (*All the King's Men*, 384).

Miller in fact makes another observation about Hardy's philosophy of aesthetics that would itself serve to undercut the argument that all we are legally allowed to find in a text is what the author consciously intended: "Hardy's abiding topic in his poems is the ability of language or of signs to be generated, to function, and to go on functioning without conscious intent" (303). "For Hardy, it is not minds that generate signs, but minds that are generated, shaped, and coerced, done and undone, by signs" (306). As I noted in the introduction to this work, what this reading of Warren's recent poetry has been looking for in the first place is not the instances of "the same ultimate psychological pressure or creative impulse" that occupied Rosenthal and Gall in *The Modern Poetic Sequence*, not a state of mind, but those signs themselves: sequentially recurring, puzzling, words.

As for what one might actually find in Hardy's poems, Dennis Taylor identifies certain sequential echoes between "the three major journey poems of *Moments of Vision*, 'The Five Students,' 'The Wind's Prophecy,' and 'During Wind and Rain,' " which, he notes, "are placed together forming a triptych at the centre of the volume" (36). In the second of these, "the present storm-driven scene is like the journey of man through an entire time-driven life in 'The Five Students,' " while the light that suddenly emerges near the end of "The Wind's Prophecy" when "every chasm and every steep / Blacken as wakes each lighthouse-shine" prompts him to ask "Is not the shock we feel at seeing this emergent light like the shock we feel in seeing the emergence of carved names in 'During Wind and Rain'?"

One could go much farther than Taylor actually does in suggesting the extent to which the poems in *Moments of Vision* are sequentially linked by pointing out that the argument of "The Five Students" (*Complete Poems*, 493), wherein the five friends journeying down the road of life are separated, one by one, by death, is anticipated by the immediately preceding poem, "The Ballet" (492), in which the dancers repeatedly come together "and then / They part," while the poet observes that each has her own life and fate: "Links in a one-pulsed chain, all showing one smile, / Yet severed so many a mile!" Unity in diversity (and among professional entertainers at that) is apparent, too, in the preceding poem, "At Madame Tussaud's in Victorian Years" (492), where a fiddler on two occasions forty years distant "bears the same babe-like smile of self-centered delight, / Same trinket on watch-chain, same ring on the hand with the bow." There is disjunction between that same smile and the rest of his face, which, "if regarded, is woefully wanner"; there is disjunction as well in the setting of his performance, the waxen figures "With their glass eyes longing they too could wake notes that appeal." "The Caged Goldfinch" (491), just before, longs too to make music: "There was inquiry in its wistful eye, / And once it tried to sing." It is as strangely juxtaposed to a disjunctive background as the fiddler, caged "Within a churchyard, on a recent grave." It may be there for the rest of its life—as, it appears, will be the fiddler. If one continued to work backward in Hardy's sequence one would find that the goldfinch peering out of its cage echoes the woman in "The Ageing House" (491) who "Would often lean / From the sunny casement / And scan the scene." Like the goldfinch, she too will grow old (as will the fiddler, for that matter) in the same setting: "But storms have raged / Those walls about, / And the head has aged / That once looked out." "The Sunshade" (490) is, likewise, a meditation on a woman's aging, and likely demise: "Is the fair woman who carried that sunshade / A skeleton just as her property is . . . ?" Fair, too, was the woman in the casement window: "A fresh fair head / Would often lean." One last instance: the skeletal sunshade, discovered after twenty years' ruin in the rain, was anticipated in "Logs on the Hearth" (489) by "the log / Of the tree we felled" now being destroyed by fire, the apple tree the poet can remember climbing with his sister. In "The Sunshade" he will compare the parasol "Here at my feet in the hard rock's chink" to the skeleton that its owner may now be, "Laid in the chink that none may scan"; while in "Logs on the Hearth" the tree (whose shape in fact resembles "the ribs of the sunshade") that the log once was makes him think of the other woman's grave (and note how the "Here at my feet" of the poem to come is anticipated by the nearness of a foot here): "My fellow-climber rises dim / From her chilly grave— / Just as she was, her foot near mine on the bending limb." The apple tree that existed in two states in "Logs on the Hearth" (before and after burning, before and after the death of the sister) becomes "The Sunshade" that once was "silked in its white or pink" (colors, in fact, of apple tree blossoms) and is now a skeleton; the transformable tree returns in "The Ageing House" as the sycamore that closes each of its two stanzas ("While blithely spoke the wind to the little sycamore tree / . . . While fiercely girds the wind at the long-limbed sycamore tree!"), and whose growth (from "little" to "long-limbed") marks the passage of time, together with the woman's progress toward death.

These poems reveal not only sequential links but links that themselves speak of juxtapositions (foot to foot, foot to sunshade, goldfinch to churchyard, fiddler to wax figures, ballet dancers to each other)—juxtapositions that uncannily resemble "the juxtaposition of unrelated, even discordant effusions" that the poems themselves are.

The discovery of sequential connections in Warren's poetry does, then, open up the possibility of similar phenomena elsewhere. Yet there is something peculiarly relevant to Warren himself about the way each of the poems read here replays something in its predecessor. It is natural to say that the revelation of such echoes enriches our understanding of his poems, but it is true, too, that at times this supplementary dimension is not, perhaps, necessarily welcome. For sometimes it can appear to take away something we thought had been there, something we thought we had liked. "New Dawn," in particular, loses something of its momentousness upon the discovery that the very

next poem parodizes the meticulous care with which the me-
chanics of the bomb was described—as well as the tragic event
itself—by reassembling those elements in a setting of so much
less apparent significance.

It is not, in fact, that Warren is consciously seeking to enrich
his poems by planting such little explosions. Indeed, he didn't
mean to do it: "Their contiguity in that volume," he has told me,
referring to the ten-foot distance that unites these two contiguous poems, "is, I am certain, a sort of accident. This, unless we
take the view that there are no accidents in life" (RPW to RPR,
7 December 1986). From slips of the tongue to dreams, Freud's
insights into the human psyche make such a view significantly
less untenable. Indeed, in "Minneapolis Story," a poem about
writing poetry ("Whatever pops into your head, and whitely /
Breaks surface on the dark stream that is you, / May do to make
a poem"), Warren himself speaks of accidents as if they had a
will of their own: "every accident / Yearns to be more than itself."

Perhaps it was just an accident—or perhaps something else is
at work here, some compulsion to repeat, to treat what has been
written (or what, given the ordering, *appears* to have been already written) as if it were a text that by its very separateness
from the poem at hand can now be abandoned, mined for material for the poem now unfolding (an illusion, of course, given
that sequence does not repeat chronology, yet a meaningful illusion of the fiction of the text we are reading). A text that could
even be imagined to have been written by someone else, for once
the poet has finished a poem he is no longer the poet who wrote
it. He is no longer its author; he is, at most, its reader.

The Seth in "Blackberry Winter" who approached his father
on horseback, thereby reenacting without realizing it the strangely anticipatory scene in the immediately preceding story in *The
Circus in the Attic*, in which another Seth dies while performing a
similar gesture, and to whom I alluded in the introduction to
this work, is the same Seth who does precisely what Warren is
doing here: he writes a text in order to become its reader: "You
do not understand that voice from back in the kitchen which
says that you cannot go barefoot outdoors and run to see what
has happened and rub your feet over the wet shivery grass and

make the perfect mark of your foot in the smooth, creamy, red
mud and then muse upon it as though you had suddenly come
upon that single mark on the glistening auroral beach of the
world. You have never seen a beach, but you have read the book
and how the footprint was there" (64). It is perhaps fitting that
it should be the same boy, for there is an intimate relation in
Warren's own life between father and preexisting text. As he
tells it in *Portrait of a Father*, "When I was about eleven or twelve,
I was idly prowling in a bookcase and happened to find, flat
against the wall behind other books in proper places, a thick
black volume. The title was *The Poets of America*. I certainly had
no particular interest in poetry, but I idly happened to open the
book. By accident—or was there a reason why the book came
open there?—it had opened to a page with the name of my father in print across the top. . . . There were several poems on
the page. His poems. The discovery was, in itself, a profound
and complex surprise. Of what nature I cannot remember" (40-
41). Profound and complex indeed, for it is a scene that keeps
repeating itself throughout Warren's poetry and fiction,[3] as if by
its recreation that complexity could be plumbed, its enigma resolved. When he restages his father's death, for example, in
"One I Knew" there, too, is a text from the father, left for the
son to find: "Later, / I found the letter, the first / Paragraph unfinished. I saw / The ink-slash from that point / Where the unconscious hand had dragged / The pen as he fell. I saw / The
salutation. It was: / 'Dear Son.' "[4] The same dying paternal hand
is itself an indecipherable text in "Mortmain" as it "Lifts in a
Spasmodic Gesture, as Though Trying to Make Contact" before
falling "Like an eyelid." In "I Am Dreaming of a White Christmas" the father's hand offers a Christmas present to his son that
the son can never open: "Will I never know / What present there
was in that package for me, / Under the Christmas tree?" The
father's text—gift, final attempt at contact, or unfinished letter—may never release its message, for it is a taciturn text, as
"To a Face in a Crowd" continually reminds Warren's readers at
the end of each of his *Selected Poems*: "the taciturn tall stone, /
Which is your fathers' monument and mark." The text is there,
but the father refuses to explain it to his son: "I could not wait
for my father to come home. When he did get there I showed

him the book. He took it, examined it, and wordlessly walked away with it. That was the last time I was ever to see it. Many years later [I learned that it was a] 'vanity publication.' I was later to learn that my sister, a little younger than I, had finally encountered the book again hidden by our father, and had simply, as she said, 'stolen' it. He had not managed to destroy it, after all" (41). (She did not really steal it, for it was given to her, as I learned when she showed to it me: it bears the inscription "To My Daughter: Mrs. H.E. Barber, Maysville, Kentucky, 1943." Warren thus exaggerates the degree to which the father seeks to withdraw the text from circulation.) The father's reticence about the poems as well as his propensity for providing his son with a text that he refuses to discuss was still apparent "some thirty years after" when Warren received a letter from him enclosing an old typescript of a poem. "Beneath the poem was the signature 'R.F.W.'. . . . But at the lower edge of the sheet were, in a scribble of old age"—that is, contemporaneous with the sending of the poem—"the words: 'Do not answer' " (42). Once more the father refuses to do more than present his son with the text (a refusal written in a "scribble of old age" that recalls "The ink-slash . . . / Where the unconscious hand had dragged / The pen"), refuses all commentary—like the Willie Stark to whom I alluded at the beginning of chapter 1 who gave Jack Burden a wink (or a blink) to puzzle over (recall that the unconscious hand's last gesture in "Mortmain" becomes the closing of an eye: "Like an eyelid the hand sank") and refused to confirm or deny its intent (" 'Boy,' he said, 'if I was to tell you, then you wouldn't have anything to think about' ").

The compulsion with which this scene repeats itself—in the novel *World Enough and Time*, for example, when Jeremiah Beaumont receives a mysterious handbill and mistakenly assumes it comes from Fort, his adoptive father (and therefore feels grateful, with "the gratitude of a good son to a father . . . grateful because Fort . . . had showed him the truth" [209])—bears an unexpected resemblance to the classical Freudian scene of repetition-compulsion itself, which is also, at it turns out, a story of a child's grief over a parent's absence. I am referring to the child (Freud's grandson, actually, though he only hints at that fact) in *Beyond the Pleasure Principle* who overcame the pain of his mother's absence by repeatedly mimicking her departure and return,

throwing a wooden reel out of sight and then pulling it back by
its string. When he cast it away he cried out *fort* ["gone"] and he

> hailed its reappearance with a joyful "*da*" ["here"]. . . . The
> interpretation of the game then became obvious. It was re-
> lated to the child's great cultural achievement . . . , the re-
> nunciation of instinctual satisfaction . . . , which he had
> made in allowing his mother to go away without protest-
> ing. He compensated himself for this, as it were, by himself
> staging the disappearance and return of the objects within
> his reach. . . . At the outset he was in a *passive* situa-
> tion . . . but by repeating it, unpleasurable though it was,
> as a game, he took on an *active* part. These efforts might be
> put down to an instinct for mastery. . . . But still another
> interpretation may be attempted. Throwing away the ob-
> ject so that it was "gone" might satisfy an impulse of the
> child's, which was suppressed in his actual life, to revenge
> himself on his mother for going away from him. . . . "All
> right, then, go away! I don't need you. I'm sending you
> away myself." [15-16][5]

Like the mother, the father in the scene Warren both lived out
and continues to retell had absented himself from the son when
he refused to discuss the text, refused to make any contact with
the son with regard to that text outside of the text itself (like a
good New Critic disdaining any such extratextual assistance—as
Warren the critic was later himself to conclude, the best evidence is not the teller but the tale: "Even if the poet himself
should rise to contradict us, we could reply that the words of the
poem speak louder than his actions" ["A Poem of Pure Imagination," 397]). Like the boy in Freud's story, Warren restages the
grief of parental inaccessibility in his accounts of a father's tantalizing textual gesture (both in his poems about his own father
and in his fictions about sons); like the Seth in his own, he does
so in the sequences read in these pages by pretending not to
have written what he has in fact written, by pretending that
there could be no connection between one poem and the next to
march across the reader's field of vision (the reader who, like the
father in "Reading Late at Night," reads in a "forever / Marching gaze") but an accidental one.[6] By pretending to depart from

the immediately preceding poem only to bring it back, against all logic of apparent subject and emotion and time of composition, in the fragments that reappear, in the *then* that returns as *now*, in the *there* (*fort*) that is now *here* (*da*):

How is it that I am *there* again?
Space and Time our arbitrary illusions: even so,
How odd that my feet fit old foot-tracks.

Notes

Introduction

1. I cite two of the better-known works of that period. Yet even more difficult of access, and not preserved by Warren in his later anthologies, were such poems as "Aged Man Surveys the Past Time" and "Toward Rationality," which Dudley Fitts at the time found unintelligible, even "after the most painful rereading" (cited in Strandberg, *The Poetic Vision*, 2). As Bedient has recently, and somewhat provocatively, observed, "Warren was schooled in, and virtually parodied, the precious rhetoric that an injured but high sensibility applies to itself as a balm. . . . Dreamily piecing together a quilt of terms and rhythms from Marvell, Yeats, T.S. Eliot, Auden, Ransom and others, the young . . . Warren pulled it up over his jutting country-boy knees, presenting himself as an invalid of virtue, a casualty of the collapse of the sublime. He had yet to see that a certain rawboned vigor (both of attitude and word) was to be his salvation" (7). Yet that raw-boned vigor had already begun to show itself as early as 1944 in "The Ballad of Billit Potts."

2. Adopting the convention observed by James A. Grimshaw, Jr., and Victor Strandberg, I will italicize *Altitudes and Extensions 1980-1984* as if it were a book, for as Grimshaw notes, it "is viewed by Warren as a new 'book' of poems similar to *Can I See Arcturus from Where I Stand?— Poems 1975* (*Selected Poems: 1923-1975*) and *Tale of Time: New Poems, 1960-1966* (*Selected Poems: New and Old 1923-1966*)" ("Editor's note" to Strandberg's "Poet of Youth," 105). The discrepancy, by the way, between the 1984 of the sequence's title and the 1985 of the book's (*New and Selected Poems: 1923-1985*) is a bit of a mystery. Warren has always put his newest poems first in his several *Selected Poems*, working his way back in time to the 1923 poem "To a Face in a Crowd," their perennial conclusion, and so there is no poem in *New and Selected Poems* more recent than those in *Altitudes and Extensions*—unless perhaps that sequence itself (together with, as I will suggest in my conclusion, the new sequences formed by selections from previous volumes) counts as a poem, a poem formed by the final decision Warren made concerning

the order in which its poems would ultimately appear. Manuscripts and notes on deposit in the Beinecke Library reveal that Warren went through several arrangements of the poems until he arrived at that final ordering.

3. Unless indicated as Warren's, italics are mine.

4. Miller, too, found that to talk about the self-referential linguistic moment leads inevitably to talking about time: "It gradually dawned on me in the course of writing . . . that each of my poems constitutes a different version of a spatial emblem of human temporality. My interpretation of the poems has led me to follow out as much this pathway of reading as the initial guiding thread of the linguistic moment. At any rate I have been led to explore the nodes of intersection between these two topics" (xv).

5. Reprinted in *New and Selected Poems: 1923-1985*, 180. Future references to poems reprinted in this volume will be given parenthetically in the text as *N & SP*.

6. This bequeathal of books between father and son works both ways. "A few years ago I was writing an essay . . . and using my father's books. I noticed at the end of every novel there was the date when he had finished it. . . . He was reading Freud, Marx, and things like that as well as poetry and history" (*RPW Talking*, 242). Indeed, this father and son perhaps come closest to communicating through the Freudian text that shuttles back and forth between them.

7. The implications of these contiguous Seths for a reading of *The Circus in the Attic* are further explored in my article "The View from the Attic."

8. Yet Justus quite correctly points out not only that such early Warren sequences as "Kentucky Mountain Farm" and "Mexico Is a Foreign Country" were both "intimations of the best work" to come but also that "sequences [were] a form which becomes more and more important to Warren in part because they are hospitable to the diverse explorations of narrative" (53). I do not know whether Justus had in mind the possibility of a narrative hidden *within* the sequence, a possibility which Warren's latest collections explore.

ONE. *Altitudes and Extensions*

1. The narrator of *All the King's Men*, for example, makes use of just such a superposition of images when he speaks of the "two you's" that being in love creates ("the one you yourself create by loving and the one the beloved creates by loving you") and of how perfect love would be the state in which they "coincide perfectly . . . a perfect focus, as when a stereoscope gets the twin images on the card into perfect adjustment"

(282). Seeing two images at once is again at issue when Jack Burden sees Anne Stanton lying supine on a bed at the same time that he remembers her floating in the water three years before, "and that scene and this scene seemed to fuse, like superimposed photographs, each keeping its identity but without denying the other" (295). A stereopticon, by the way, is prominently displayed on several occasions when Jack visits Willie's widow Lucy Stark. Yet it would appear that this is precisely what Warren's sequentially linked poems invite us to contemplate: a stereoscopic, binocular reading. Particularly in this instance, where one poem allows us to view the two-inch glass window and the bifocals of the immediately preceding poem through its own binoculars. On the significance of Warren's loss of his left eye see Watkins, 54-56, and Singal, 342-344.

2. And has been persisting, perhaps, for some fifty years. In "The Return: An Elegy," from *Thirty-Six Poems* in 1935 (and reprinted in the *New and Selected Poems: 1923-1985*), the poet, returning home on the train for his mother's funeral, is "Locked in the roaring *cubicle* / Over the mountains through darkness hurled." Within the *Thirty-Six Poems* the word is once again associated with his mother's death in "Letter of a Mother," where "The son, defined upon the superscription, / Inherits now his *cubicled* domain, / And reads."

3. The narrator of Warren's 1977 novel *A Place to Come To* (who will later make love to a woman who echoes the sentiment "Wind and Gibbon" expresses: " 'I've taken up reading Gibbon—oh, what lovely, crystalline lava flowing over all the centuries' " [385]) bespoke a similar fascination: "As suggested by the plaster casts at Pompeii of men who died even in some obsessive private concern, no doubt more than one citizen of the doomed city, who, as he entered upon the long dark slide toward bliss, didn't even miss a beat as the ashes fell" (207).

4. My argument that there is something significantly new about "Myth of Mountain Sunrise" (that the father finally begins to speak) is paralleled by Victor Strandberg's observation that the ending of *Altitudes and Extensions* is in "direct contradiction [with] those of all Warren's previous volumes of poetry. Up until this volume of his eightieth year, every published collection has ended in an image of full darkness or declining light" ("Poet of Youth," 103).

5. The associations of taciturnity, stone, and previous generations go back a long way in Warren, not only to "To a Face in a Crowd," but to "Kentucky Mountain Farm" (from the 1920s but reprinted in *New and Selected Poems*): "we . . . have seen stand and pass / Stubbornly the taciturn / Lean men that of all things alone / Were, not as water or the febrile grass, / Figured in kinship to the savage stone."

6. Quoted here from the more accessible 1978 edition of Ransom's *Selected Poems*, where the poems' order of appearance has been changed.

TWO. *Rumor Verified*

1. The extraordinary attachment Warren has developed for paternal eyes is especially evident in his novels: Willie Stark's mysterious wink in *All the King's Men*; the dying Hans Meyerhof's eyes that "glittered with astonishing brilliance, as though" under the effect of "some commanding thought" that Adam Rosenzweig knew could not have been there, in *Wilderness* (119); or the stricken Sunderland Spottwood's eyes in *Meet Me in the Green Glen*, which made Murray Guilfort think that "Something might be there, if only he could read it" (44). Similarly, as we will see in *Now and Then*, in "Last Laugh" young Sam Clemens, staring at the corpse of his father, is unable to "make terms with the fact / Of the strangely prismatic glitter that grew in his eye." In "Mortmain," first published in *You, Emperors, and Others: Poems 1957-1960*, his father's dying gesture, the right hand lifting "in a Spasmodic Gesture, as Though Trying to Make Contact," descends like a closing eye: "Like an eyelid the hand sank, strove / Downward, and in that darkening roar, / All things . . . / Were snatched from me, and I could not move, / Naked in that black blast of his love."

2. In "Penological Study: Southern Exposure," in *Incarnations*, Jake the convict suffers a similar fate: "inside his gut, / The pumpkin grows and grows." That the speaker in the poem identifies Jake with his father becomes apparent in this juxtaposition: "Jake is awake. Oh, Warden, / Keep that morphine moving, for your father is not really dead, he // Is trying to get out of that box he thinks you put him in." In the companion poem "Internal Injuries," the vegetable growth in Jake's "gut" is answered by a floral one in the poet's own (as the horse-apple that killed his father from within in "Reading Late at Night" was to be answered in "Paradox of Time" by the flowering century plant): "meaning / In my guts blooms like / A begonia, I dare not / Pronounce its name."

3. Death in the darkness at the foot of the stairs is what the lovers in "Picnic Remembered," originally in *Eleven Poems*, "did not know" though "half understood": "How darkness darker staired below."

4. And, obviously, about the role of the unconscious in the literary critic—or at least his interest in verbal echoes that resonate in the structure of the literary text.

5. Sequential echoes also in fact exist. A few have been found by Richard Sayce and Marianne S. Meijer, though not yet between each pair of essays. I have, on the other hand, found substantial echoes uniting each of the fifty-two symmetrical pairs several of which are discussed in "Montaigne's Larceny" and "The 'Oblique Gaze.' "

6. The *Essays* appear in three books (of fifty-seven, thirty-seven, and thirteen chapters each), each of which display these symmetrically placed verbal echoes.

7. Quotations are taken from Donald Frame's translations.

THREE. *Being Here*

1. Jeremiah Beaumont, in Warren's novel *World Enough and Time*, once expressed very nearly the same sentiments about his spelunking experience: "So I lay there, and breathed the limey, cool, inward smell of earth's bowels. . . . It is a smell cleanly and rich, not dead and foul but pregnant with secret life, as though you breathed the dark and the dark were about to pulse" (315). "Pregnant" here is a word pregnant with more meaning than Jeremiah might realize, as I suggest in "The Beech, the Hearth, and the Hidden Name."

2. The same association of images underlies the characterization of both victim and executioner in *Brother to Dragons*. Thomas Jefferson regrets that his nephew Lilburne Lewis had not been killed at birth, and—as did Jason Sweetwater in *At Heaven's Gate* when he described the unseen fetus—spoke of the *wizened* quality of that newborn's face: "It was a parcel of flesh / That my sister's body ejected. . . . / You know an infant's face, wizened and seamed / . . . the wizened mark is not the mark / Of new possibility, but is / Prefiguration of the face of vile age, / . . . malign / Calligraphy" (42). In the murder scene, just before Lilburn raised his axe, the slave boy "wanted, in the end, / To curl on the meatblock, draw his knees up little, / And squinch his eyes" (87), as if he wanted to become a fetus, his knees drawn up in the fetal position, his eyes squinched shut like the "hunched," "squinting"-eyed Indian mummies that Sweetwater found so much resembled fetuses in *At Heaven's Gate*. And when the slave was dead, burned and buried, but then unburied by a hound, what's left to be discovered by the sheriff is "a parcel . . . / Wrapped in a rag, his handkerchief" of bone to which "some shred of flesh / Yet clings"—hauntingly like the "parcel" of flesh that was once, in Jefferson's eyes, Lilburn himself (thus twice named on the same page, 42). In *Audubon*, there is yet another "hunched" Indian with something strange about his eye: "The Indian, / Hunched by the hearth, lifts his head, looks up, but / From one eye only, the other / An aperture below which blood and mucus hang" (*N & SP*, 216).

3. In the forthcoming *The Taciturn Text: The Fiction of Robert Penn Warren*. In "The Fictive Fetus in *The Cave*," which has appeared in print, I explore Isaac Sumpter's attempt to read the name his father gave him.

4. The *W* in *Wilderness* was also a wound in the thigh, branded painfully onto Mose's skin (217).

FOUR. *Now and Then*

1. A fact confirmed by Warren's sister, Mrs. Mary Warren Barber, in conversation with me 31 January 1988: "We called him 'Daddy-Bob.' "

2. By strange coincidence, a father's imagined death in Warren's novel *Band of Angels* coincides with *his* deliverance from a horse-apple that had been building up inside him for years. When Hamish Bond told his mother she was lying when she bragged about how many slaves she owned before she married his father, his henpecked father suddenly " 'burst out laughing. The laugh was awful. . . . Maybe now [Hamish comments] that I got him free of the horse-apple of a lie he had lived with all that time, maybe there wasn't anything to live for now. Maybe he just dried up and blew away' " (183).

3. "Picnic Remembered," from *Eleven Poems on the Same Theme* (1942), reprinted in *New and Selected Poems: 1923-1985*, bespeaks a long-standing fascination with the paradox of *then* and *now*: "The *then*, the *now*: each cenotaph / Of the other, and proclaims it dead" (Warren's italics). A cenotaph, literally an "empty tomb," is "a sepulchral monument erected in honour of a deceased person whose body is elsewhere" (*Oxford English Dictionary*). In "Picnic Remembered" two lovers wonder whether they are perhaps already dead and their souls elswhere—perhaps, as Victor Strandberg argues, back in Eden: "Here . . . the immediate result of the Fall is a divided self, the better half of which harkens directly back to paradise, leaving the postlapsarian self behind it as an empty shell that must carry on as best it can in the fallen world" (*Poetic Vision*, 54). The cenotaph that each is for the other (body for soul, and vise versa, or each half of the divided self for its other half) would have been a peculiarly apt metaphor for the textual echoes that haunt Warren's most recent sequences and attests to the deep unity, over all these years, of Warren's thought. For each poem is a cenotaph—an inscription, an epitaph—of the other "and proclaims it dead." As I said earlier (concerning "Orphanage Boy" and the poems that precede and follow it), poems eat other poems. The poems in sequence, like the divided self that Strandberg reads in Warren's earlier poetry, are never entirely *there*. Part of each poem is always somewhere else, in the poems on either side. Each denies the reality and meaning of its predecessor, undercutting it with the restatement, often ironic and even parodic, of some of the latter's most significant elements.

Afterword

1. James Justus notes the parallel between these two passages (86), though he thinks it is the injured woman who is speaking about the begonia blooming inside. This reading would strengthen the parallel between her and the dying con, but it seems to me that these words in "The World Is a Parable" are actually spoken by the narrator. For whoever speaks them also says "Oh, driver! / For God's sake catch that light." In the immediately following "Driver, Driver," the driver is again

addressed, presumably by the same speaker, but it is now clear that he is driving not an ambulance but a cab: "Driver, driver, hurry now— / . . . The traffic begins to move, and that fool ambulance at last, // Screaming, screaming, now arrives." Though the injured woman may be in a hurry to reach the hospital, the poet who witnesses all this is in just as great a hurry to escape from the awful scene.

2. As best I can tell, selections made from collections earlier than *Now and Then* in the 1985 *New and Selected Poems* do not display these contiguous echoes, though it is apparent that Warren did some radical rearranging of his selections from *Promises*. The *Selected Poems* of 1976 and 1966 had both reprinted all the poems of *Promises* except for "The Necessity for Belief." But in 1985 twenty-eight more were omitted, and the remaining ten appear in very different order: "School Lesson Based on Word of Tragic Death of Entire Gillum Family" and "Founding Fathers, Nineteenth-Century Style, Southeast U.S.A.," now conclude the sequence (and appear side by side, their first words echoing each other: "*They weren't* so bright, or clean, or clever"; "*They were* human, they suffered"). "Lullaby: Smile in Sleep" and "Lullaby: A Motion Like Sleep," once separated by sixteen poems, are now appropriately contiguous (though the first no longer follows, as it once appropriately did, the sequence "Infant Boy at Midcentury"). While it is rare for Warren to change the order of a reprinted sequence, this is not the first time he has done so. The 1966 and 1976 *Selected Poems* put "The Letter About Money, Love, or Other Comfort, if Any" in the "Garland for You" sequence in *You, Emperors* in second place instead of sixth. And the 1944 *Selected Poems* completely mixed up the order of the *Eleven Poems on the Same Theme* as well as separated several of them with intervening poems.

3. Its appearances in the fiction are the subject of my *Taciturn Text*.

4. Warren repeats this story in *Portrait of a Father* (78-79).

5. That the boy said *fort* was Freud's interpretation of what was in fact a "long-drawn-out 'o-o-o-o' " (14). Freud, in a strange aside, wonders why it "never occurred to him to pull it along the floor behind him . . . and play at its being a carriage [*Wagen*]" (15). Now in "What Was the Promise That Smiled from the Maples at Evening?," a poem in *Promises*, Warren happens to have done precisely this, uncannily (if unconsciously) fulfilling Freud's unfulfilled desire (the desire that his grandson play choochoo with the reel and the string), by making a string-dragged train of cars represent the ultimate parental absence (and here he goes even farther than Freud desired, in as much as he did not say he wanted the boy to represent his absent mother by this other game):

> Children gravely, down walks, in spring dark, under maples, drew
> Trains of shoe boxes, empty, with windows, with candles inside,

Going *chuck-chuck*, and blowing for crossings, lonely, *oo-oo*?
But on impulse you fled.

For later, the lighted boxes so gravely led here, pulled by a string and accompanied by a child's *oo-oo*, reappear as their luminescent graves:

Then sudden, the ground at my feet was like glass, and I say
What I saw, saw deep down—with their fleshly habiliments rent,
But their bones in a phosphorus of glory agleam, there they lay,
Side by side, Ruth and Robert.
"We died only that every promise might be fulfilled."

6. As accidental as the mark on another beach (recall that Seth's mud had become a beach—"the glistening auroral beach of the world," as well as the one where Friday's footprint appeared) in "Aspen Leaf in Windless World" that the sea foam scrawled with its teasing possibility of "a message there for you to decipher" that may have been nothing more than "the joy of its . . . intricate rhythm"—an intricacy that is itself precisely what is at issue in this instance, for the immediately preceding poem is, from its very first line—"Beautiful the intricacy of body!"—a celebration of intricacy too.

Appendix
The Order of Warren's Poems

Now and Then: Poems 1976-1978
American Portrait: Old Style
Amazing Grace in the Back Country
Boy Wandering in Simms' Valley
Old Flame
Evening Hour
Orphanage Boy
Red-Tail Hawk and Pyre of Youth
Mountain Plateau
Star-Fall
Youth Stares at Minoan Sunset
Dream
Dream of a Dream
First Dawn Light
Ah, Anima!
Unless
Not Quite Like a Top
Waiting
The Mission
Code Book Lost
When the Tooth Cracks—Zing!
Sister Water
Memory Forgotten
Waking to Tap of Hammer
Love Recognized
The Smile
How to Tell a Love Story
Little Black Heart of the Telephone
Last Laugh
Heat Lightning
Inevitable Frontier
Heart of the Backlog
Identity and Argument for Prayer
Diver

Rather Like a Dream
Departure
Heat Wave Breaks
Heart of Autumn

Being Here: Poetry 1977-1980
October Picnic Long Ago
Speleology
When Life Begins
Boyhood in Tobacco Country
Filling Night with the Name: Funeral as Local Color
Recollection in Upper Ontario, from Long Before
The Moonlight's Dream
The Only Poem
Platonic Drowse
Grackles, Goodbye
Youthful Truth-Seeker, Half-Naked, at Night,
    Running Down Beach South of San Francisco
Snowshoeing Back to Camp in Gloaming
Why Have I Wandered the Asphalt of Midnight?
August Moon
Dreaming in Daylight
Preternaturally Early Snowfall in Mating Season
Sila
Empty White Blotch on Map of Universe
Function of Blizzard
Dream, Dump-heap, and Civilization
Vision
Globe of Gneiss
Part of What Might Have Been a Short Story, Almost Forgotten
Cocktail Party
Deep—Deeper Down
Sky
Better Than Counting Sheep
The Cross
Truth
On into the Night
No Bird Does Call
Weather Report
Tires on Wet Asphalt at Night
Timeless, Twinned
What Is the Voice That Speaks?
Language Barrier
Lesson in History
Prairie Harvest
Eagle Descending
Ballad of Your Puzzlement

Antinomy: Time and Identity
Trips to California
Auto-da-Fé
Aspen Leaf in Windless World
Acquaintance with Time in Early Autumn
Safe in Shade
Synonyms
Swimming in the Pacific
Night Walking
Passers-by on Snowy Night

Rumor Verified: Poems 1979-1980
Chthonian Revelation: A Myth
Looking Northward, Aegeanward: Nestlings on Seacliff
Blessèd Accident
Gravity of Stone and Ecstasy of Wind
Law of Attrition
One I Knew
Small Eternity
Basic Syllogism
Sitting on Farm Lawn on Sunday Afternoon
Going West
Nameless Thing
Rumor Verified
Sunset Scrupulously Observed
Minneapolis Story
Mountain Mystery
Convergences
Vermont Thaw
Cycle
Summer Rain in Mountains
Vermont Ballad: Change of Season
Questions You Must Learn to Live Past
After Restless Night
What Was the Thought?
Dead Horse in Field
Immanence
The Corner of the Eye
If
What Voice at Moth-Hour
Another Dimension
Gasp-Glory of Gold Light
Snow Out of Season
Redwing Blackbirds
Crocus Dawn
English Cocker: Old and Blind
Dawn

Millpond Lost
Summer Afternoon and Hypnosis
If Ever
Have You Ever Eaten Stars?
Twice Born
The Sea Hates the Land
Afterward
Fear and Trembling

Altitudes and Extensions 1980-1984

Three Darknesses
Mortal Limit
Immortality Over the Dakotas
Caribou
The First Time
Minnesota Recollection
Arizona Midnight
Far West Once
Rumor at Twilight
Old Dog Dead
Hope
Why You Climbed Up
Literal Dream
After the Dinner Party
Doubleness in Time
Snowfall
New Dawn
The Distance Between: Picnic of Old Friends
True Love
Last Walk of Season
Old-Time Childhood in Kentucky
Covered Bridge
Re-interment: Recollection of a Grandfather
Last Meeting
Muted Music
The Whole Question
Old Photograph of the Future
Why Boy Came to Lonely Place
Platonic Lassitude
Downwardness
Interlude of Summer
The Place
First Moment of Autumn Recognized
Paradigm of Seasons
If Snakes Were Blue
Little Girl Wakes Early
Winter Wheat: Oklahoma

Youthful Picnic Long Ago: Sad Ballad on Box
History During Nocturnal Snowfall
Whistle of the 3 A.M.
Last Night Train
Milton: A Sonnet
Whatever You Now Are
Wind and Gibbon
Delusion?—No!
Question at Cliff-Thrust
It Is Not Dead
Sunset
Myth of Mountain Sunrise

Works Cited

Works by Warren

"Images on the Tomb. III. Evening: The Motors." *Fugitive* 4 (September 1925): 91.

Thirty-Six Poems. New York: The Alcestis Press, 1935.

Understanding Poetry: An Anthology for College Students (with Cleanth Brooks). New York: Henry Holt, 1938.

Night Rider. Boston: Houghton Mifflin, 1939.

Eleven Poems on the Same Theme. Norfolk, Connecticut: New Directions, 1942.

At Heaven's Gate. New York: Harcourt, Brace, 1943.

"Pure and Impure Poetry" (originally 1943), in *New and Selected Essays*. New York: Random House, 1989.

Selected Poems, 1923-1943. New York: Harcourt, Brace, 1944.

All the King's Men. New York: Harcourt, Brace, 1946. Rpt. New York: Bantam Books, 1974.

"A Poem of Pure Imagination: An Experiment in Reading" (originally 1946), in *New and Selected Essays*. New York: Random House, 1989.

The Circus in the Attic and Other Stories. New York: Harcourt, Brace, 1947.

World Enough and Time. New York: Random House, 1950. Rpt. New York: Vintage Books, 1979.

Band of Angels. New York: Random House, 1955.

Promises: Poems 1954-1956. New York: Random House, 1957.

The Cave. New York: Random House, 1959.

You, Emperors, and Others: Poems 1957-1960. New York: Random House, 1960.

Wilderness: A Tale of the Civil War. New York: Random House, 1961.

Flood. New York: Random House, 1964.

Incarnations: Poems 1966-1968. New York: Random House, 1968.

"Notes on the Poetry of John Crowe Ransom at His Eightieth Birthday" (originally 1968), in *New and Selected Essays*. New York: Random House, 1989.

Audubon: A Vision. New York: Random House, 1969.

Meet Me In the Green Glen. New York: Random House, 1971.

Or Else—Poem/Poems 1968-1974. New York: Random House, 1974.

A Place to Come To. New York: Random House, 1977.
Now and Then: Poems 1976-1978. New York: Random House, 1978.
Brother to Dragons: A Tale in Verse and Voices/A New Version. New York: Random House, 1979.
Being Here: Poetry 1977-1980. New York: Random House, 1980.
Robert Penn Warren Talking: Interviews 1950-1978. Ed. Floyd C. Watkins and John T. Hiers. New York: Random House, 1980.
Rumor Verified: Poems 1979-1980. New York: Random House, 1981.
Chief Joseph of the Nez Perce. New York: Random House, 1983.
New and Selected Poems: 1923-1985. New York: Random House, 1985.
Portrait of a Father. Lexington: Univ. Press of Kentucky, 1988.
New and Selected Essays. New York: Random House, 1989.

Works about Warren

Bedient, Calvin. *In the Heart's Last Kingdom: Robert Penn Warren's Major Poetry.* Cambridge: Harvard Univ. Press, 1984.
Bloom, Harold. Review of *New and Selected Poems: 1923-1985* by Robert Penn Warren. *New York Review of Books*, 30 May 1985, pp. 40ff.
————. "Sunset Hawk: Warren's Poetry and Tradition." In *A Southern Renascence Man: Views of Robert Penn Warren*, ed. Walter B. Edgar. Baton Rouge: Louisiana State Univ. Press, 1984.
Burt, John. *Robert Penn Warren and American Idealism.* New Haven: Yale Univ. Press, 1988.
Clements, A.L. "Sacramental Vision: The Poetry of Robert Penn Warren." In *Critical Essays on Robert Penn Warren*, ed. William Bedford Clark. Boston: G.K. Hall, 1981.
Harmon, William. "Three Italians Visit Monticello." In *Robert Penn Warren's "Brother to Dragons": A Discussion*, ed. James A. Grimshaw, Jr. Baton Rouge: Louisiana State Univ. Press, 1983.
Justus, James. *The Achievement of Robert Penn Warren.* Baton Rouge: Louisiana State Univ. Press, 1981.
Runyon, Randolph Paul. "The Beech, the Hearth, and the Hidden Name in *World Enough and Time.*" *Southern Literary Journal* 17 (fall 1984): 68-81.
————. "The Fictive Fetus in *The Cave.*" In *Time's Glory: Original Essays on Robert Penn Warren*, ed. James A. Grimshaw, Jr. Conway: Univ. of Central Arkansas Press, 1986.
————. *The Taciturn Text: The Fiction of Robert Penn Warren.* Columbus: Ohio State Univ. Press, 1990.
————. "The View from the Attic: Robert Penn Warren's *Circus* Stories." *Mississippi Quarterly* 38 (spring 1985): 119-35.
Snipes, Katherine. *Robert Penn Warren.* New York: Frederick Ungar, 1983.
Stitt, Peter. "The Grandeur of Certain Utterances," in *Homage to Robert*

Penn Warren: A Collection of Critical Essays, ed. Frank Graziano. n.p.: Logbridge-Rhodes, 1981.

———. Review of *New and Selected Poems: 1923-1985* by Robert Penn Warren. *Georgia Review* 39 (fall 1985): 648.

———. "Robert Penn Warren: Life's Instancy and the Astrolabe of Joy." *Georgia Review* 34 (winter 1980): 711-31.

Strandberg, Victor. "Poet of Youth: Robert Penn Warren at Eighty." In *Time's Glory: Original Essays on Robert Penn Warren,* ed. James A. Grimshaw, Jr. Conway: Univ. of Central Arkansas Press, 1986.

———. *The Poetic Vision of Robert Penn Warren.* Lexington: Univ. Press of Kentucky, 1977.

———. "Robert Penn Warren's Worst Book." Paper presented at the symposium "Robert Penn Warren: A Hometown Symposium," October 1987, Austin Peay State University, Clarksville, Tennessee.

Watkins, Floyd C. *Then and Now: The Personal Past in the Poetry of Robert Penn Warren.* Lexington: Univ. Press of Kentucky, 1982.

Other Works

Fraistat, Neil. "Introduction: The Place of the Book and the Book as Place." In *Poems in Their Place: The Intertextuality and Order of Poetic Collections,* ed. Neil Fraistat. Chapel Hill: Univ. of North Carolina Press, 1986.

———. *The Poem and the Book: Interpreting Collections of Romantic Poetry.* Chapel Hill: Univ. of North Carolina Press, 1985.

Freud, Sigmund. *Beyond the Pleasure Principle.* Vol. 18 in *The Standard Edition of the Complete Psychological Works of Sigmund Freud,* ed. James Strachey. London: Hogarth Press, 1953-74.

———. *The Interpretation of Dreams,* trans. and ed. James Strachey. New York: Avon Books, 1965.

———. "The Uncanny." In *Studies in Parapsychology,* ed. Philip Rieff. New York: Collier Books, 1963.

Hardy, Thomas. *The Complete Poems of Thomas Hardy,* ed. James Gibson. New York: Macmillan, 1976.

Hoffman, Daniel. "Poetry: After Modernism." In *Harvard Guide to Contemporary American Writing,* ed. Daniel Hoffman. Cambridge: Harvard Univ. Press, 1979.

Miller, J. Hillis. *The Linguistic Moment: From Wordsworth to Stevens.* Princeton: Princeton Univ. Press, 1985.

Miner, Earl. "Some Issues for Study of Integrated Collections." In *Poems in Their Place: The Intertextuality and Order of Poetic Collections,* ed. Neil Fraistat. Chapel Hill: Univ. of North Carolina Press, 1986.

Montaigne, Michel de. *Oeuvres complètes,* ed. Albert Thibaudet and Maurice Rat. Paris: Gallimard, Pléiade, 1962.

———. *The Complete Works of Montaigne,* trans. Donald M. Frame. Stanford: Stanford Univ. Press, 1957.

Perkins, David. *A History of Modern Poetry: Modernism and After*. Cambridge: Harvard Univ. Press, 1987.

Ransom, John Crowe. *Selected Poems*. New York: Knopf, 1978.

———. *Two Gentlemen in Bonds*. New York: Knopf, 1927.

Rosenthal, M.L., and Gall, Sally M. *The Modern Poetic Sequence: The Genius of Modern Poetry*. Oxford: Oxford Univ. Press, 1983.

Runyon, Randolph Paul. "Montaigne's Larceny: Book III's Symmetrical Intertexts." In *The Order of Montaigne's Essays*, ed. Daniel Martin. Amherst, Mass.: Hestia Press, 1989.

———. "The 'Oblique Gaze': Some Evidence of Symmetry in Montaigne's *Essais* (1:1-6, 57-52)." In *Essays in European Literature for Walter A. Strauss*, ed. Alice N. Benston and Marshall C. Olds. Manhattan, Kans.: Studies in Twentieth Century Literature, 1990.

Singal, Daniel Joseph. *The War Within: From Victorian to Modernist Thought in the South, 1919-1945*. Chapel Hill: Univ. of North Carolina Press, 1982.

Stauffer, Donald A. "Portrait of the Critic-Poet as Equilibrist." In *John Crowe Ransom: Critical Essays and a Bibliography*, ed. Thomas Daniel Young. Baton Rouge: Louisiana State Univ. Press, 1968.

Taylor, Dennis. *Hardy's Poetry, 1860-1928*. New York: Columbia Univ. Press, 1981.

Ward, William S. *A Literary History of Kentucky*. Knoxville: Univ. of Tennessee Press, 1988.

Whitman, Walt. "On the Beach at Night." In *Complete Poetry and Selected Prose*. New York: Library of America, 1982.

Index of Warren's Works

General Index

Library of Congress Cataloging-in-Publication Data

Runyon, Randolph, 1947-
  The braided dream : Robert Penn Warren's late poetry / Randolph
Paul Runyon.
    p. cm.
  Includes bibliographical references.
  ISBN 0-8131-1722-4
  1. Warren, Robert Penn, 1905-   —Criticism and interpretation.
I. Title.
PS3545.A748Z864   1990   89-48187
811'.52—dc20